D0506966

LANDSCAPE DESIGN
An International Survey

LANDSCAPE DESIGN

An International Survey

Edited by Ken Fieldhouse & Sheila Harvey

Coordinating Researcher Jennifer Hudson

THE OVERLOOK PRESS
WOODSTOCK, NEW YORK

ACKNOWLEDGEMENTS

The Editors should like to express their gratitude to the many people throughout the world whose interest and enthusiasm made this book possible. This includes both those whose work is featured here and those who kindly submitted schemes that we were regretfully unable to include for a variety of reasons. Thanks also to the many individuals who have freely supplied advice on selecting designers and for drawing our attention to specific schemes. We are especially indebted to Jennifer Hudson for the dedication, determination and tact she brought to the enormous task of gathering in the material and information without which this book could not have been produced. Finally, thanks to Elizabeth Thussu of John Calmann & King for guidance, encouragement and providing this opportunity; and to Chris Hodder for typing the manuscripts. Special acknowledgement is also due to Peter Walker for permission to use material from his article, 'Solana, A Corporate Landscape with Buildings' on pages 108-111.

PHOTOGRAPHS

The publishers and Editors would like to thank the landscape practices and designers featured for their cooperation and the submission of material for inclusion in this publication. The following credits are given with thanks to the photographers whose images have been used:

Rick Alexander (*122 left, 123*); Blanc de Birges (*127*); Bruns Nurseries, Hamburg (*38*); Paul Buchard/Struwing (*168, 169, 171*); Karl D. Buhler, Comet Photo AG (*112, 113*); Martin Charles/Derek Lovejoy Partnership (*100, 101, 102, 103*); Ellen Dawson (*146*); Stuart Davidson (*75*); Jacques Dufresne (*66, 67*); Jay Faber (*76*); Gabriel Figueroa Flores (*28, 29*); J. Gollings (*178*); Jim Hendrich (*110, 111*); Haruo Hiroto (*46, 47*); Industrie und Werbefotografie Nord GmbH (*45 top left*); Aaron Kiley (*122 right*); Balthazar Korab (*90, 91*); Clive McDonnell (*34, 35, 36, 37, 39*); Mike McKee (*107*); Fujjitsuka Mitsumasa (*40 bottom left and right, 41*); John Neubauer (*147*); Office of Public Works (*244*); Ole Roe/Roe Foto A/S (*141, 182, 183*); Helke Rodemeir (*166, 167*); Smith & Co./Peter Hall (*218, 221*); David Soliday (*74, 78 bottom, 79*); Uli Steltzer (*153 left*); Oscar Thompson (*132 top right, 133 bottom*); David Walker (*6, 86, 87, 88, 89, 106, 108, 109*); James Wilson (*84*); Robin Winogrand (*20, 21*).

First published in 1993 by
The Overlook Press
Lewis Hollow Road
Woodstock, New York 12498

Copyright © 1992 Ken Fieldhouse and
Sheila Harvey

All rights reserved. No part of this publication may be reproduced or transmitted in any form or by any means, electronic or mechanical, including photocopy, recording, or any information storage and retrieval system now known or to be invented without permission in writing from the publisher, except by a reviewer who wishes to quote brief passages in connection with a review written for inclusion in a magazine, newspaper, or broadcast.

Library of Congress Cataloging-in-Publication Data

International landscape design / edited by Ken Fieldhouse and Sheila Harvey.

    p.cm.
Includes index.

    1. Landscape architecture. 2. Landscape design. I. Fieldhouse, Ken. II. Harvey, Sheila, 1938-

SB472.157 1993
712--dc20

ISBN 0–87951–474–4

92-23782
CIP

Contents

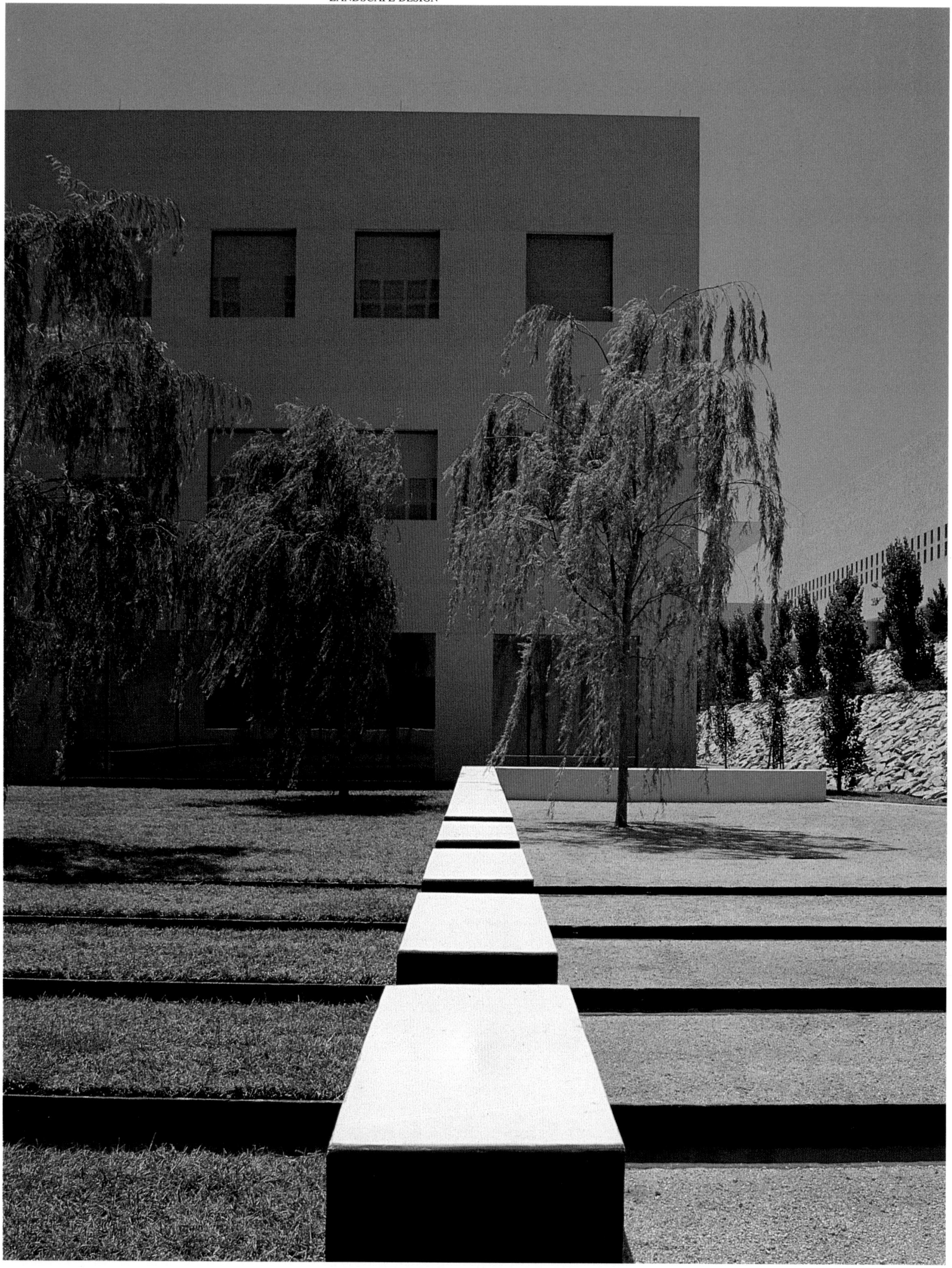

Introduction

The extent to which landscape architecture forms part of our surroundings has not always been appreciated. Other design disciplines such as architecture, interiors, textiles, furniture, and fashion have received frequent public attention from publishers and press. This book is an attempt to redress the balance.

One of the established tenets of landscape design has been that it should recognize a sense of place – the '*genius loci*' of earlier times. It is often this awareness that sets landscape architecture apart from other creative disciplines, together with the fact that through its understanding of the need for the careful integration of the natural and man-made, landscape design can respond positively to the challenges of an ever more demanding world and of its finite resources. We feel that most, if not all, of the schemes included in this book achieve this, either implicitly or explicitly.

In recent years, a greater public awareness of the environment has strengthened the role of landscape design, enabling it to forge essential links with nature, even in hostile situations. Landscape is perhaps the only discipline linking sustainability of nature with the civilizing interests of humankind.

Nowadays landscape design is seldom the result of individual patronage. It has become a more complex process, often with corporate bodies or government committees as the major clients. Such clients require a greater measure of accountability in landscape planning and see the investment in landscape in terms of image and marketing value, benefit to the workforce, and resource auditing. Some of our examples show how landscape architects can respond to these pressures so that landscape design should not be seen as something set apart from the community and business life. Design in landscape usually requires considerable vision and faith, as the time scale from first thoughts to effective maturity may be measured in terms of decades rather than months.

Landscape architecture does not fall into such clearly defined movements as, for example, architecture or fine art. Its strength and weakness in recent years lies in the fact that it has not been subject to the same proliferation of rigid styles. There are, of course, some minor themes, such as the natural design movement of the last two decades, and also attempts to interpret the modernist philosophy found in architecture. But there is little solid evidence of substantial contemporary design theory underlying the schemes reviewed for inclusion in this book. This is one of the weaknesses of current landscape practice, evidenced by a mixture of somewhat unconvincing styles, components and work practices which have materially influenced design solutions. In the right hands, however, this freedom from theory can produce exciting results, and we have included examples here which show that landscape design can rise above mundane or predictable responses.

Opposite: Solana (see pages 106-111).

It remains to be seen how this design process will stand the test of time, even with effective management and maintenance, which is essential to the viability of all landscape projects. Far too many promising schemes fail when there is a lack of understanding or interest in the continuing performance of the initial landscape investment. This is a foolish waste of resources. It has not always been possible to assess properly this aspect in all the schemes illustrated. Many are at an early stage of development. It also became apparent that some contained future maintenance plans within the initial design process, whereas others were not able to enforce conditions for various reasons, often economic.

This book offers an opportunity to explore the creativity and diversity apparent in much contemporary landscape work throughout the world. It also provides a fascinating means through which the reader can make comparisons of both the differences and similarities to be found in landscape activity in many varied situations. Apart from geographical, cultural and social influences, client interest and user involvement in the design process have proved to be important and often rewarding.

We have kept a very open mind in the selection of designs and designers. Neither popular acclaim (and recognition) nor eminence within professional circles have necessarily determined our selection, although it is fair to say that a large proportion of the schemes illustrated within this book have been designed by professional landscape architects. However, this has not been a major criterion for inclusion and indeed, in some parts of the world, the use of the distinct term 'landscape architect' could prove problematic.

Landscape design, in common with all serious disciplines, has a basis of history and tradition on which to draw. Many practitioners and writers have explored this rich territory in great detail and, while acknowledging these foundations, our purpose here is to examine the present and the future. Therefore we have deliberately limited selection to post-1980 schemes, although the necessarily long-term process involved in landscape development means that some schemes may have originated years previously, and that they will continue to mature. The very nature of landscape inevitably links the past with the future.

It may be helpful to comment on what we have *not* tried to do. There are specialist subject areas of exclusion such as reclamation and housing, although a few unusual and intriguing examples have crept in. Private and historic gardens and parks have also not been included as these have been amply covered elsewhere, and their inclusion would have helped to proliferate unnecessarily the widely held notion that landscape design is solely about gardens and gardening.

Costs have been excluded on the grounds that it is impossible to arrive at a common basis of comparison for all projects. Particularly, this refers to differential rates of inflation in the last ten years, and difficulties in equating costs expressed per unit area when compared with those described on a commodity or work practice basis. Interpretations of what to include or exclude will vary enormously. Relative costs of materials and labour within specific countries or regions of those countries are far more valuable than a spurious global comparison. The purpose of this book is to encourage a creative view of landscape and each designer must decide what is appropriate and possible within specific circumstances. Successful landscape design is not necessarily dependent upon extensive funding. However, where appropriate, the percentage cost breakdown between 'hard' and 'soft' landscape is given, although this should be approached with some caution as the line of delineation between the two has been determined by the various designers.

Sources were as wide and varied as possible, using a network of contacts in conjunction with personal knowledge, experience and current literature. Inevitably, some schemes have been presented in more detail than others, but it was considered important that as wide a range of cultures and geographical areas as possible be included. Selection has taken into account design solutions that stand out as exemplars either in part or as a whole. Sometimes small sections of a scheme had immense appeal and deserved inclusion, whereas overall the project proved of less interest. Where this has happened, comment has generally been restricted to those parts illustrated. We have made no attempt to compile a definitive compendium of current work, neither is the coverage geographically comprehensive. Rather it is a personal selection based on best-known evidence and subject to availability of relevant material.

Landscape architecture can so often be seen as part of a team or multi-disciplinary process. Over the years, there has been an ebb and flow in the influence of landscape designers on their fellow professionals. Currently this influence is strong and, in our opinion, can only be for the general good at a time when the sustainability of the environment and maintaining or enhancing the quality of life are proving intractable problems. Nevertheless the practice of landscape architecture should not be considered as simply a question of problem solving, but also of opportunities seized and realized. The projects in this book demonstrate, on the whole, the ability to create stimulating landscape out of problem-solving situations.

In an age when it is fashionable to condemn planners, architects and engineers, landscape architects have emerged relatively unscathed, without being accused of creating unbearable urban environments or debasing the images of countryside. But as they are drawn steadily into the development process, they will not be able to remain immune from criticism unless the highest principles of design and management are observed. The greatest achievements for landscape architecture lie in the future, but practitioners will need to prove their capabilities to meet the rapidly changing conditions and requirements. Otherwise those with less creative or ill-formed skills will step in.

Project users rather than just the commissioning client now have a more significant place in the design process. They are voicing genuine concerns and interests in their surrounding environment, whether for work, leisure, or at home. Landscape design has an immense opportunity to respond to this interest and to expand this crucial aspect of our relationship with the world that surrounds us. Truly creative landscape on whatever scale and in whatever context remains far too rare an event.

Today there has perhaps never been a better opportunity for landscape design to flourish, nor perhaps a greater need. If this book encourages a fresh look at the subject and offers encouragement to those who doubt the value of excelling in landscape design, then our endeavours will have been successful.

Parc Sausset (see pages
48-53)

1

Leisure & Recreation

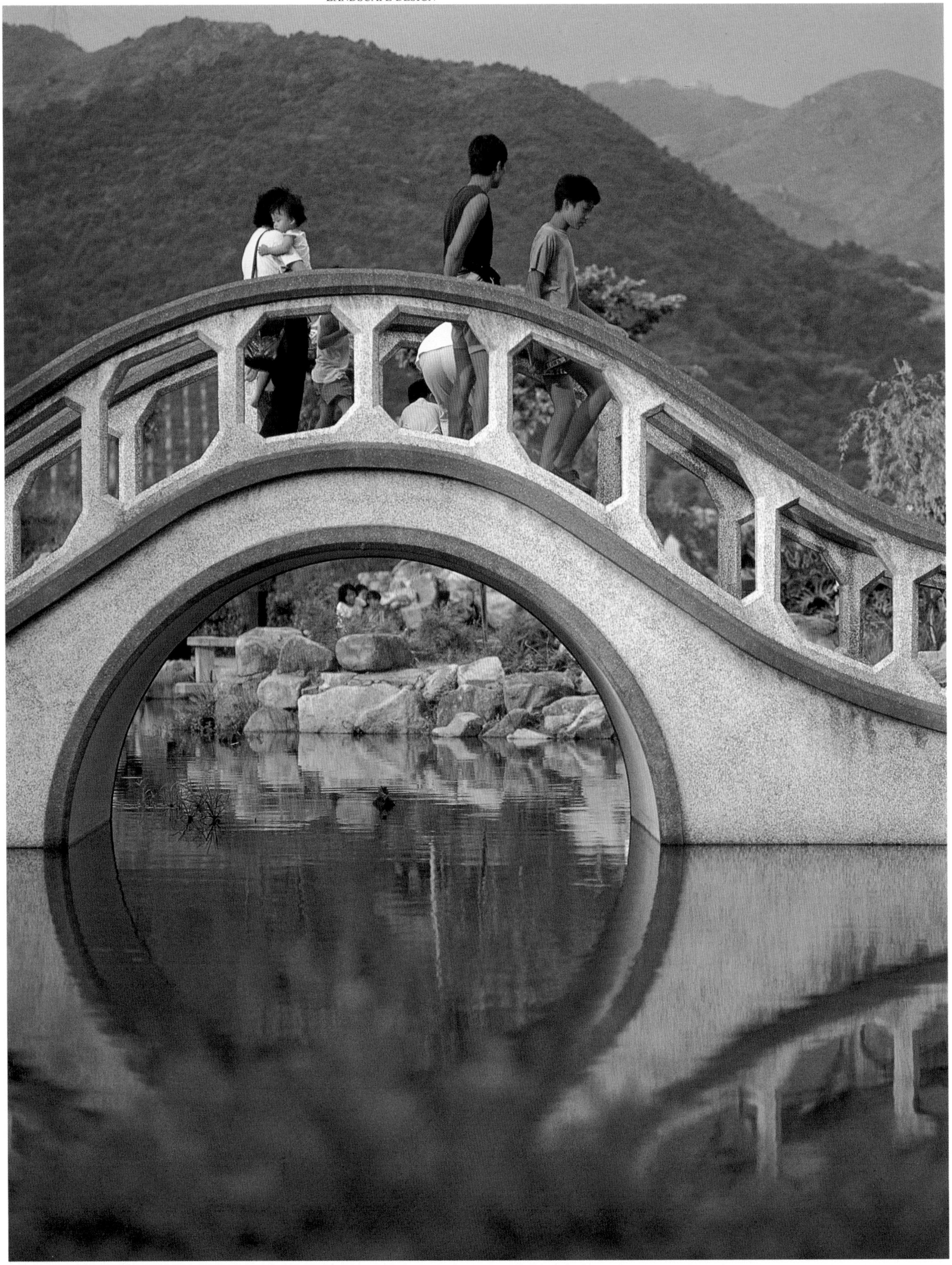

1.1

BRIAN CLOUSTON AND PARTNERS,
HONG KONG LTD.
Sha Tin New Town, Hong Kong

Sha Tin Park

Sha Tin was designated as a new town in 1974 with a target population of 750,000. It was built on a combination of reclaimed land and flat platforms on the steep hillsides above the valley of the Shing Mun River. The river was 'retrained' into a straight outflow running through the centre of town to Plover Cove. Both banks were designed for recreational use. The town park, now known as Central Park, is adjacent to a cultural complex, government offices, and commercial centre. It has river frontage of approximately 1000 metres (3280 feet) and varies in depth from 80 to 120 metres (262 metres 6 inches to 393 feet 8½ inches). When design work started in 1981, the site was virtually flat ground reclaimed by the tipping of mainly soft excavate from the surrounding hills.

One of the difficulties to be faced was the narrow linear shape of the valley and also the fact that, since Sha Tin has become one of the densest settlements in the world, very heavy use was anticipated. The park was therefore designed for passive rather than active recreation. A series of interlinked spaces of contrasting character separated by dramatic landforms and free-standing walls help to absorb people and offer a sense of retreat from the high density surroundings. The intention was to design a lively and varied park to stimulate its prospective users. An examination by the landscape designers of existing Hong Kong parks showed that users were mainly adolescents and young adults, that parks were an escape from often cramped family homes, and that the predominant activity was the taking of posed photographs of friends and lovers.

Various oriental principles were applied to the design, such as 'borrowed landscape' – the directing of views outwards to absorb the surrounding landscape. The park's structure sets up a system of pedestrian routes and a series of individual gardens, alternating between the 'yin' qualities (informal/earthy/intimate) and 'yang' qualities (formal/hard/robust). This juxtaposition of opposites – rest and movement, soft and hard – sets up a rhythm and lends pace to the design.

The site would be imposed on by the surrounding development were it not for its location in a steep-sided valley containing a number of isolated conical hills of volcanic origin. A strong, exciting landform for the park echoes the strong landforms seen from it, and forms enclosure and acoustic barriers at the western and eastern ends. It also creates an illusion of space by dividing the long thin site into a series of intimate landscape areas.

The oriental design principle of 'borrowed landscape' absorbs the background of the hills.

The Tropical Garden and the Moon Bridge - a traditional feature repeated in this design.

Start on site: May 1983
Handover: February 1990 (opened to the public in September 1988)
Site area: 10 hectares (25 acres)

The Chinese garden is
an interpretation of
the gardens of
Suchow.

Although the park's areas are linked into the riverfront promenade, emphasizing its
length and narrowness, the promenade is never allowed to dominate the structure. There are
six of these individual 'gardens'. In the Tropical Garden, an 8-metre (26-foot 3-inch) waterfall
cascades down the side of a 15-metre (49-foot 3-inch) hill and runs through still pools under
moon bridges and past pavilions on rocky crags to a reflecting pond. It is then recycled
through two rising mains back up to the top of the hill. This landscape was designed as
backdrop for photographic compositions, an ironic reversal of the eighteenth-century English
gardens where landscapes were composed as interpretations of paintings.

The theme of the Western Play Area is an American fort, which is appropriately difficult
to assail. (Nearly everything to do with the United States is highly revered in Hong Kong.)
Probably the most rigidly structured garden is the Display Garden, designed to allow the
maximum number of people to enjoy the maximum number of plants. This garden is enclosed
by free-standing walls and formal hedges and is intended for strolling. It is planted with
geometrically patterned beds, bonzai, a rockery, pergolas and groves of trees and shrubs.

The riverfront promenade links the various areas of the park.

The Eastern Play Area features a custom-built fishing junk.

1, main plaza
2, amphitheatre
3, fountain pools
4, adventure playground
5, water garden
6, waterfall
7, ravine
8, lotus pool

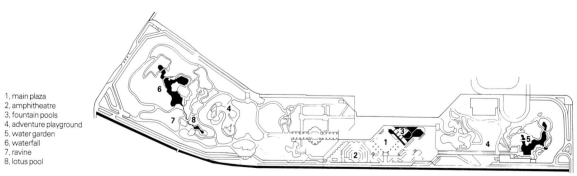

general layout

The Town Plaza is the crossroads for the park and a central square for the town. As well as a gushing water feature, it has an open view to the river, the town and the hills beyond. It contains a bandstand, refreshment facilities and a bridge over the river. The Eastern Play Area is a mirror of the Western one, but features a Chinese fort with reproduction battering rams and assault ladders. There is also a custom-built, 'authentic' fishing junk, converted for use as a play structure and located at a point which would have been on the shoreline of the former fishing bay.

An interpretation of principal features from the gardens of Suchow makes up the Chinese Garden. A central water body presents a sequence of framed views varying in scale and content. Trees and shrubs have typically muted flower colours.

Traditional features throughout the gardens include moon bridges, pantiled pavilions, moon gates, serpentine walls and inscriptions on gateways and in individual gardens. Innovative features include the tensile structure over the bandstand, a membrane capable of withstanding winds up to 257.4km per hour (160mph); the waterfall created with gabions, which is Hong Kong's highest man-made fall; the irrigation system designed to use treated sewage effluent; bamboo shuttered finish to retaining walls; and importations from Thailand, the Philippines, Singapore and China of a wide range of plant species rare or new to Hong Kong. The circulation system takes full account of Sha Tin's comprehensive pedestrian and cycleway system. It provides a major riverside route linked to adjacent open space between the town centre wall and a pedestrian bridge across the 150-metre (492-foot) wide river.

Clouston has created an exciting, multiuse park, providing much-needed facilities for individual leisure time and a refuge from the crowded urban environment. Inspired by Hong Kong itself, the design has achieved an effective combination of tradition and novelty.

View of the Aviary Garden, showing the extensive use of water features.

Opposite Water cascades down between rocky crags, to be recycled back up to the top of the hill.

19

Conceptual drawing, showing the layout of the garden.

An early concept model, showing a variation of the sun-dial with tall water wall.

The Ruhegarten is one of a series of solar gardens that together constitute the Enz Garden in the Hohewiesenpark along the River Enz in Pforzheim, site of the 1992 State Garden Show of Baden Württemberg in south-west Germany. The Knoll Landscape Practice won the competition for this project sponsored by the city of Pforzheim.

The designer of the Ruhegarten, Robin Winogrond, had to take into account the Garden Show's overall theme of solar energy and sun. She also wished to acknowledge Pforzheim's status as a world centre for jewellery design. The resulting concept uses technological processes and materials such as glass, brushed steel and cast bronze to combine with the natural elements of water and sunlight to produce a jewel effect in the landscape. Combining art and technology posed particular problems, especially the inherent conflict between the artistic and technical uses of the materials. These had to be considered along with practical landscape requirements, such as weather and vandal proofing, which exceed the normal engineering standards demanded. At the same time, construction techniques – including surface finishes, mounting systems, joints – were not allowed to detract from the desired visual effect. Initially, Winogrond set out to design a fountain which isolated two basic landscape materials, water and sunlight, so that through the interaction of these elements, the public could perceive their essential nature. A series of experiments showed that combining glass and metal with water 'dematerializes' the hard substances so that the user experiences both the elusive and dynamic qualities of water and light. The final design solution took the form of a sundial which will show the movement of the sun over the course of a day or indeed a year.

The visitor approaching the Ruhegarten will find four gold metal walls enclosing a basin of water. The three main elements of the scheme stand within the basin. The first of these is a large curved wall of sandblasted, 1.5-centimetre (6-inch) glass, measuring approximately 2 x 2.5 metres (6 feet 6 inches x 8 feet 2½ inches). The design etched on its surface acts as a screen, projecting images both of reflected water and of radiated and reflected light. The second is a tall, thin plane of 16mm (¾-inch) laminated glass, turquoise in colour, approximately 6 x 4.5 metres (19 feet 8 inches x 14 feet 9 inches), again with a special surface treatment to enhance visual quality. The third element is a curved metal rod which spills free-falling water over the turquoise panel. Other structural elements in this predominantly hard landscape are specially designed brushed stainless steel feet to support the glass walls, bronze cast walls with a reflective finish and light green Italian quartz stone pavers (30 x 30 centimetres/11¾ x 11¾ inches).

1.2 *Ruhegarten, The Enz Garden*

ROBIN WINOGROND, S. KNOLL
LANDSCAPE ARCHITECTURE
Landesgartenschau, Pforzheim, Germany

There are three cradle-like bench seats where visitors may sit and contemplate the effects of light and water. These are of steel rod and perforated steel sheeting, designed to support the sense of a dynamic, ephemeral environment and, of practical importance, specially finished with a coating which permits minimal heat conduction. Trellis supporting *Hedera helix*, the only soft landscape element of the design, also adds a touch of coolness and is designed as a geometric extension of the walls.

It is too early at the time of writing to gauge public reaction to Winogrond's Ruhegarten. However, the use of hard materials to create an ever-changing landscape with water and light is appropriate in a city dominated by industry and technology. The willingness of the landscape architect to experiment with materials like metal and glass and to collaborate with metal workers, the glass industry and technologists helps to expand the profession's profile. In this case, the result is a living and mobile sculpture which aims, perhaps paradoxically, to produce a calm and meditative landscape.

A human model is introduced to indicate the scale of the design.

Start on site: Autumn 1990
Handover: Autumn 1991
Site area: 8 metres square
(26 feet square)

The site-designed timber play structures which have been adopted for usage by other local authorities.

1.3 *John Knight Memorial Park*

DENTON CORKER MARSHALL
PTY LTD.
Canberra, Australia

The client for this project was the National Capital Development Commission (NCDC) which was established by the Australian Federal Government in 1958 with powers to plan, develop and construct the city of Canberra as the capital of the Commonwealth of Australia. By 1988 this function was considered complete and the Australian Commonwealth Territory (ACT) Planning and Land Management Act introduced new responsibilities for both Commonwealth and Territorial Governments.

The rapid growth in population within the Canberra ACT up to the late 1960s resulted in the strategy for satellite settlements, known as the 'Y-Plan'. This plan linked three new major population centres to the existing city of Canberra. Each new town sits in its own valley and is linked to Canberra by a system of river/creek corridors. Belconnen New Town is linked to this system via Lake Ginninderra. John Knight Memorial Park, named after an environmentally sympathetic senator, was developed as a result of this increase in population to function as a district park, sited conveniently between the urban fabric of Belconnen and the green corridors of the 'Y-Plan'.

An evocative compositional view of colour and light in the landscape of the park.

Start on site: 1980
Handover: 1989
Site area: 14 hectares
(34½ acres)

A sinuous timber boardwalk snakes through the vegetation at the water margin.

Elevations of the island play structure.

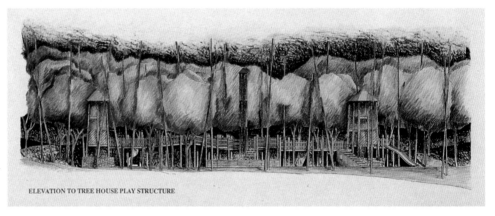

ELEVATION TO TREE HOUSE PLAY STRUCTURE

Randomly placed boulders contrast with the stepped waterfall, which matches the adjacent footpath.

The park has evolved in a series of phases over nine years. The brief demanded a natural parkland setting within the context of specific engineering requirements, including a lake feature to be a settlement pond for storm water run-off from Belconnen before it entered the Murrumbidgee River. Shallow rock and difficult landfill conditions influenced the design, and civil and hydraulic engineering sub-consultants were crucial participants in the development team.

The site consists of a northern valley, which is predominantly native in character, and a southern valley with a more exotic 'village green' character, separated by a substantial woodland ridge in between. The northern valley is deeply cut and has been developed as a series of water gardens, expressing an allegory of a river – springing from the mountain and flowing to the sea. It is a place for strolling, sitting, and meditation.

The southern valley, on the other hand, is designed to encourage community activities within a broad area of open, irrigated lawns, framed by stands of exotic trees and backed by belts of native trees, which screen the park from nearby roads and buildings. The western edge of the park is bounded by Lake Ginninderra and a promenade was designed to weave along the shore line. This promenade is not only for walkers but also for cyclists, who use the park extensively. Exposure to the prevailing north-west winds from across the lake was a major problem, solved in part by creating an island with a shelter belt on its windward side. The line of the promenade is defined by large silver poplars, but willows and casuarinas are also included along the water edge to provide contrast in form, colour and foliage, as well as offering some shelter from the wind off the lake.

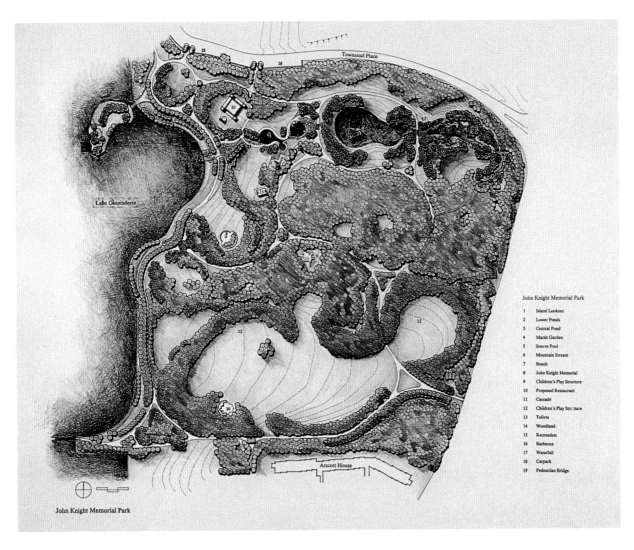

John Knight Memorial Park

1   Island Lookout
2   Lower Ponds
3   Central Pond
4   Marsh Garden
5   Source Pool
6   Mountain Stream
7   Beach
8   John Knight Memorial
9   Children's Play Structure
10 Proposed Restaurant
11 Cascade
12 Children's Play Structure
13 Toilets
14 Woodland
15 Recreation
16 Barbecue
17 Waterfall
18 Carpark
19 Pedestrian Bridge

John Knight Memorial Park

Master plan of John Knight Memorial Park, with Lake Ginnindera on the left.

The lake serves to screen out water pollutants from the surrounding urban area. As water quality was not consistently acceptable for swimming, the lake edge was designed to discourage swimming. The foreshore was finished with a hard-edged promenade and an informal edge of river-washed pebbles and rock outcrops.

In general, the designer has encouraged a comfortable, naturalistic feel to the park, particularly through the gently curving lines of paths and the plant species selected in the scheme. The rapid establishment of a native aquatic ecosystem and 'natural' foreshore has been enlarged in later phases to include creeks, ponds and bog-gardens, incorporating granite boulders over concrete construction. Where appropriate, irrigation has been included to grass areas to encourage adequate establishment.

As the park has evolved through its various development phases over the nine year period, it has increasingly been adopted by the local community and now has an important educational and interpretative role. Semi-formal play is also encouraged by timber play structures, which have been accepted as a 'standard of excellence' by the recently formed public works department. John Knight Memorial Park is an example of how well landscape and engineering principles can harmonize in a quest for scenic quality. The financial split, with 60 per cent given over to hard landscape, is evidence of the dominance of the construction and engineering requirements, but the maturing planting does not appear to have been under-specified. It may lack evidence of a strong creative statement, but the visual and functional elements result in a successful district park which provides diversity of interest and apparently meets with local approval.

At night the waterfall is an illuminated feature.

Diamond-patterned paving and pools: the flow of water can be altered to produce a variety of effects.

The monumental structures at the highest point in the park make it a landmark locally.

1.4

HEADS CO. LTD.
Nishinomiya New Town, Japan

Nacion Plaza

Nishinomiya Najio New Town is currently being developed on a 243-hectare (600-acre) hillside site just north of Nishinomiya City. Its planned population is about 12,000. Based on the theme of 'a community responsive to the five senses', the Housing and Urban Development Corporation plans an ideal environment that will stimulate its inhabitants to devote their leisure to artistic and literary pursuits. Located in the hillside residential district of the new town, Nacion Plaza is to serve as a multi-use, outdoor space for local people. It is one of the earliest sections of the new town to be completed and is intended to play an overall role in the creation of the community. The developer is taking great care to organize the space and design of its facilities so that it will enhance the community scheme.

Two roads divide the plaza into three zones, the design of which is based on the themes of 'viewing', 'socializing', and 'playing'. The highest section is, naturally, the viewing zone, which makes full use of its altitude to open up the surrounding views. Its monumental structures mean that it also acts as a landmark providing a focal point in the new town. The second sector has a highly flexible arrangement capable of accommodating a wide variety of social events, including an area that can be used as a stage for live performances.

At the lower end of Nacion Plaza is the playing zone. Although wooden climbing frames and other playground facilities have been installed, the area acts as a gateway to the entire plaza and is an extensive paved space that can be used in many ways. The difference in altitude from the other two zones means that it can be exploited in terms of water supply, sewage and drainage provision. The southern edge of this zone contains a monument symbolic of the Nacion district. Appropriately, given the name, monuments by a Spanish artist are also being installed in the plaza.

Lighting equipment, shelters and handrails are all made of stainless steel and are intended to be both functional and decorative. The solidity and oppressiveness of the concrete wall that forms a framework to the site's spatial composition are ameliorated by its chipped surface. Flat paving laid in a diamond pattern is constructed of imitation stone and quartzite. The complex flow of water and lighting can be controlled to present Nacion Plaza in many ways and to accentuate seasonal foliage changes.

Almost all parks constructed by the Housing and Urban Development Corporation as part of its New Town, together with other community projects, are handed over to the municipal government after completion. Future management of Nacion Plaza will be in the hands of Nishinomiya City. Because of this it was essential that from the initial planning stage local administration, corporation and designers should work closely together to plan the park's facilities, design and management. In this case, the process has gone ahead smoothly for both planning and implementation. Nacion Plaza is highly visible not only from the main roads and surrounding residential districts, but also from the Chugoku and other highways outside the area. For this reason it has become a symbol and major landmark for the new district.

Plan of the plaza, showing the relationship of the three zones.

Start on site: June 1990
Handover: May 1991

The park features a straightforward formula of generously proportioned pathways, gently undulating contours, strong bands of planting and water.

The Tenochtitlan sculpture, by Olaguibel, evokes the Aztec heritage of the valley of Mexico.

1.5 *Parque Tezozomoc*

GRUPO DE DISENO URBANO
Azcapotzalco, Mexico City, Mexico

In the mid-1970s, a substantial area of land was miraculously made available in the heart of overcrowded Mexico City for a new park. It was a rectangular block within a mixed industrial and working-class residential district which was also one of the most polluted areas of the city. Great things were expected of this park, which had an immediate catchment area of over one million people. The site had few encouraging properties, but the landscape architects quickly turned the apparent problems into a creative opportunity.

Introducing an historical dimension by recreating the topography of the fifteenth-century Valley of Mexico, the designers produced a strongly organized zonal plan which they laid over the contours. The straight lines of the zone plan gradually softened in the concept stage to blend more comfortably with the flowing contours.

Along with symbolic links to the past, the designers were also keen to produce a park of direct relevance to urban city dwellers. While reminding them of the historical context and ecological evolution, the park meets modern needs through sports facilities, an open-air auditorium, cafeteria, gymnasium and extensive pathways and cycle tracks.

The park development was executed in four years. The topography was formed by spoil conveniently excavated from the new subway under Mexico City. The large central lake is supplied by purified water (aerated on site) from a nearby effluent treatment plant and this water is also used for irrigation throughout the park. A municipal nursery was set up specifically to supply horticultural stock for the park, as well as for nearby urban forestry projects. The free-form lake is lined with clay which has been covered with asphalt and sealant. The paths are also in asphalt and dressed with red, crushed volcanic stone. At important intersections small-unit, red concrete tiles are used.

The park was a substantial undertaking and the principles governing the urban design practice probably helped transform the derelict site to the healthy, mature and popular city park seen today. Grupo de diseno urbano is an interdisciplinary design association which set up a project team of specialists including fine art, economics and systems engineering. In this instance an important dimension was the involvement of the local community in the development process. Almost a decade after completion, the park is a well-established part of the wider Mexico City landscape, attracting between five and twenty thousand visitors every weekend. It is used for all kinds of public ceremonies and group or community activities.

Cities worldwide, old and new, need the vitality of renewal in their urban landscape structure, just as in sewers or roads. This park has made a substantial impact, is maturing well and appears to belong to its neighbourhood. The designers have also been conscious of the need to utilize limited resources to achieve this composition.

A powerfully grouped sculpture is strategically located on an island in the lake.

Start on site: 1978
Handover: 1982
Site area: 28 hectares
(70 acres)

The visitor route
crossing the valley.

1.6 *The Field of Battle*

PROPERTY SERVICES AGENCY
DEPARTMENT OF THE ENVIRONMENT
East Sussex, UK

The Battle Estate, site of one of England's most famous historic battles, was acquired for the nation in 1976 by the Department of the Environment (DoE) with the help of US funding. Still in existence were ancient trackways, the slopes where the opposing Norman and English forces clashed and the hillock and water courses depicted in the Bayeux Tapestry, together with modern remains of scrub, marshes, forest and grazing land. In 1979, English Heritage (then known as the Department of Ancient Monuments and Historic Buildings) asked the landscape architects of the DoE Property Services Agency to advise on the implications of allowing visitors access to 15 hectares of the Field of Battle, which until then could only be viewed from a raised terrace walk, as it was private farmland.

The initial brief was simply to provide arboricultural and horticultural advice, but this expanded to include all aspects of visitor use and circulation. Landscape work was carried out at the same time as the long-term excavation and restoration of the site and buildings and the general provision of visitor facilities. The work was started in phases in 1980, 1982 and 1985. However, the resulting piecemeal approach meant that the design evolved over several years, thus avoiding drastic changes and allowing the landscape architect to work with rather than against nature.

Pat Bullivant, the landscape designer, sought to make the visitor aware of a sense of place, both in relation to the English rural landscape and to its own particular history. Nature conservation was also an important factor. The major issues for the design brief were public safety, land management, visitor access and amenity planting. Although public safety was a priority, site clearance was limited to obvious hazards and eyesores. Existing thickets of bramble and gorse were retained, with dead wood, rotting stumps and, where possible, hollow trees. The emphasis was on native planting that would encourage wildlife: oaks, hawthorn and willow with wild cherry, crabapple, dog rose, hazel, holly, guelder rose and alder buckthorn for variety. A path was cut out of the gorse covering the hillock, sturdy steps were built, new bridges spanned the field ditches and stiles, fencing and gates were provided. These were of oak, not only durable but oconomic at the time because of a surplus of pit props after a lengthy miners' strike.

The new 1.6-kilometre (one-mile) visitors' route around the battlefield, finished in 1981, leads them around the position of the opposing forces, showing at first hand the ground conditions in which the battle was fought. New planting was used to screen intrusive views of vehicles and buildings. The route also traces a green path through a meadow rich with a succession of wild flowers, creating an atmosphere of timelessness, before leading via the steepest slopes beside the abbey ruins to the spot on the hill where King Harold was killed. The field itself was formerly grazed by sheep and is presently cut for hay twice a year. New fencing means that grazing could still be an economic option.

One of the ancient
trackways showing new
edge planting.

Implementation: Phased 1980, 1982, 1985
Handover: Final handover in 1987 (open
to the public in 1981)
Site area: 15 hectares (37 acres)

Looking back across the valley from the abbey ruins.

The gradual approach to design, evolving over several years, allowed for continuity and made the best possible use of limited capital resources. Unfortunately, the final handover of the site coincided with a hurricane in October 1987, which did considerable damage to new fencing and young planting and this has taken some time to restore. Neither was there provision for future management of the site in the contract with the Property Services Agency. Nevertheless, the objective of combining an experience of history through a sense of place with nature conservation has been achieved with the minimum of upheaval, a factor greatly appreciated by the local people. Meanwhile, both the abbey and the Field of Battle continue to be popular destinations for visitors.

The Field of Battle seen
from the Long Terrace.

Planting in front of
Sleeping Beauty's
Castle.

1.7 *Euro Disney Magic Kingdom*

DEREK LOVEJOY PARTNERSHIP
Marne-la-Vallée, France

Disney theme parks have been successfully developed in the United States and Japan over the past 35 years. Euro Disney has now introduced this combination of theme park and resort complex into Europe. The Magic Kingdom will occupy 55 hectares (136 acres) of a 1,943-hectare (4801 acre) development site 32 kilometres (20 miles) to the east of Paris, acquired by the Disney Corporation. This development zone, known as Marne La Vallée, comprises low-grade arable land. The French Government agency, EPA agreed to assist in funding for an extension of the rail and road infrastructure – the new high-speed train (TGV) will now stop at Euro Disney.

The overall site masterplanning and design of hard landscape elements such as footpaths, retaining walls, bridges and fake rockwork was carried out either by the in-house Euro Disney Imagineering or by specialist outside design consultants. The Derek Lovejoy Partnership was employed to design and detail the soft landscape works: soil treatments, planting and mulching. (Disney particularly wanted to employ Europeans for their knowledge of indigenous plants.) The Partnership saw the brief as a challenge to create what will arguably be the most strongly theme-related planting designs in any European park. Access to Euro Disney Imagineering's project headquarters outside Paris enabled design ideas to be developed with the approval of, and in association with Disney's own 'show producers'. In fact, upwards of ten departments had to be made aware of the Derek Lovejoy Partnership's design intentions before the landscape drawings could be finalized.

In some cases it was difficult to meet the show producers' exact requirements since they often had no horticultural experience, but exhaustive searches of major plant nurseries throughout Europe helped the Partnership to meet the show producers' expectations. In addition, the soft landscape design proposals had to be coordinated with an unusually large number of complex services – such as those operating rides and special effects within the park. This often meant liaising carefully with consultants located as far away as Colorado to ensure the proper co-ordination and integration of the landscape design works. The entire design process leading to finalization of full working drawings and specifications had to be completed between November 1989 and December 1990.

The project called for the creation of a wide variety of landscape settings to support the themed areas and rides within the Magic Kingdom. These settings create illusions from jungle through to desert using living plant materials and carefully selected mulches, including different coloured sands, shattered rock and pine needles. The entire theme park is separated from the French plain by a carefully graded earth berm up to 20 metres (65 feet) high. In addition to this, the park itself is sub-divided by secondary berms which define the five main attractions or 'lands'. The berms themselves have been heavily planted with trees and shrubs to further strengthen their effect and to create appropriate back-drops to the different themed areas.

One of the main technical problems the Partnership had to overcome was to decide on the most appropriate soil treatments necessary to accommodate the enormous variety and range of plants needed for the park. The soil stockpiled for re-use displayed certain deficiencies in structure and composition and the Derek Lovejoy Partnership recommended that trial beds

Bedding construction
and tree planting in the
Forecourt area.

Start on site: 1990
Handover: 1992
Site area: 55 hectares (136 acres)

Perspective sketch of the mountain trails in Autopia, used by DLP to communicate design intentions to various interested parties within the Disney Corporation.

should be established on site to test the various prescriptions for amelioration put forward by the consultant soil scientists. Detailed specifications were also drawn up and contract drawings prepared showing exactly the type of treatment each planting bed within the park should receive. The long term success of the scheme will depend as much as anything on the correct preparation of soil for the different plants specified.

Another central issue was that planting had to be appropriate to themes representing for example, the tropical jungles of the Caribbean, the deserts of North Africa and the primeval forests of Jules Verne's futuristic world. However, in this instance the park is not located in Florida, Los Angeles or even Tokyo, but in the relatively severe climate of the North French plain. Indeed, certain 'essential' plants such as cacti and banana palms will have to be planted in specially designed underground containers and removed from the site during cold weather. To ensure a mature and impressive landscaped backdrop to the park's illusions, over 10,000 carefully selected trees and 200,000 shrubs will be planted throughout the park. A major part of the Partnership's commission was to visit the nurseries of Europe to procure the special plants essential for 'theming' the different lands within the park. It also enabled the firm to compile a comprehensive database of plant sources and availability throughout Europe which will undoubtedly be of value to future projects. Plants selected include unusually clipped yew trees with square heads which are planted on the immaculate grass slopes sweeping up to the centrepiece of the Magic Kingdom, the Sleeping Beauty Castle. Mature weeping beeches, and distorted, deformed trees and shrubs are set in a cinder-like mulch for the gardens of the Phantom Manor. Swamp cypress and monkey puzzle trees set off the space-age architecture of Discoveryland, while giant tree rhododendrons (7-8 metres; 23-25 feet) from Germany act as an evergreen sub-canopy within the jungle areas of Adventureland. Rhododendrons may seem like an unlikely choice for a jungle, but their sinuous stems, glossy leaves and heavy exotic blooms may be an effective northern substitute for normal jungle plants. Ground cover plants include miniature bamboos, ferns and mosses especially effective in creating the 'jungle illusion'.

Planting alongside the tracks to the car journey known as Autopia has been designed in the form of chevrons, and bands of different coloured groundcover plants create the illusions of distance and speed. The use of colour, shape and form have been important in relating planting

Master plan of
Euro Disney – the
Magic Kingdom.

The Entry Forecourt area at the time of the opening of Euro Disney.

View of Fantasyland, with Fleur-de-Lys box hedging, which was grown in advance.

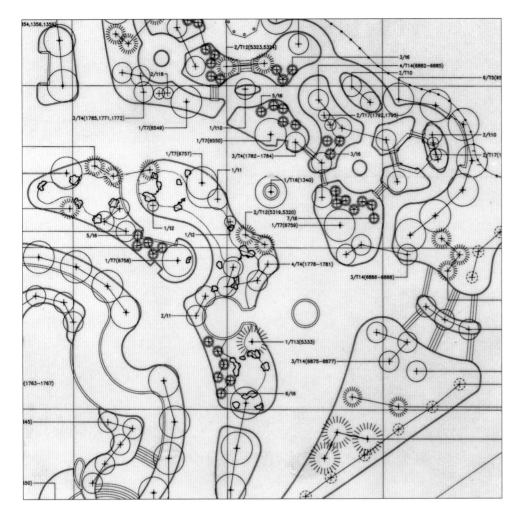

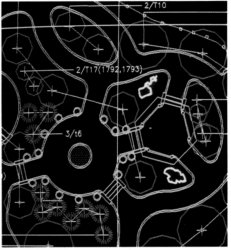

CAD – generated plan
of part of
Discoveryland and
Autopia.

CAD – generated tree
plan of part of the Entry
Forecourt Sequence.

to illusion throughout the theme park showing great imagination by the designers. The Derek Lovejoy Partnership specified that box hedging should be grown well in advance of the park's opening so that it could be transported fully grown into position – for example, the Fleur-de-Lys in Fantasyland was prepared for over eighteen months in Germany prior to being transported to the Magic Kingdom.

In order to complete the design work within the specified period the Partnership set up a special team of six principals and six support staff with its own studio based in their London office. A newly installed CAD facility came into its own, enabling the team to coordinate their work accurately with service drawings prepared by other consultants, for example with the computer controlled irrigation systems designed by a company based in Colorado and now installed throughout the park. Special graphics and programmes were designed by the project's CAD Manager so that the designers could communicate their intentions as clearly as possible to Euro Disney Imagineering and eventually to the landscape contractors who will implement the works. The final design package – 110 A0 drawings at 1:200 scale, together with construction details and a full specification was then translated into French by API, Euro Disney's French landscape support team.

Through careful planning and management throughout the plant procurement and design process the Practice feels that it has risen fully to the challenge of fulfilling the demanding requirements of the client's design brief for the Magic Kingdom. The inevitable wear and tear of such concentrated visitor use will test not only the success of the design itself but also the careful maintenance planning by Euro Disney.

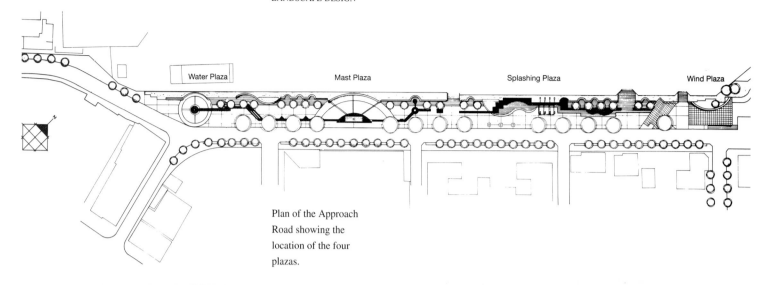

| Water Plaza | Mast Plaza | Splashing Plaza | Wind Plaza |

Plan of the Approach Road showing the location of the four plazas.

Children enjoying one of the water features in the Splashing Plaza. Hard landscape detailing of steps, paving and planters follows the curved lines of the design.

Aerial view which shows the patterns and colouring used in the design of the Water Plaza, together with some of the sculptural features.

1.8

MITSURU SENDA AND
ENVIRONMENT DESIGN INSTITUTE
Yokosuka, Japan

Approach Road to Mikasa Park

Mikasa Park is one of Yokosuka's landmarks, but the approach road to it is dominated by educational facilities and blocks of high-rise flats. The city authorities are planning a 10,000-metre (32,808-foot) seaside promenade park and the approach road is to act as a prototype for the construction of the entire promenade. EDI's design team of Senda, Mori and Sakuma wished to create a scheme that would symbolize the town's history and culture, its technological industries and relationship with the sea. They also had to take into account the conditions pertaining to the route as a whole. Another important element was the need to provide a space which would enhance the everyday surroundings of the neighbourhood residents.

The intention was to create an integrated space, 26 metres (85 feet 4 inches) in width, comprising the carriageway and footpath, but municipal restrictions required that the footpath was completely separated from the 13-metre (42-foot 8-inch)-wide road. The introduction of innovative elements relating to choice of materials, colour treatments and layout of sculptural features was initially misunderstood by the client, but most of EDI's proposals were eventually accepted and differences with the client resolved.

The overall site area is 7,500 square metres (80,732 square feet), 480 metres (1575 feet) long by 28 metres (92 feet) wide in the main section. A stream was constructed along the 300-metre (984-foot 3-inch) straight section of the approach road. Four plazas, each differing in character, with monuments, sculptures and landscape facilities, were placed along the stream. These symbolize various aspects of the town's life and history; for example, in the Mast Plaza, a ship's mast echoes the commemoration of a Second World War battleship in the park itself. The paving is gently sloped and bounded by a low curved and decorated wall to add to the feeling of being on a ship's deck. The others are the Water Plaza, the Splashing Plaza with water jets in which children may play and, nearest to the sea, the Wind Plaza. For the paving and hard landscape elements, Italian serpentinite, Chinese pink granite and concrete blocks add colour and texture, while the principal vegetation consists of camphor and Chinese tallow.

A theme of circles and semi-circles incorporated into the design softens the otherwise harsh line of the road itself and adds a sensation of width to a narrow space. These shapes are formed by the curves of steps into the water of the Splashing Plaza, by the semi-circular layout of the Mast Plaza or by simply depicting wave or flower designs in the paving layout through the use of different coloured paving materials. These designs are seen most effectively from above and can therefore also be appreciated by those who work or live in the high-rise buildings lining the road.

The designers feel that the use made of what is essentially a footpath from one point to another entirely validates their design concept. Pedestrians take time to enjoy the sculpture and stream as they walk along, children play freely in and with the water and there is every indication that the Mikasa Park Approach will succeed as a symbol of Yokosuka.

The Approach Road Park, showing its relationship to the road, the sea and adjacent buildings. The Mast Plaza can be seen in the foreground, backed by a curved and painted wall.

Start on site: July 1986
Handover: March 1987
Site area: 7,500 square metres (80,731 square feet)

1.9 *Aquatop*

MAREILE EHLERS, TRÜPER
AND GONDESEN
Travemünde, Germany

Travemünde is a popular resort on the north-German coast, close to an important ferry port linking Germany with Scandinavia. Located on the sea front, the covered swimming pool dates from the 1960s. The local board for tourism commissioned an improvement scheme to upgrade the pool and surrounding features. Glass structures were added to the front of the building to give it a fresh appearance and a major new attraction was the addition of a roof-top water shute descending by a circuitous route into the pool. The landscape architect's brief was to improve the quality of the key spaces surrounding the building: a roof terrace alongside the pool; a lower plaza, which in turn leads to the beach promenade, and the beach itself. The swimming-pool terrace and plaza form a public area giving access to the building, but also affording panoramic views over the estuary of the Trave River and Lübeck Bay.

The plaza was conceived as part of the beach promenade and as a forecourt to the main entrance, an area for gathering and street performance. A restaurant/café opens onto this area and the layout encourages visitors and passers-by to stop here. The design hinges on a formal arrangement of hornbeam trees, which in time will achieve a closed canopy, while the grid is interrupted by colourful flagstaffs, information boards, lighting fitments, sun umbrellas and randomly placed reclining chairs. Some of these chairs are fixed to the ground while others are deliberately mobile and discreetly stored at night to avoid theft. The dense shrub planting dating from the 1960s was removed and the area given over to an attractive finish in reddish sand-textured Dutch brick paviors. Only on the sunnier southern side, away from the beach, has a softer edge been introduced, with clusters of trees over gently undulating lawns.

The major upper terrace is approximately four metres (13 feet) above the plaza and looks over the beach promenade to Lübeck Bay. Access is from within the building. On this terrace, the designer has attempted to play on the theme of wave patterns spreading from the pool to the outdoor space. The 'waves' are inserted as mosaics of granite stones within a flat surface of white concrete slab paving. Gently curved planting beds owe their origin to the shape of sand dunes found on this coastline. The lines of the 'waves' flow through the beds and are symbolized as small depressions within the vegetation, covered with beach gravel and planted with blue-leafed grasses. The choice of plants has been made to reflect the coastal quality of the area. *Hippophae rhamnoides* was avoided on this roof terrace, due mainly to its invasive rooting character, but *Salix purpura 'Nana'*, *Salix repens argentea* and *Pinus mugo mughus* form the bulk of the terrace planting. Inevitably, the scale and location of planting within the terrace area is severely restricted through weight limitations and demands on irrigation and drainage.

The uneasy and contrasting lines in paving and fixed seat arrangements do not obviously encourage use.

Aerial view showing the relationship of the different levels and zones.

Start on site: November 1990
Handover: June 1991
Site area: 243 hectares (600 acres)

The roof terrace with
the tower and water-
shute slide on the right.
The lower plaza can
just be seen on the left.

A plan view of this project gives a misleading impression of the various elements. The functions of plaza (at promenade level) and raised terrace are quite separate. The contrast in treatment between the two levels is not so apparent to the visitor. The concept of 'waves' in the paving extending from the building, along with 'dune' islands of planting is fascinating, but would benefit from being stronger in practice to balance the scale and presence of the adjacent architecture. The firm line of seats and light fitments is a strangely uneasy solution within the flowing shapes. One also wonders whether, over time, the maturing hornbeam trees within the plaza will obscure the view from the terrace.

The generously proportioned plaza seems to fit well with the function of a seaside area to stroll, gather, sit or view the surroundings. It is a pity that the brick paving could not have been continued as far as the junction of the promenade and beach. Having taken a reasonably imaginative route the designer would have succeeded in producing a scheme of even greater distinction if fully exploiting this appreciation of the site and functions.

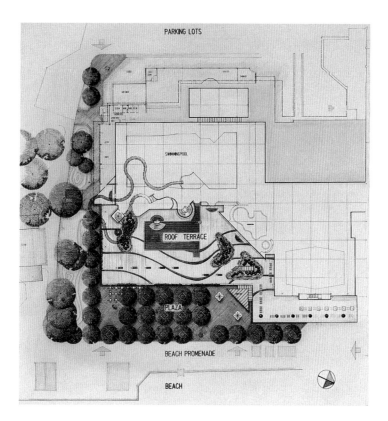

Plan view showing the various levels and zones.

Looking from the main entrance of the swimming pool towards the sea. Some of the relaxing chairs are fixed in position, others can be moved and stored.

The paving patterns in granite extend uninterrupted through the vegetation.

Cosmos plaza with
Toyama airport in the
background.

The tulip monument
refers to the plant's
cultivation locally.

1.10 *Toyama Airport Sports Plaza*

KEIKAN DESIGN INC.
(TOKYO BRANCH)
Toyama City, Japan

The construction of a sports plaza near the runways and terminal of Toyama Airport was commissioned in 1986 by the Japanese Ministry of Construction, the Environmental Pollution Service Corporation and Toyama Prefecture. The client (the Environmental Pollution Service Corporation) wished to enliven and improve the area with a modern facility that included a much-needed leisure centre. A sports complex with gymnasium and track is part of the site.

As is common practice in Japanese landscape projects, symbolism is important and the landscape architect was asked to design a park that would be representative of both the airport terminal and Toyama City itself. Keikan Design's main goal was to make the park part of the lives of the terminal users and local population, making best use of the natural and human resources available. Images of Toyama reflected in the design concept are Mount Tateyama, the flow of the Jintsu River, the Tonami Plains, the Koshi Pine Groves and the famous local tulips. An added dimension was that the design will also be seen from the air.

The park is divided into different areas, or plazas, whose geometric shapes are a softer version of those seen in the airport itself. These plazas relate to nature or tradition, as can be seen from their names: Rainbow, Green, Cosmos, Grove and Angel. The latter, based on an old folk tale of an angel who came down to earth for a while and left angel clothes in the branches of a pine tree, is in the traditional Japanese style with rocks carefully arranged in sand to represent a beach, planted with pine trees. The Cosmos Plaza focuses on a spiral effect created with two-colour paving to represent the flow of the Jintsu River and the eternal circling nature of the cosmos. A stone tulip monument has been erected in its centre, a reminder that tulips are grown commercially in this area in spring. Perhaps the most spectacular part of the design is the Rainbow Plaza. Placed in a striped paving are seven-colour pipes of different heights and shapes, rather like old-fashioned giant candy sticks to Western eyes. These pipes function as sprinklers in summer and, as a result of the very cold weather, and frequency of snow, generate steam in winter, lending an air of mystery to the plaza. Even when snow covers the striped paving, the bright colours of the pipes add life and warmth to their surroundings and show even more clearly the contrast between artifice and nature.

Seasonal colour is an integral part of Keikan's scheme with a green carpet in summer, red and orange in autumn and white for winter. Hard materials used include brick, washed pebbles, ceramic tiles, cast-stone concrete slabs and gas pipes. Except for during the winter snows, there are always some flowers in bloom. Hedges of *Boxus mycrophylla* (Japanese box) enclose the flowerbeds and, although yet to reach maturity, add winter interest. The back-drop to the whole design is the Tateyama Mountain, an ancient landmark in contrast to the modern site. The landscape designer compares it to a gold leaf Japanese screen, with the park as the natural theme with which such screens were traditionally decorated.

The modern airport complex, with its park and leisure centre, has proved an exciting addition to the lives of the local people, who are free to use the park in whatever way they please. The landscape architect hopes that his design will be seen as forward-looking while observing tradition, and that it will project an image of modern Toyama as well as providing enjoyment, repose and peace to those using the airport.

The Rainbow Plaza features multicolour pipes of different heights and shapes.

Start on site: April 1989
Handover: December 1989
Site area: 6 hectares (15 acres)

47

A railway footbridge over the Bassin de Savigny, constructed in pinewood, is designed to carry pedestrians and horses towards the forest.

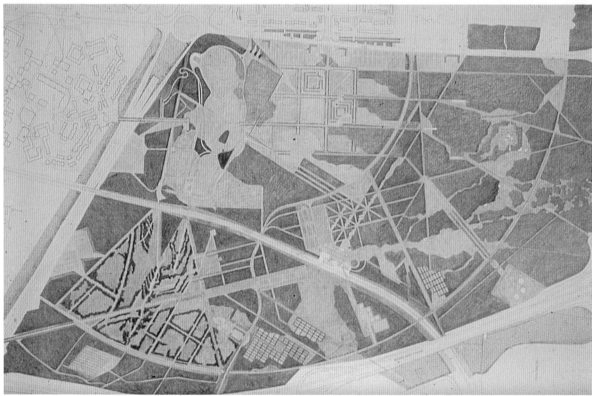

Master plan of the park in the pre-project phase, 1980.

1.11 *Parc Sausset*

MICHEL AND CLAIRE CORAJOUD
Paris, France

On the north-east outskirts of Paris, between Charles de Gaulle and Le Bourget airports, lies a rich agricultural plain where maize and corn were once produced. By 1980, changes in agricultural requirements left the Seine Saint Denis Department with 200 hectares (495 acres) of unused land on its hands. It was decided that a regional park should be created and it says much for the Department Council that, by September 1981, the designers Michel and Claire Corajoud were able to see work start on site.

The client's main requirement was that the park should be adaptable to as many uses as possible and that the planning brief should allow for the development and satisfaction of needs and uses not apparent today. It was also suggested that the old forest of Bordy, cleared over many centuries to create cornfields, should be reconstituted in spirit if not in its original form. Specific problems faced by the designers were the unplanned growth of suburbs in eastern Paris and the destruction of the site's unity over the years by railways and roads. Fortunately, in spite of the proximity of the two airports, noise is not a problem, since Parc Sausset is sufficiently distant from them and outside the noise cone they create.

View of one of the railway paths as it passes under a planted bank which crosses the park from north to south to finish in a terrace overlooking the park.

Start on site: September 1981
Handover: In progress
Site area: 200 hectares (494 acres)

The artificially created marsh provides a habitat for aquatic plants and birds.

The designers knew that it was important to restore the unity of the area and to reconcile the suburbs with the park, so that it became a natural extension of them. Since the Corajouds did not wish to interfere with the good quality soil of the French plain by extensive ground modelling, vegetation was to be the main element of the park's structure, providing form and relief in an essentially flat area. Two-thirds of the site were to be turned into woodland and meadows, while the individual areas of the park were to be linked with vistas, glades and an extensive network of footpaths, which has the effect of drawing people from one area to another.

A railway station is situated in the middle of the park and around it the four landscape types chosen by the designers are arranged. The re-creation of the forest was a priority, since its area dominates the plateau and was designed to provide variation in scale, shelter from the wind and to hide the source of road noise. The latter aim has been achieved by planting thick clumps of mixed evergreen and deciduous trees. A system of axes directs the eye to distant views, contrasting with intimate zones that have been created by glades and planted slopes. Species were chosen for appropriateness to the area and for speedy growth: oak, beech, ash, scots pine, maple, hornbeam, wild cherry, lime and alder. Homogeneous clumps are surrounded by other species, with edges composed of three levels of shrubs which vary in density. To gain as much growing time as possible, 300,000 trees were planted in the first phase of work in 1982. They will require thinning and are protected during establishment by a temporary enclosure.

The rising ground to the south of the park lends itself to the installation of children's play equipment.

An open area of meadowland lies immediately below the forest plateau, with both agricultural and horticultural planting. The third area is in the form of a grove with a children's farm. Finally, an urban park marks the interface with the city of Aulnay bordering the west line of the park. An existing pond has been enlarged to form a lake and an adjacent swamp is now an ornithological reserve, sheltering many aquatic birds. In order to protect the wildlife, it has been made inaccessible to the public but can be viewed from two terraces and a high esplanade.

Landscape styles to be found within the park are the *patte d'oie* ('goose foot'), one of the principal axes that provides the main entrance to the urban park from the south, copses, hedges and groves, interspersed with slices of cultivated land. Sand paths and rustic masonry contrast with steel structures, such as the pergola, which acts as an access route to the park as well as supporting climbing plants. It also defines two small squares: one for young children, with a giant sand bucket, the other for adults to play *boules*. Advantage has been taken of mounds and banks in the southern area of the park to install play equipment for children, such as long slides. A yew labyrinth has also been planted in this area but is still immature. Furniture has been carefully designed to form an urban link where the park and town merge. It is important to remember that, although five phases have been completed, work on Parc Sausset is still in progress, with a sixth underway and a seventh on the drawing board. Nevertheless, it is now possible to gain some idea of its future appearance and for the client to see the results of its financial outlay. There is still much to be done but users have already taken over the park's different spaces, and associations have been formed to protect areas such as the swamp and the historic groves. The decision to keep the planning as flexible and open as possible means that Parc Sausset can evolve according to the needs and requirements of its users. The people of the region are already demonstrating that a regional park adds a quality to life not obtainable from neglected farmland and uncontrolled urban sprawl.

The steel pergola in the urban park. As well as supporting climbing plants, it separates recreation areas for adults and children.

Opposite One of a series of ladders linking the avenues with the higher ground. This one is shown before the installation of the handrail.

An arrangement of
stones is used to mark
out garden areas
between paths with
trees and fallen leaves.

For over 300 years, Imari has been famous in Japan for the manufacture of traditional pottery, based on the plentiful supply of natural resources from the Kurohige Mountain and the surrounding area. However, when modern industry began to destroy the character and culture of the town, it was decided that action should be taken to restore the balance.

Although Imari pottery and ceramics can be purchased in Tokyo, it was considered essential for the survival of the industry that tourists should be attracted to Imari itself. The way ahead was, paradoxically, to bring back the craft-based enterprise of earlier years, emphasizing the special characteristics of Imari products. The alternative was bleak – to be just another small industrial town, mass-producing its wares for a largely indifferent market. Zen's philosophy in tackling this problem was to be both economical and inspirational. A ceramic park was to be created as both a showcase and a museum for the pottery trade, as well as, of course, an attraction for visitors to the area.

Mountains of discarded pottery and firing rejects were reused to provide the foundations for the park. The plan was to create the park from recycled ceramics and locally available materials. It was to be very much a home-made park, involving anyone and everyone who wished to contribute. Many retired potters came to help, each representing a small family business that had been in existence for generations and had perhaps been overshadowed by modern mass-production methods. As well as contributing broken materials for the construction work, they were able to advise on traditional ideas and techniques. At first, the older generation found it difficult to grasp the new concept of a ceramic park but it was not long before a dialogue between the generations was established. Traditional kilns, studios and workshops employing traditional techniques and materials were used by Zen to create the modern park. A wall was turned into a mosaic artwork by imaginative use of pieces of discarded pottery and other old materials.

1.12 *Nabeshima Ceramic Park*

ZEN ENVIRONMENTAL DESIGN
Imari City, Japan

A mosaic wall is softened by the use of curves.

The park contains a museum with collections of old tools, models of kilns and similar artefacts, while an old workshop has been recreated. An open-air exhibition park has been developed, as well as an area where visitors may try their skill at creating pottery works. The park's spectacular natural surroundings add greatly to its attraction, particularly in a country where nature and its seasonal changes are so much appreciated. Ceramic Park has succeeded in bringing tourists back into the town. Since its opening, visitor numbers have increased tenfold and pottery sales have risen considerably, encouraging potters to experiment with new designs in some cases. What was a rather enclosed and conservative industrial area is now opening out, showing and sharing its skills, and in turn becoming receptive to an exchange of ideas and innovative concepts.

The local population is enthusiastic about its new park, which is seen as an appropriate symbol of the area and its industry, creating harmony between new and old and perhaps helping Imari to face the twenty-first century positively. In contemporary high-technology Japan, the reassertion of traditional methods, carefully blended into a forward-looking scheme, is heartening. Even more important is the involvement of ordinary people of all ages in creating Ceramic Park, especially the contribution of the elderly and retired to the future of their town.

A typical park street, again showing use of locally available materials and the relationship to planting.

An open-space area has been created from old ceramics, with mosaic benches, paving and sculptural shapes.

Start on site: 1983
Handover: March 1986
Site area: 15,000 square metres
(161,463 square feet)

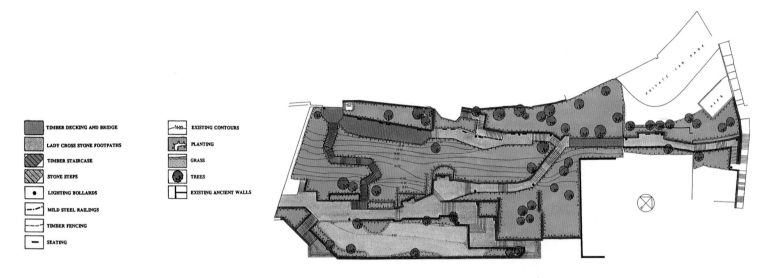

TIMBER DECKING AND BRIDGE

LADY CROSS STONE FOOTPATHS

TIMBER STAIRCASE

STONE STEPS

LIGHTING BOLLARDS

MILD STEEL RAILINGS

TIMBER FENCING

SEATING

EXISTING CONTOURS

PLANTING

GRASS

TREES

EXISTING ANCIENT WALLS

Timber, sandstone, brick and reconstituted stone copings are the principal materials used at the site. The mild-steel railings were designed by the landscape architect for the site.

This view along the 45-degrees slope illustrates the way in which the stairs and platforms carefully interlock and become an important new feature in this urban landscape.

1.13 *Hanging Gardens*

ANTHONY WALKER AND PARTNERS
Newcastle-upon-Tyne, UK

The site of this park lies along the line of a short section of Newcastle's old city walls. It had long suffered neglect and, at the time of appraisal, was a crumbling and derelict plot which had been passed by in recent phases of the city development. Nevertheless, the land immediately raised the interest of the designer, not only because of its historic associations, still apparent in the masonry and foundations, but also because of the challenge posed by the 45-degree slope. The brief supplied by the client, Tyne and Wear Development Corporation, called for an urban park which recognized and retained existing historical features, particularly the remains of the city wall. Public access had to be improved through the construction of footpaths, steps, ramps, bridges and retaining walls. The site overlooks the River Tyne and gives impressive views of the river and the main city bridges. The client required that the site should link with the adjacent riverside walk along the north bank of the River Tyne, which connects several long flights of steps running between the quayside and the higher level of the castle area. Otherwise, the Development Corporation (a government-sponsored authority independent of local government councils), which was charged with commercially revitalizing this specific urban area, sensibly gave an open brief to the designers to exploit the site in the most exciting way possible. Taking advantage of this, the designers have avoided viewing the slope and site conditions as a constraint, inhibiting the expression of design appropriate to an attractive and utilized urban park. Instead, the changes in level have been perceived as a dramatic experience emphasized by cantilevered walkways and viewing platforms.

On excavation, the steep slope proved to be fairly unstable, with many of the old walls due for inclusion in the design solution proving to be unsafe. The excavations also revealed remains of defunct buildings, foundations and unexpected cavities. These required new, sound foundations in order to be retained and soil-stabilization fabric mats were introduced on other slopes. This process required ingenuity and cooperation between designers and contractors during the whole contract period. It also explains why 85 per cent of the landscape contract costs were given over to hard treatment, much of which undoubtedly disappeared into footings and retaining walls. The designers' vision was for planting to cascade down a series of horizontal platforms linked by steps. The trees include weeping willow, ash, oak, flowering cherries and poplars, planted with flowering and scented evergreen shrubs and herbaceous plants. Due to the steepness of the slopes, everything was done by hand.

Gleefully and affectionately acclaimed in the local press as Newcastle's answer to the hanging gardens of Babylon, this scheme is a tribute to the ability of a designer to make something significant out of an unprepossessing subject. The appeal of this scheme surely lies in this, rather than in a particularly enlightened client or substantial resources for rehabilitation and landscape development. Many eyesores of worn-out neighbourhoods could disappear, with a similar enlightened policy, linked to the sensitivity and enthusiasm of a designer. In time this scheme will settle into its locality, and already it appears to be finding favour with the public, who visit the rapidly regenerating quayside environment, particularly at weekends. A heavy responsibility rests with the Tyne and Wear Development Corporation who maintain the hanging gardens, to prevent a gradual decay settling back into this public space, while simultaneously enabling the whole scheme to mature and blend with separate parts of the riverside walk.

The success of the scheme lies as much in the geometry of the retaining walls and timber platform as in the planting on the bank. A bridge over the River Tyne can be seen in the background.

Start on site: January 1989
Handover: November 1990
Site area: 0.6 hectares (1½ acres)

The rushing, spray-driven water in a simulated boulder-strewn stream at the head of the pool contrasts with the shallows gently flowing around the large spherical boulders.

1.14

BOFFA MISKALL PARTNERS
Manukau City, New Zealand

Manukau Court

Manukau City Council's brief for this plaza was to provide a focus and major feature within the city centre by creating an attractive space which would encourage people to gather within it. The designers were particularly conscious of the strong cultural connections that Manukau has with Polynesia and wanted this identity to be evident in the design. The surrounding existing buildings presented a major challenge, as it proved difficult to relate the components of the proposed Manukau Court to their varied scales and functions. Additionally, road access, parking and ground drainage proved to be major constraints that had to be resolved in the early planning of this large, pedestrianized court.

Apart from creating a defined space to attract people, the design needed to be capable of being extended and integrated with adjacent buildings and the spaces between them. Although the circular design of the court does not relate to any individual building, the striking geometric pattern of paving and terraces has effectively drawn the buildings together into a cohesive whole. The surface pattern uses a simplified motif often found in Maori wood carvings, the spiral shape adapted to emphasize and direct movement within the square. The herringbone paving uses a common South Pacific weaving pattern and the striking sitting stones were inspired by the unique South Island Moeraki Boulders. These geological curiosities were formed some 60 million years ago on the seabed by the accumulation of lime salts around a core. The boulders were subsequently buried in soft mudstone and were eventually revealed by the weathering of the sea. The simulated boulders are 60 centimetres (23½ inches) in diameter and constructed in reinforced concrete. The designers introduced the boulders as an alternative to traditional, bench-type seats. Both boulders and terraces are constructed of precast concrete units coated in a local aggregate, glued to the surface of the concrete. The colour reflects the dominant earth colours found throughout this region of New Zealand.

Water flows around the boulders, and a series of water jets at the head of the pool, set in among boulders, creates an impression of a white-water mountain stream. The recycled pool water also captures surface run-off from the extensive paved areas. The profile of the pool is a very gentle slope leading to a maximum depth of 30 centimetres (11¾ inches). This encourages children and adults alike to explore freely the world of the Moeraki Boulders. Conceived as neither sculpture, fountain nor decorative pool, this simple composition combines the delights of all in a relaxed but symbolic manner. The designers have seen possibilities beyond the simple compartments so often planned in public space.

On one side of Manukau Court, shade canopies suggest a series of sails, characteristic of Auckland, the City of Sails. They add another, valuable, three-dimensional element to the design which otherwise is very dependent on the striking boulders and ground-level patterns.

Manukau Court is popular for relaxation and the design anticipates varied use by a wide range of people at different times of the day and evening.

Commissioned: Assessment in 1983 led to full commission in 1984
Implemented: March-December 1986
Site area: Approximately 11,000 square metres (118,406 square feet)

The aerial view of the Court clearly shows how the firm lines in paving and terrace flow outward from the pool to meet the buildings and fill the space in between.

A geological curiousity, the Manukau Boulders, provided the inspiration for the pool feature.

Opposite Strong, confident planting helps frame the Court, particularly where the surrounding buildings do not enclose this space. Native cabbage tree (*Cordyine*

australis) and flax (*Phormium tenax*) create a well-ordered composition. Irrigation is provided by an automatic system installed throughout the development.

Trees and shrubs are held back largely to the periphery of the court, but in time will give a welcome framework of mass and shade.

The scheme has succeeded in drawing on an individual source in a sensitive way, without crudely apeing the original inspiration. It is an unusual expression of public-space design and avoids the pitfall of being yet another uninspiring example of international style. The proof of its appeal appears to be in the way Manukau Court has been adopted in the first few years. The city council frequently organizes outdoor events, particularly utilizing the amphitheatre, and allowing the shops fronting the court to take fresh or expanding roles reflecting the needs of those gathering within and visiting the city square.

Paving and structural detailing with museum and fountain basin in the background.

Plan of Grand Mall Park, showing the strict geometrical planting arrangements.

1.15

TOKYO LANDSCAPE
ARCHITECTS INC.
Yokahama City, Japan

Grand Mall Park

Night view of the
meandering stream in
the lower level plaza
with illuminated
planting.

First opened in 1859, with a European settlement, the international port of Yokahama has perhaps been more open to Western influences than most Japanese cities. Yokahama Bay City is a huge development still in progress in preparation for the twenty-first century, for which Grand Mall Park forms a symbolic focus. It is surrounded by office, residential, civic and cultural buildings and forms the hub of the city's administrative centre. The mild climate lends itself to the designers' intention that the public should be able to relax in this open space both by day and in the evening and at all seasons of the year. Located at the end of a pedestrian mall, it also acts as a round-the-clock park, bringing life and relaxation to a busy urban district. The various elements of the Grand Mall are intended for casual or specific use, individual recreation or large-scale organized events.

The landscape designers decided that the site's linear position in front of the City Art Museum called for a symmetrical layout. The resulting scheme combines a formal forecourt to the museum with small pocket-park plazas flanking the formal area. Closest to and in direct parallel with the museum's frontage are two identical basins separated by a low stage structure and edged with water jets. Water is an important element in the design, which also reflects Yokahama's proximity to the sea. Embedded in the formal paving in front of the basins are solar-powered light sources. At night, the combination of the illuminated pavement and edge lighting to the basins' cascades provides a powerful dramatic effect, referred to by the Japanese as *Yakokai* or 'night shining sea'. To add to the drama, ninety-six speakers have been set into the ground, relaying the sounds of waves and wind. Extending the marine analogy, lighting for the amphitheatre and outdoor stage was based on a lighthouse. Separating this plaza from the road, symmetrically planted trees form a shady area for strolling.

At either side of this 'grand' entrance space, a series of stepped areas and planted terraces drop down to street level. These, although generally similar in layout, have varying arrangements of detail: cascades tumbling down steps into streams, meandering in one pocket-park, straight in another; seating; small garden structures; coloured paving patterns; neat angular lawns, and more trees again symmetrically planted into the paving.

Grand Mall Park provides a busy and growing city development with an elegant frontage for its art museum and also enables its users to retain some contact with nature in the middle of an urban environment.

The effect of the
'Yakokai' ('night
shining sea') is
produced by
illuminated pavements
and fountains.

Start on site: April 1990

1.16

GILLES VEXLARD AND LAURENCE
VACHEROT, LATITUDE NORD
Parc de la Villette, Paris, France

Le Jardin du Jardinage

When in August 1982 a competition was launched by the government-sponsored Établissement Public du Parc de la Villette for a new park in the Île-de-France, north east of Paris, Gilles Vexlard's submission was a strong contender for the prize. As is well known, the competition attracting some 800 entries was won outright by the Swiss-French architect Bernard Tschumi. However, once the park was under construction, three thematic gardens were planned within the park to be designed by other designers, one of these being Latitude Nord's Jardin du Jardinage – Sequence 3. (The other two are by Alexandre Chemetoff and Kathryn Gustafson.) Vexlard's garden is centrally situated, just to the north of the Grand Hall and south of the canal, and is bounded to the north by the meandering Promenade Cinématique and to the south by an avenue of trees forming the southern perimeter of a circular grass prairie. This circle, bisected by the canal, is one of the geometric shapes incorporated into Tschumi's design for la Villette and delineated by lines of trees.

The designers see the Sequence 3 garden as a product of the site's geography, a cultivated meander locked between two walkways and shaded by standard trees. The programme required the creation of recreational space for the public. Because of the non-traditional nature of la Villette's overall concept, a traditional garden seemed inappropriate. Instead the site aims to embody the idea of gardening, with, however, only a minimal amount of actual gardening and plant-growing taking place. The Jardin du Jardinage is seen as a showcase for exhibiting the results of gardening, having more in common with a garden centre or flower market than the vegetable patch. Certain elements associated with gardening, such as the individual relationship between gardener and garden, and the gardener's own mental constraints, such as using lines and rows, had to be changed. Although the soil's type, slope and exposure (or lack of it) to the sun limited the options available, particularly in this latitude, Vexlard wished to open out the whole concept of domestic gardening. Logical patterns were to be substituted for random choice: the most efficient combination for the best crop results being quadrangular forms.

The site posed some contradictions that had to be faced: it was a shaded area that should have been in the sun; a domestic space in a public place; a collective purpose for an individual activity; complex shapes which ideally should be simple; and, despite its location at the centre of the park, a lonely spot. Latitude Nord set about dealing with these problems. A climbing vine has been installed at la Villette's highest point to restore horizontality, while the ground level has been managed by a counterpoint of terraces which break down and amplify the cinematic walkabout slope. (Tschumi's view of cinema as a twentieth-century art has

An example of the
planted terraces.

Start on site: July 1987
Handover: March 1988
Site area: 1500 square metres
(16,146 square feet)

View of the garden from the Promenade Cinematique, a reference to the designer's interest in film.

Site plan, showing the curving pathway.

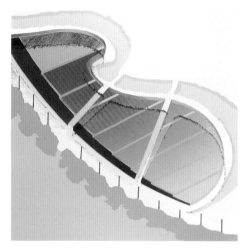

inspired his vision of the park as a sequence of filmic images, although whether or not the cinema is still an appropriate symbol for the twenty-first century is open to debate.)

Elements such as layout, rows, fountains, poles refer back to gardening, reflecting the regular order of the plants, while perennials or ferns have started colonizing the terraced walls and the planting joint at the foot of the enclosing wall. The southern slope is planted with box. There are various references to filmic qualities. On each of the walls supporting the terraces, marble-mouthed fountains spew water into gutters (from where it is recirculated) and are illuminated at night. All the walls are capped with Carrara marble. The posts have an inclination of 4 degrees and are linked by rust-proof cables capable of supporting climbing plants: some of them are topped with mirrors intended as a decoy or lure. Black concrete paving marked with aluminium joints is designed to absorb the sun. The basics, perforation of soil exposing earth, holes in walls exposing water, empty rows exposing light are present. Colour and volume have yet to be added in containers and bunches to combine with rhythms, steps and shade to create layers of complexity and finally justify the care invested in this well-ordered garden for the next century.

In relation to la Villette's general programme of development, the Jardin du Jardinage will also be used as an outdoor exhibition space for the nearby Gardening House. It has already become an active and dynamic space enjoyed by visitors. Whether ordinary members of the public appreciate the garden in terms of its theoretical concept remains to be seen.

CAD-generated visualization, showing how metal and cable pergolas will be covered by the planting, providing a horizontal dimension.

1.17 *Shinagawa Ward Park*

AI LANDSCAPE PLANNING CO. LTD.
Tokyo, Japan

The rock-strewn torrent
of channelled water
contrasts with the
mirror-like reflections
of the calm open water.

This district of Tokyo is primarily commercial and industrial, interspersed with residential apartments. It has suffered severely from industrial pollution and the impact of traffic and highways. Population density is very high and Shinagawa has until recently offered very little open space or an effective policy to green the existing urban area, compared with many other districts of Tokyo.

The client, Shinagawa Ward Office, determined to improve the image and the environment of the district by creating a new urban park. Apart from providing a much-needed open space, the brief expected the designer to establish a link with the marine past which Shinagawa has gradually lost in its industrial and commercial growth.

For many centuries, Shinagawa had a close relationship with the sea and the designer has attempted to recapture this through an unusual programme of water features. In particular, a sculpture of three whales recalls a piece of local history, when the whales strayed into Shinagawa Bay in the nineteenth century. The sculpture is also a fountain, symbolizing both the water spouts from the whales and also the close affinity with the sea. The fountain is programmed to give different water displays, including spray mist, a candle and a powerful jet. The pattern is repeated in twenty-minute cycles, resembling spouting whales in the sea. The smooth flow of water is deliberately interrupted to emphasize the unpredictability of the sea – from maelstrom and chaotic rushing water, to more tranquil displays. The landscape architect felt that it was important to show the many faces of the sea to an urban population increasingly divorced from contact with it, even though the sea is close by.

This marine theme is seen in the whole park, which is in the shape of a corridor 1000 metres (3281 feet) long. Essentially a green oasis for neighbourhood recreation and relaxation, Shinagawa Park tends to turn its back on the surroundings with screening mounds and a 'green belt' of planting around the perimeter. There was also a requirement to provide sports facilities and greenways threading through the park to link up the formal and informal elements.

The strongest and most remarkable feature of the park is the lake, which also draws its inspiration from the sea. Sea water is used, of which 15,000 tons is stored and purified in a tank. Following the cycle of the tides, the purified water fills the lake and is then allowed to drain to the sea at the time of the ebb tide. It is a conscious effort to increase awareness of the natural environment in the residents of Shinagawa. 3000 tons of natural stones have been used to create the shoreline. With such an emphasis on the sea and hydrological engineering, it is hardly surprising that 70 per cent of the available budget has been used on hard landscape.

So often urban park design in whatever culture, attempts to impose external values on the physical landscape. Here it is an unusual design statement, in which the landscape architect has used dramatic licence in an attempt to encourage visitors to the park to rediscover their connections with the local natural environment. It is a touch of theatre. That it succeeds must be partially measured by the fact that it is proving very popular with the client and residents, and that the values of adjacent properties have increased significantly since the park opened.

The mist-like quality of
the fountain fascinates
visiting children and
contrasts with the more
furious cycle in the
water programme.

Start on site: 1982
Handover: 1987
Site area: Approximately 10 hectares (25 acres)

The design of the Tin Han Temple Park called for great sensitivity in integrating the functional temple complex.

1.18

DENTON CORKER
MARSHALL PTY LTD.
Tsuen Wan New Town, Hong Kong

Tsuen Wan Parks and Playgrounds

One of Hong Kong's first new towns, developed in response to mass migration from post-war China, Tsuen Wan suffers from incredible housing densities unrelieved by landscape architecture. DCM was faced with two very separate sites of limited size left over after major engineering works. The situation was further complicated by geotechnical constraints, poorly coordinated mass service lines (a result of fast track new town development), a total absence of topsoil and natural vegetation, and a minimal budget. Not surprisingly, civic and geotechnic engineers were involved in all stages of design and hydraulic engineers contributed to the development of water features.

The Hong Kong Government's brief required a wide range of sometimes conflicting uses. These included all-weather sports pitches, a five-a-side football pitch, an historic temple site, an amphitheatre, and informal play areas, all on a site of 8500 square metres (91,496 square feet) with a 3-metre (10-foot) level change in two directions across the site. The design scheme contained two parks, consisting of the temple site and the Kwok Shui Road site, which is effectively a roof garden over an underground mass-transit station.

The designers faced a range of cultural and technical problems. The integration of a functioning temple complex called for great sensitivity, while dense planting at a depth of only 60 centimetres (23½ inches) on the roof of the station with a very restricted load tolerance required considerable technical skills. Added to this was the difficulty of service access to the site because of steep slopes to the north. The hot, humid climate makes shade desirable, but cooling breezes from the west and south are to be encouraged. Heavy storms bring high rainfall during the summer months and structures need to be strong enough to withstand typhoons.

Faced with what seemed like an impossible site, DCM's only option was to develop a flexible response for the multi-functional spaces, using a dense green oasis and colour to enliven an otherwise grey landscape, based on concrete, to which the designers were limited by availability of construction skills and materials. It was therefore decided to incorporate cheap, hard-wearing, but high-quality detailing using materials that could be thoroughly understood by local craftsmen.

A strong, brightly coloured design vocabulary was employed for the detailing of minor buildings, pergolas, walls and seating. The use of simple, easily read geometric forms (based on Confucian symbols of squares, circles and triangles) became a unifying device for the many disparate elements within the design.

Primary colours have been used for structural features to enliven the otherwise grey landscape.

Start on site: 1984
Handover: 1985
Site area: 8,500 square metres (91,496 square feet)

Pergola and shade
garden in the Tai Wo
Han Park.

An illusion of space has been created through winding walkways, using levels and
dense planting for spatial differentiation. Structures are deliberately playful, in the style of
Takafumi Aida's toy block houses, to provide contrast with the drab reality of Tsuen Wan.
They are also designed for minimum maintenance and, of course, to withstand the rigours of
the climate. All retaining walls are in-situ concrete with Shanghai plaster rendered in different
tones, with ceramic tiles and acrylic paint for external use. Paving is generally of precast,
exposed concrete aggregate with varying tints. Topsoil is extremely scarce in Hong Kong, so
soils fabricated from a mixture of decomposed granite gravel and commercial conditioners are
used for planting beds. The humidity of the climate ensures that plants grow very quickly so
that mulches are unnecessary.

DCM feels that it has satisfactorily achieved all of the brief's requirements within budget
and programme, with a final 70:30 ration of hard to soft landscape. As the main open space in
Tsuen Wan New Town, it has no competition and is well used, although there have been
minor problems with vandalism. For instance, quality light fittings have been stolen, while poor
quality replacements have been left untouched. However, the citizens of Tsuen Wan may
now enjoy a number of green oases within this harsh urban environment, described by the
designers as the ultimate concrete jungle.

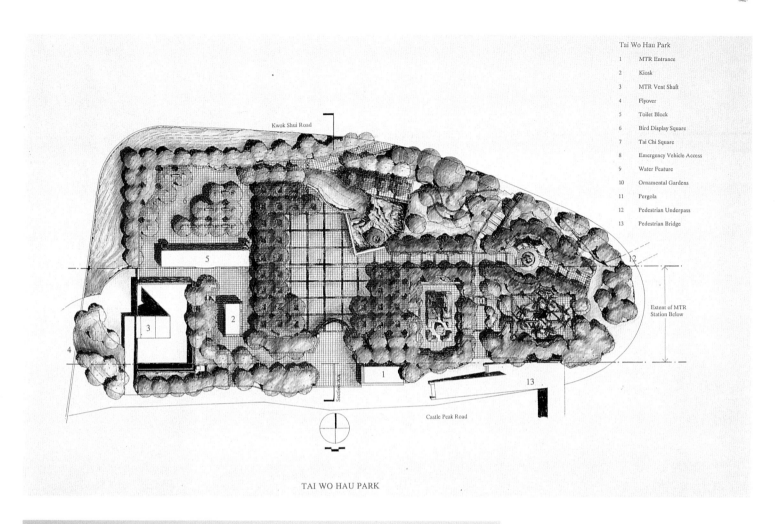

Tai Wo Hau Park

1   MTR Entrance

2   Kiosk

3   MTR Vent Shaft

4   Flyover

5   Toilet Block

6   Bird Display Square

7   Tai Chi Square

8   Emergency Vehicle Access

9   Water Feature

10   Ornamental Gardens

11   Pergola

12   Pedestrian Underpass

13   Pedestrian Bridge

TAI WO HAU PARK

Plan of Tai Wo Hau Park.

View of the Tai Wo Hau Park gardens over the mass transit railway station, with their dense planting.

1.19 *Charleston Waterfront Park*

SASAKI ASSOCIATES INC.
Charleston, South Carolina, USA

Hard-detailing of seats, lamps and railings along the promenade echoes old Charleston, while below the sea wall are the salt marsh grasses.

Charleston is a small and coherent community with a history of maritime commercial activities. Over the years, shipping facilities have been relocated and the old port has fallen into disuse and decay. In 1970 the newly elected Mayor, Joseph P. Riley, Jnr, started a campaign to restore prosperity to the old docklands and create a waterfront park for the recreation of Charleston's citizens, as well as for tourists. He launched ten years of fundraising and planning, commissioning a design team from Sasaki Associates, led by Stuart Dawson, to prepare an urban-design master plan for the historic waterfront area.

After a five-hour walk through Charleston, led by Mayor Riley, the Sasaki landscape team drew up the following list of overall goals for the new park. These were to:

- *provide impetus for investment in urban revitalization.*
- *create an important open space for residents and visitors.*
- *enhance awareness of the historic, cultural and geographic significance of Charleston's waterfront.*
- *create a dynamic environment appropriate to the colonial architecture of the historic district.*
- *protect and enhance the sensitive marine ecology of the tidal river's edge.*
- *eliminate parking, overhead utilities and unnecessary streets on the site.*
- *provide a diversity of activity and plant materials that would respond to the seasonal variation of the climate.*

Before construction could begin, however, two new parking areas had to be created to relieve parking pressure on the site itself. Also, the poor soil conditions of the site necessitated a temporary fill with 2.7 metres (9 feet) of sand and wick drains for two years to stabilize the existing soil. This technique, although known in Europe, was relatively new in the US at the time. Briefly, wicks made of filter fabric were placed on a 1.5-metre (5-foot) grid covering the entire site and then covered by a 4.5-metre (15-foot) layer of soil. The extra weight squeezes the water from the soil, which is then drawn up by the wicks and drained into the river. This technique drains soft organic soils and consolidates their construction-bearing capacity.

A sea wall had to be constructed below the promenade to protect the site from the tidal river. The Coastal Council was concerned that the existing marsh grasses should remain undisturbed during the process. Inevitably, the salt marsh was affected during the removal of debris from the site and construction of the sea-wall foundations. However, following preliminary work the salt marsh was reconstructed and expanded to almost double its original area. Before the park was built, people were able to walk into the marsh from the shore, disturbing habitats and leaving rubbish. The design of the park separates park users from the marsh, although it is still possible to get close to the marsh along the sea wall and on the pier, while protecting the marine ecology of the marshland.

An unexpected set-back occurred with the destructive arrival of Hurricane Hugo only six

Local citizens take advantage of the promenade's facilities.

Start on site: January 1981
Handover: May 1990
Site area: 5 hectares (12 acres), including salt marsh

months before completion of the park was scheduled. Most of the planting was destroyed, but the careful design and engineering methods employed in the construction process ensured that other park elements remained intact. It says much for the determination of all involved that planting and repairs only postponed the opening by three months.

The historic and cultural context of schemes is always of importance to Sasaki Associates and this was a prime consideration in Charleston. Dawson knew that he had to maintain the broad view of the Cooper River and at the same time blend with the residential scale of the old city streets behind the park. This was to be achieved by leaving the water's edge uncluttered and planting the side of the park nearest to the city with hundreds of trees and nine small gardens. The intention was to evoke the traditional courtyards of many Charleston homes, just as the restoration of the neglected waterfront should rekindle the public's fascination with the sea.

To emphasize the relationship between city and sea, a 360-metre (1200-foot) promenade runs along the river, separating a community park from the restored salt marshes. The paved promenade has Charleston-style benches, decorative railings and lighting, and is lined with palmettos. The park area consists of two raised lawns which can be used for informal recreation and are separated from the promenade by a cast-stone seat wall. Cast stone – a form of cast concrete incorporating materials such as sand, rock, water and cement to simulate the colour and texture of limestone – was used because it is easy to cast, is less expensive than real stone, stronger and of greater density. This makes it more durable in a marine environment.

Probably the best-known sight is the Pineapple Fountain, Charleston's symbol of welcome and hospitality. This is situated between the recreation areas and is surrounded by formal bedding. The bowls of the fountain are manufactured from cast stone, while the central leaves are sculpted in bronze. The garden is surrounded by wisteria-covered trellis on three sides, with the fourth open to embrace the river view.

The historic city is now linked by the park with the waterfront, reuniting town and sea.

The Pineapple Fountain is seen here in its setting of formal raised bedding, flanked by lawns, with shade trees on the inland perimeters and palms lining the promenade. The pineapple – symbol of friendship and welcome – is a motif used frequently in Charleston itself in architectural details.

Opposite Aerial view
of Charleston and the
Waterfront Park
showing salt marshes,
pier and the
relationship of the city
to the Cooper River.

Diagrammatic plan of
the Charleston
Waterfront Park
showing flow of
movement and visual
direction from town to
sea.

General view of
Charleston Waterfront
Park, showing the
Vendue Fountain in the
foreground, with lawns
for informal recreation
and the riverfront
promenade.

On the city edge of the park, small, individually designed gardens are shaded by four rows of live oaks. The gardens are enclosed by holly hedges and each has its own distinctive benches, paving and central figure. The main entrance to Charleston Waterfront Park from the city is marked by the Vendue fountain, leading to Vendue Plaza. The plaza has more of the Charleston benches, bluestone paving and interpretive plaques describing four centuries of local history. From the plaza, the visitor is again drawn back to the coolness of the sea by a 120-metre (400-foot) wharf, with shade structures and porch-style swings, which is effectively an extension of the plaza. Deepwater fishermen are catered for by a 90-metre (300-foot) fishing pier across the end of the wharf, parallel to the shoreline and promenade.

Sasaki's achievement reflects the commitment of both designer and community. Careful, long-term planning has produced a master plan that has caught the spirit of old Charleston and given the city a contemporary park, catering for many tastes. Allowing the old city to expand through a series of gardens, gradually opening out into wider expanses of open space until the waterfront is reached, has successfully reunited the town and sea. However, major technical considerations had to be faced, such as closing an existing street which effectively separated the proposed park from the city. It says much for the persuasiveness of the design team and the vision of the mayor and the community that this was accepted. There is a depressing tendency for landscape design to take on a bland, international flavour but Dawson was determined that this should not happen here, that Charleston Waterfront Park should quite obviously relate to Charleston. All the evidence suggests that this aim has been achieved. Although it is perhaps too early, especially in a period of world-wide recession, to gauge the scheme's success in terms of investment impetus to Charleston, it has certainly revitalized a run-down area. In terms of amenity value, both the mayor, as client, and the general public have responded enthusiastically to their new park.

1.20 *Michinoku Lake Wood Park*

A detail of the ceramics, glass and stone used to create highly original patterns in the paving.

TAKANO LANDSCAPE
PLANNING CO. LTD.
Miyagi Prefecture, Japan

Lake Wood Park is situated in the north of Japan where the climate is very cold with a lot of snow in winter. The site is surrounded by beech forests covering the mountain sides in well-known and respected countryside. The client, a government construction department, wanted to create a lakeside park, sympathetic to the natural beauty and history of the region, which is an important centre for some of the oldest cultural traditions in Japan. The project was first considered in 1979 but took nearly five years to get on site. To understand the unusual nature of this project, one must relate it to the context of historic and contemporary Japanese garden design. Certain elements found in this park will be familiar, such as the reliance on boulders, but the greatest departures are in the enormous scale of the open area and the scarcity of plants within the centre of the park.

The landscape architect has attempted to give the park a sense of spaciousness to enhance visitors' awareness of the presence of nature. This is achieved through various subtle interpretations of a theme, radiating outward from the ground under one's feet to further views of tree-covered mountain slopes. The major source of inspiration for the repeating theme was the spiral of the ammonite-shell fossil. The focal point is an enormous basin in the shape of the ammonite shell, moulded subtly in stones laid in grass. The spiralling terraces are also deliberately reminiscent of the area's rice fields. Within this pattern, there are various smaller and more intricate designs within the floorscape, often reusing the ammonite shape.

The area is renowned for pottery, and ceramics have been extensively used in the detailed paving design. Broken ceramic pieces of many colours have been bedded alongside stone fragments in concrete, like a complex and incomplete mosaic. The placing of stones is a very traditional part of Japanese garden design. The landscape architect has boldly developed this principle on a scale which is unusual in Japan. There are sixty stones with the largest weighing approximately 70 tonnes. They were selected after several months' search of the nearby mountains. The search for and transport of the stones proved the most difficult aspects of the project. Size, colour and texture were all carefully assessed and each stone precisely positioned.

The rock garden within the park, like so many more traditional examples of Japanese garden design, is rich in symbol. In particular, the spiral and the far-flung stones record the continuing progress of time and the passage of the seasons. Each season produces different colours and length of shadow thrown by the stones, depending upon the height and position of the sun. The large stones on the west side are positioned to frame the rays of the setting sun. This is an intriguing design, which would find a place or parallel in many cultures. It also has a timeless quality about it. The restraint in form and materials is matched by the intricacy of pattern. Creativity in landscape is as much about a light touch as a heavy hand of intervention. Given the care and attention for which the Japanese gardeners are rightly famous, this composition of the late twentieth century will still delight in a hundred years or more.

The large stones are positioned to frame the rays of the setting sun.

Start on site: 1984
Handover: 1989
Site area: Approximately 10,000 square metres (107,642 square feet)

Plan view: the detail was worked out adjacent to the site using a one-tenth scale model.

One of the finely detailed ammonite paving patterns in which glass marbles add extra sparkle.

Some of the largest stones placed on the periphery of the coiled-shell pattern.

Contextural view.

84

Solana (see pages
106-111)

2 *Corporate & Commercial*

2.1 *IBM Federal Systems Division Facilities*

THE OFFICE OF PETER WALKER
Pasadena, Texas, USA

The water parterre, with radiating and curvilinear paths stretching out into the surrounding pine wood.

This project is the first phase in a master-plan in which IBM will bring together within one building complex all its services for the United States National Air and Space Administration (NASA). This phase involves a large crescent-shaped building, parking and extensive associated grounds, located on a level flood plain which is covered with open pine forest. When complete, the masterplan anticipates a second crescent-shaped building, constructed as a mirror image of the first. The office of Peter Walker was drawn in to the project only after the architects CRSS had already designed the postmodern building and its adjacent, rectilinear parking facility.

The geometry of the central axis and concentric paths in part draws inspiration from the building shape, and in part from the traditional Southern plantation manor house. It recalls a time of slow-moving gracious living, and a landscape of great spaciousness. This contrasts poignantly with the urgency and vastness of NASA. The designer in this minimalist landscape is, in his own words, exploring the formal qualities of flatness and horizontality. The pattern, which is largely expressed in two dimensions through decomposed granite footpaths, is of such an immense scale that it not so much subjugates the surrounding landscape, but embraces it. Walking one of the concentric paths, the curve is hardly apparent.

The curvilinear form is matched in both architecture and landscape.

Start on site: 1985
Handover: 1986
Site area: Phase I 12 hectares (30 acres)

The flat, regular water
channels contrast with
the marching ranks of
trees in the pine
woodland.

A view back along the
axial radiating path
towards the cupola-like
porch and terrace.

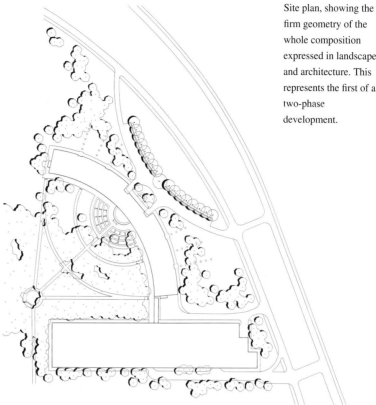

Site plan, showing the firm geometry of the whole composition expressed in landscape and architecture. This represents the first of a two-phase development.

The gently curving path, as an outpost of the building, threads through the margins of the pine wood.

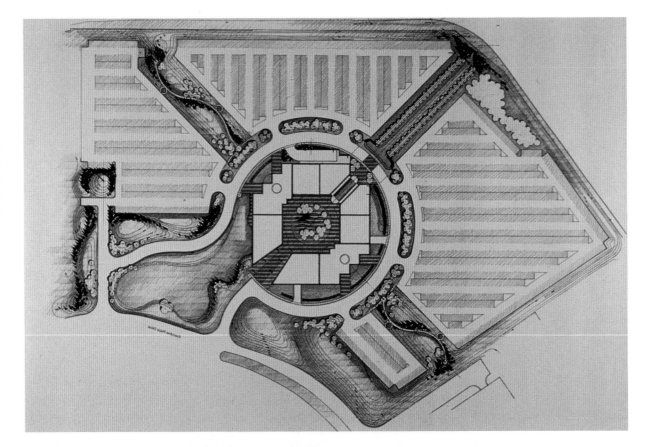

Site layout drawing, showing the plaza at the centre and linear planting radiating from the building into the campus.

The undulating grass-and-brick ribbon design, viewed from an upper floor of the office building.

The linear park radiates out from the autocourt within the U-shaped block.

2.2 *Regent Court Office Building*

RANDALL METZ, JOHN GRISSIM
AND ASSOCIATES
Ford Motor World Headquarters
Campus, Dearborn, Michigan, USA

The world headquarters of the Ford Motor Company is situated in Dearborn, Michigan. Regent Court is a 12-storey, 'U'-shaped office building on the Ford campus serving various divisions of the company. It encloses a central space creating a potentially bleak environment. In conjunction with the client, the landscape architect laid down some basic requirements for Regent Court. These included a scheme that would be attractive both at ground level and from all office levels, combining colour and year-round interest; that would integrate with the architecture and function as an autocourt, yet provide a visually inviting space, with or without activity. The client became very involved in the design process, showing great faith in the landscape firm's ability to develop an appropriate design for his site, and supported all design ideas put forward.

Working closely with the architects, Randall Metz went for a strong and simple design concept that responded to the architecture of the building and extended the park setting of the adjacent campus into Regent Court. Linear parks radiating from the office building break up the parking areas and link the building's entrance to the park both visually and physically, providing both a focal point and a pedestrian oasis at the hub. To assist in the design process, computer-generated shadow studies and microclimate models were developed.

Since the autocourt or plaza at the centre of the scheme was to be viewed from different levels, bold patterns, warm colours and plant material were used to modulate the scale of the building, provide texture and seasonal interest. The size of the building dictated the need for mature trees and the project designer personally selected 40-year-old Ginkgo Biloba trees. Chosen for their hardiness, architectural form, and brilliant yellow autumn colour, these were shipped from Princeton nurseries to Michigan with 300-centimetre (10-foot) root balls and transplanted.

The paved surface of the court leads into three-dimensional brick and grass ribbons which undulate to emphasize depth and shadow. They also provide perspective and create a sense of motion. The hard landscape of the plaza is constructed from wire-cut, clay-brick pavers in two colours, set into asphalt bedding on 15 centimetres (6 inches) of reinforced concrete. The side walls are clad with polished 'absolute black' granite. All drainage, both surface and subsurface, is designed to function with minimal visual impact. The simple design approach ensures that landscape maintenance is also minimal and can easily be handled by the Ford Motor Land Development Corporation's in-house maintenance staff.

This unusual approach to the design of an autocourt has met with a very positive response from its users. Regent Court encloses its plaza like a spider at the centre of a vast web, represented by the linear parks radiating from it to the natural confines of the campus. As the visitor is drawn into the court, the undulations and planting echo in miniature the larger scale of the campus landscape surrounding it. Conversely, the intimate landscape of the plaza opens out to the grander scale of the lawns and tree-covered hills. No one can be more aware of the continuing battle between the motor car and the environment than the Ford Motor Company. In commissioning this landscape scheme for its Regent Court Office Building, the company has made a positive attempt to come to terms with the problem within its own organization.

Flat and undulating strips with tree planting are shown in relationship to the building.

Start on site: Spring 1989
Handover: Autumn 1990
Site area: 14 hectares (34 acres)

91

The oval pergola, cafeteria patio and planted roof can be seen in the foreground. The surface car park is beyond the curtillage of the site.

Below Detail of landscape materials on the road frontage, with the metal frame encouraging vertical growth.

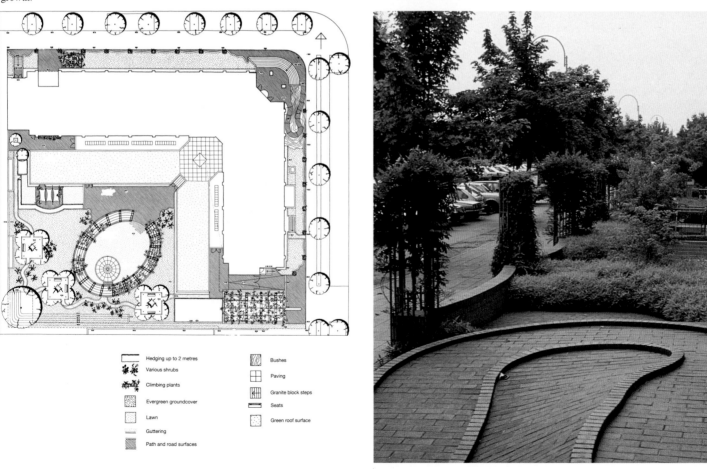

	Hedging up to 2 metres		Bushes
	Various shrubs		Paving
	Climbing plants		Granite block steps
	Evergreen groundcover		Seats
	Lawn		Green roof surface
	Guttering		
	Path and road surfaces		

2.3 R and V Versicherung, Administration Building

KARL BAUER
Karlsruhe, Germany

This office development is like many to be seen on street corners in cities around the world. It was destined to remain undistinguished until a landscape architect persuaded the client, an insurance company, to abandon the development plan to use the site for ground-level car parking for occupants of the adjacent building. Instead the client was convinced that an outdoor green space was a better, if more expensive, investment. As a result, the car park for the development is now underground, completely hidden beneath a new verdant courtyard. Access is via a ramp covered with an arched tubular metal frame, over which climbers are rapidly becoming established.

The adjacent seven-storey administrative building dominates the site, closing it off from the road on the east and north sides. This leaves the site open on the south and west, drawing sunlight into the main courtyard. The architects changed the interior spatial and functional layout of the building, so that the cafeteria, classrooms and the superintendent's residence are located on the ground floor, overlooking the garden. The courtyard is sub-divided by an oval pergola into three zones: cafeteria patio, designed to encourage users to spill outside; the lawn, with a glass pavilion for shelter, and the surrounding garden, with pathway and smaller spaces framed by dense planting of shrubs.

The soil depth is 40 centimetres (15¾ inches) and a specially prepared growing medium has been incorporated. To overcome the restrictions on size and height of plants caused by the limited soil depth, the designer has created a living wall of greenery (*Wisteria sinensis*) enfolding the oval pergola. This attractive vertical dimension helps sub-divide the garden while also strongly linking with the main point of egress from the building. The principal materials include red/blue paviors for the pathway beneath the pergola and patio area; a yellow-tone brick capped with red for the dwarf walls to marry in with the building materials, and yellow-grey gravel for the pathways within the garden beyond the pergola and as edging. Ground-cover planting includes *Vinca minor* and *Sasa pumila*, with lavender and sedum planted on the single-storey rooftop. The court is served by fixed-point irrigation of rainwater, but the rooftop has no extra water supply.

Although the original development proposal was fundamentally revised, the client has expressed his pleasure at the result and sees it as an excellent precedent for similar projects in the future. The outdoor areas are well used by the employees. The scheme demonstrates the huge visual and practical advantages of persuading a client to look beyond the most obvious solution. In this case, placing the car park underground has released a resource of immense value, which is now greatly appreciated by client and employees alike. The capital cost is higher, but the result must enhance the value of the total investment. The landscape design is sensible, not overly complicated and appears to make the most of what would otherwise be a very 'average' development.

Plants are rapidly covering the tubular metal structure over the entrance to the underground car park.

Start on site: May 1982
Handover: October 1985
Site area: Courtyard 1475 square metres (15,877 square feet); total landscaped area: 4430 square metres (47,685 square feet)

The illuminated
fountain provides a
feature for the night-
time plaza.

2.4 *Plaza Tower One*

HARGREAVES ASSOCIATES
Englewood, Colorado, USA

Situated only a short walk from an earlier Hargreaves project, Harlequin Plaza, is Englewood's Plaza Tower One. It comprises a courtyard and fountain for a 22-storey office building and low-rise retail development built on a 2.8-hectare (7-acre) site, being an early phase of a 32.4-hectare (80-acre) mixed development plan. The design of associated spaces includes retail space along parking garages, soft and hard plazas, a major fountain feature, an eating terrace and an associated public park fronting Interstate Highway 25.

The client is the real-estate arm of a major oil company whose intention was to install several hundred research scientists in the building, with remaining space leased on the open market. The client required a design that provided amenities for employees, tenants and the general public, while remaining compatible with the overall goals of the mixed-use master plan and art programme. The high-rise building and parking garage were to be used to frame two sides of the public plaza, which would be open to the 'friendly' side of the street but protected from the interstate highway and adjacent major arterial road.

The central feature of the landscape design is the Chevron fountain which, apart from being decorative, is an expression of the release of kinetic energy stored in oil shale below the earth's surface, a reference entirely familiar to the geologists working in the office building. The fountain is thus intended as a metaphor for the confluence of cultural and natural forces. It bisects the public space into a paved plaza for restaurant use and a grassy park with mountain view and water noises. In Harlequin Plaza, too, Hargreaves bisects the space, but with a colourful wall; he also made use of the mountain view as a distant focal point. The paved plaza flanks the retail façade and disguises vehicle circulation within its paving scheme. The second sector is green and meadow-like, with informal planting to frame views of the foothills of the Rocky Mountains. Sweeping seatwalls are designed to reflect the curving line of the street and its trees, and to act as protective barriers.

The fountain itself is composed of layers of river granite echoing the layers of the earth's substrata, cracking open along the top ridge to emit torrents of water and steam. Apart from its metaphorical nature, it also creates a stimulating and enjoyable environment. Its huge granite slabs seem to erupt from the rift between the formal paved plaza and informal 'meadow'. One side of the fountain responds to the symmetry of the building's entry and provides a reflective backdrop for the plaza's allée of trees and flowers. The images are multiplied in the deep emerald-green, polished-granite surface. The other side allows asymmetry and curvature to predominate on the side of the plaza with the softer, mountain view.

An eating terrace on the second storey incorporates evergreen and deciduous planting for various sun and shade exposures and offers seatwalls and benches built into planting walls. A large circular lawn, with concentric bands of paving forming a 'target' pattern, has been created for seminars and lunchtime gatherings. It also provides a space for art installations. More intimate meeting places have been created around the perimeter. Both plaza and terrace provide open space for daily lunchtime users, while the fountain creates a strong focal image appropriate to the nature of the building's major tenant.

This shows the relationship of the spiral and the 'target' lawn with the lower block.

Start on site: 1984
Handover: 1986
Site area: 2.8 hectares
(7 acres)

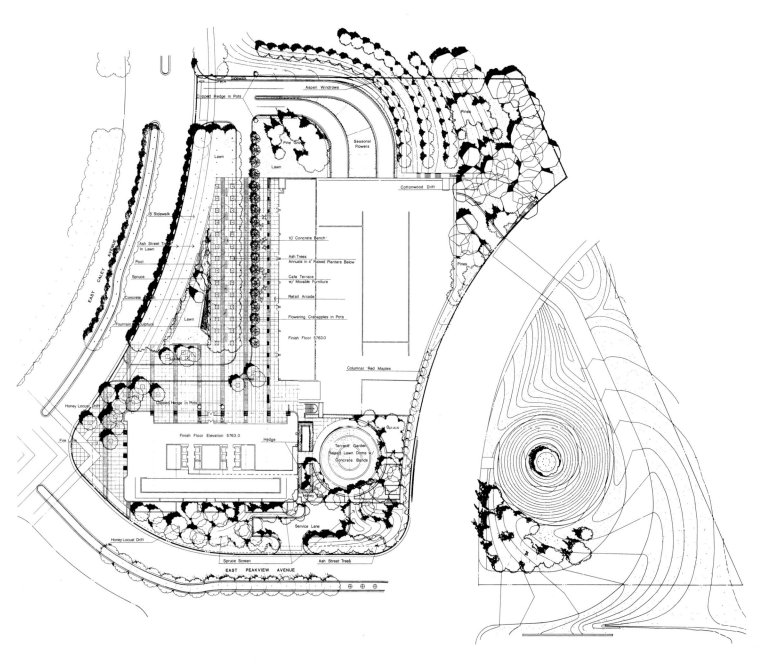

Located across the frontage road and developed with this project is Spiral Park. Its earthen spiral bears an obvious relationship with the 'target' lawn. Spiral Park was developed with a minimal budget by using fill excavated during construction. The fill has been shaped into a mound with a spiral configuration, rising above the busy traffic of Interstate 25, Yosemite Bridge and the frontage road. The spiral path up the mound unwinds the 'target' pattern of the eating terrace lawn and links these two public spaces firmly together. The spiral can be seen by thousands of motorists as well as the pedestrians who wind their way up to its crown of aspen trees.

Spiral Park has evolved into a mysterious local feature with many interpretations: it obviously exerts an effect on the imagination, a feature of Hargreaves' design philosophy. It also demonstrates that thousands of left-over highway spaces could be made far more interesting than is usually the case. This project is a multi-spatial, multi-expression landscape in the Hargreaves style, to be used, enjoyed and interpreted by people. Meanwhile, the fountain, entirely designed by landscape architects, has been officially designated a public artwork.

Day-time view of
fountain slabs and
foaming water.

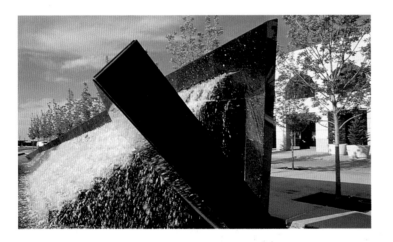

Reflections in the
fountain 'wall' nearest
the building.

Aerial view of the plaza
showing the narrow
shape and its proximity
to the road.

The relative scale of the black sculpture figures, bisecting wall and the distant mountains can be seen here.

The planted strip reinforces the bright colour scheme and the use of elongated reflections.

2.5

HARGREAVES ASSOCIATES/SWA GROUP
Greenwood Village, Denver, Colorado, USA

Harlequin Plaza

It is increasingly recognized that the landscape designer has an important contribution to make in the initial planning stages of any development scheme. Harlequin Plaza demonstrates that an imaginative and innovative designer can make a crucial difference to the final result, even when called in at a rather later stage in the process. Built over a two-storey car park in Greenwood Village, Colorado, the John Madden Company's speculative office building offered little scope for green landscape, except for a view of the Rocky Mountains in the west. All major decisions about the three- and four-storey, mirrored-glass building has been taken before the landscape architect was called in. Thus the shape of the 'courtyard' it enclosed was entirely predetermined. The client's objective was to create a setting for his large collection of Italian sculpture and a strong identity for his buildings within the often monotonous environment of Denver's suburban sprawl. Hargreaves Associates took a bold decision here to produce an abstract design rather than geometrically defined formal spaces. Since the designers believe that landscape should relate to people, the plaza was designed as a stage set for special after-working-hours events as well as for daily users, creating a sense of place. This was an adventurous approach in view of the daunting nature of the site in an area usually deserted at night.

Against all odds, landscape was made to play a primary role in the plaza with the buildings as backdrop. A black-and-white terrazzo with a distorted diamond-shaped paving pattern, forms the basis of the design. Instead of trying to mask or minimize the intrusion of vents and chillers from the garage below, Hargreaves has turned them into a feature. Providing them with angled tops turned them into sculptural elements which, together with the brightly coloured walls that bisect the plaza and reflective panels, create a strong sense of energy and movement. Similarly, a boiler flue becomes a skewed black tower.

The only section of the courtyard strong enough for soil and water loading is a strip 12 metres (40 feet) wide by 60 centimetres (2 feet) deep, running lengthways down the centre of the site. This has allowed for the creation of a central oasis with banks of bright red petunias, willow trees, long benches and a linear fountain whose jets diminish as they move westwards. The elongated effect this produces draws the eye to the view of the Rocky Mountains. Reflection has been used to create space, and sky and clouds are seen mainly as images. In a way, nature in the form of the mountains has been kept at a distance by this design. The focus of the linear strip is a natural vista which could be seen as complementary to, or an ironic comment on, the artificiality of the scheme. Small patches of lawn have been established at the entries to the buildings, rather like green doormats. Finally, black sculptural figures were placed by the client like chessmen on a crazy board. Not surprisingly, nearly all of the landscape budget was spent on hard landscape materials.

The predominantly black, white and red design with its sensation of great energy has achieved a theatricality worthy of the Italian Commedia dell'Arte, a source of inspiration to Hargreaves and an appropriate one for the Italian interests of its owner. The aptly named Harlequin Plaza has, in fact, become the setting for local festivals and performances. The community has adopted the plaza as a major public space and makes heavy use of it in the evenings and at weekends – perhaps a unique achievement for an office-park development.

Overall view of the plaza showing the red wall and terrazzo.

Start on site: 1980
Handover: 1982
Site area: 4650 square metres (50,000 square feet)

2.6 *RMC International Headquarters*

DEREK LOVEJOY PARTNERSHIP
Thorpe Park, Surrey, UK

When Ready Mix Concrete (RMC), a large international company trading mainly in concrete products, wished to construct a new headquarters building on green-belt land, objections were raised and there was a public inquiry. There was particular concern about a listed Georgian house and stable block, together with a nineteenth-century Arts and Crafts house. The land falls entirely within London Metropolitan green-belt designation, and partly within the Thorpe Park conservation area. From the landscape and visual assessment of the site and its surroundings undertaken for the inquiry, DLP was able to show that due to the local topography and vegetation, the zone of visual influence of the new proposals was limited to a maximum of 1000 metres (3280 feet).

Having successfully presented its case, RMC showed its sensitivity to the needs of the environment by insisting that the landscape for the new building should above all be in sympathy with the conservation area and the green belt. Car parks, entrance roads and service areas should all be positioned to respect the conservation area. Luckily, plans for the extension of the adjacent Thorpe Park lake system also necessitated the demolition of modern utilitarian buildings which had marred the site and setting of the historic buildings.

In order to fulfil the client's wishes, DLP made an early decision that landscape should be the major element of the site, and central to this decision was the concept of a vast roof garden. Close collaboration with Edward Cullinan Architects produced a single-storey construction for the new offices which are built around enclosed courtyards. The architects also helped to develop the technical specification required for the roof gardens. Dual-level formal gardens in a parkland setting link the three listed buildings, which have been carefully restored. Existing trees were retained and the outside of the new building is designed to mimic the original walls that surrounded the garden of Eastley End House.

At 4500 square metres (48,439 square feet), the RMC headquarters has one of the largest roof gardens in Europe. Great care was required on the part of landscape architects, architect and structural engineers to estimate the correct loading for the roof structure. The architectural design of the roof uses an 'upside-down' roof construction, so that Styrofoam insulation board was the foundation for landscape works. Materials were kept as light as was consistent with the required strength, waterproofing and insulation. A topsoil depth of 45-50 centimetres (1 3/4 -19 5/8 inches) was specified for shrubs and 25-30 centimetres (9 7/8 -11 3/4 inches) for grass. Good drainage is essential to a successful roof garden and, on the RMC building, a land drain maintains free drainage to outlet gullies positioned at the edge of the building and covered with loose pebbles for easy access.

View of the roof gardens and existing buildings for conservation.

The Moorish design of Fern Court provides light and visual interest for staff within the new building.

Start on site: January 1989
Handover: January 1990
Site area: Roof – 4500 square metres (48,439 square feet)

Aerial view showing the layout of the site and buildings, and its relationship to access roads, car-parking and the Thorpe Park lakes.

Top A detail of the roof garden and the design of the courtyard below. Access ladders from one to the other can be seen.

The roof area is mainly laid to lawn with substantial shrub gardens at the outside edges to reduce wind speeds and improve the microclimate (they also serve to hide the perimeter handrail). Hardy species such as juniper, cotoneaster, pyracantha and escallonia were selected because of the strong, cold winds experienced in this area. Large glass-reinforced-plastic plant containers placed on the roof's perimeter contain clipped yew hedging, 'ball-headed' topiary and conical holly trees, imported from Italy. A temporary nursery was established on site so that plants purchased 18 months in advance could knit together. The result was a well-established one-metre (3-foot 3-inch)-high hedge. Each container is linked to the automatic irrigation system. Because of the extensiveness of the roof gardens, the water for irrigation is supplied by a borehole rather than mains. Shrub areas are fed by trickle lines and grass by flush-mounted, plastic pop-up sprinklers. The roof gardens have been split into zones that can be controlled separately by the maintenance team during watering operations and individually adjusted according to variations in weather conditions.

There are three courtyards, each with a different theme. The design for Eastley End House Court includes a formal pool which reflects the fine Georgian architecture of the house, clipped box parterres, Yorkstone paving and gravel paths. It provides a formal setting appropriate to the house. Meadlake House was once the stable block to Eastley End House and is now used as an accommodation suite. Its courtyard comprises a series of gardens influenced by Vita Sackville-West's gardens at Sissinghurst: each is a different colour (yellow, white, pink and blue). Clipped yew hedges enclose herbaceous borders and lawn and the planting is designed to create colour throughout the year. The court provides a relaxing and pleasant area for guests and staff. Fern Court is designed in Moorish style with light pavings, water channels and shade-loving plants. While ceramic tiles and grey sawn-Cornish-granite edgings (all with buffed finish for slip resistance) help to achieve the desired effect of providing light and visual interest for the interior of the new office building.

Covering the office roofs with hedged gardens set with pavilions, follies and gazebos, together with the courtyards, effectively returns the entire site to landscape within the original garden walls. The fact that 40 per cent of the landscape costs was allocated to soft landscape emphasizes the importance of planting in this scheme. As a result, the new low buildings in no way dominate the site and the overall effect is of a formal garden to the Georgian house.

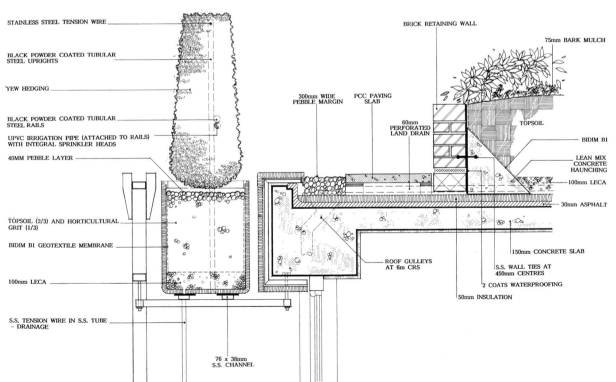

STAINLESS STEEL TENSION WIRE

BLACK POWDER COATED TUBULAR
STEEL UPRIGHTS

YEW HEDGING

BLACK POWDER COATED TUBULAR
STEEL RAILS

UPVC IRRIGATION PIPE (ATTACHED TO RAILS)
WITH INTEGRAL SPRINKLER HEADS

40MM PEBBLE LAYER

TOPSOIL (2/3) AND HORTICULTURAL
GRIT (1/3)

BIDIM B1 GEOTEXTILE MEMBRANE

100MM LECA

S.S. TENSION WIRE IN S.S. TUBE
- DRAINAGE

76 x 38mm
S.S. CHANNEL

BRICK RETAINING WALL

75mm BARK MULCH

300mm WIDE
PEBBLE MARGIN

PCC PAVING
SLAB

60mm
PERFORATED
LAND DRAIN

TOPSOIL

BIDIM B1

LEAN MIX
CONCRETE
HAUNCHING

100mm LECA

30mm ASPHALT

ROOF GULLEYS
AT 6m CRS

150mm CONCRETE SLAB

S.S. WALL TIES AT
450mm CENTRES

2 COATS WATERPROOFING

50mm INSULATION

Edge detail of roof
garden with pebbles
covering outlet gullies.
Eastley End House is
reflected in the formal
courtyard pool below.

Section drawing,
showing construction
detail of the roof garden
at the edge of the
building.

103

A polished stone
arrow points the way
into the building.

Detail of granite support
for one of the pavilion
columns.

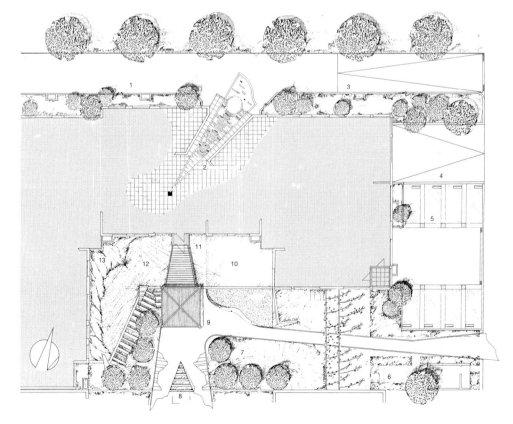

2.7 *Courtyard for Business Park*

BERND KRÜGER AND
HUBERT MÖHRLE
Stuttgart, Germany

Stuttgart Business Park was set up in 1985 to bring together firms working in the computing and communications industries and Krüger and Möhrle were commissioned to design a courtyard within this 'media city'. Its purpose was to provide creative contact between people working in similar fields and to create a stimulating environment that would, it was hoped, promote the development of individual companies through cross-fertilization of ideas.

Krüger and Möhrle believe that landscape design should always be an integral part of its social and physical context and that contemporary solutions must be found for the design problems posed by a multicultural society. In considering this particular project, they realized that the Stuttgart Business Park's colourful, 'high-tech' architecture had to be matched by the landscape design. They elected to achieve this through the bringing together of different and unrelated design features within the small space available, relying on form, function and choice of materials to create the desired effect. They hoped that the landscape would challenge its users to think critically about the limits and dangers of technological progress.

The central focus for the design is an airy glass pavilion, supported by a variety of steel structures, one of whose functions is to provide shelter from the rain. The foot of the thinnest support, made of pink tubular steel, is in the form of a massive needle in polished granite, a reference to Max Bill's monumental sculpture in Zurich's Bahnhofstrasse. Many themes are concentrated in this small space: pool, beach, pond, projecting bow-window, artificial surface areas patterned to stimulate the user's interest. For instance, a gently swaying gangplank leads out from the foyer with a water-permeable surface designed to give training shoes extra drive.

A pool planted with reeds beside the building helps raise ecological awareness by offering an insight into the lifecycles of plants, frogs, dragonflies and other organisms. It also improves the microclimate. The adjoining terrace is constructed from bands of light and dark coloured granite reminiscent of a piano keyboard. An arrow pointing into the building is made of polished natural stone remnants set together, while at the pool's edge is a suspended wedge, also of granite, cut and polished to show its layered structure. The pool and a 'beach' were added to fit the image of the development and to stimulate the imagination. Cherry trees planted to suggest a Swabian orchard unfortunately stand in highly maintained lawns instead of the planned flowering meadows, thus diminishing the intended contrast with the buildings.

The juxtaposition of the technical with the natural within the landscape design of the courtyard is to remind the technologically-minded site users of the natural elements. Effective use of colour has been made to create unity between architecture and landscape on the site. 'High-tech' buildings require a special response in the design of their open spaces necessitating interdisciplinary cooperation between ecologists, urban planners, architects, artists and landscape architects. Most vital of all if the scheme is to be a success is the involvement of the user. The success of the whole concept is such that there are already 230 firms on site with 2200 employees occupying 50,000 square metres (538,213 square feet) of office space.

A view of the courtyard, framed by the building, showing the glass pavilion.

Start on site: 1985
Handover: 1987
Site area: 1000 square metres
(10,764 square feet)

105

The gravel and lawn unifies the objects so you see both the separation of the objects and the continuity of the ground plane.

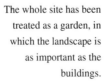

The whole site has been treated as a garden, in which the landscape is as important as the buildings.

2.8

Solana

PETER WALKER AND PARTNERS
LANDSCAPE ARCHITECTURE INC.
Westlake and Southlake, Texas, USA

The symbolic relationship between the species-rich prairie and the totality of the development has been a success.

Opposite Sharp edges or lines in the landscape organize the space and bring together architecture and landscape within the total composition.

Westlake and Southlake do not fit easily into the stereotype image of Texas. Hilly rather than flat, green instead of brown, they are towns (population 4000) dotted with thick stands of post oaks and pecan trees. They are now the location for a new corporate office park known as Solana or 'place in the sun'. Adjacent to Dallas-Fort Worth International Airport, Solana consists of a marketing centre and regional headquarters for IBM, a village centre with restaurants, shops, office buildings and a hotel, plus approximately ten sites for future 'high-tech' tenants with a projected 20,000 employees.

The buildings and roads were laid out so as to preserve the uplands, some 122 hectares (300 acres) of pastureland and the flood plain. In this prairie landscape, where summers are hot, winters are dry and cold, and winds are often harsh, water and natural vegetation are precious. The existing topography, including creek beds, and the established vegetation both helped to determine the siting of the building 'compounds' on broad meadows. Given a planning development restraint of five storeys, buildings are seen against a generous, wider landscape. The entire site has been treated as an extended garden, in which the landscape is as important as the buildings and, in the words of Peter Walker, big ideas have not been crowded out by narrow expediencies. The design team was charged with creating a place for buildings without destroying the sense of place. In meeting this, a bold approach has achieved a composition of great distinction.

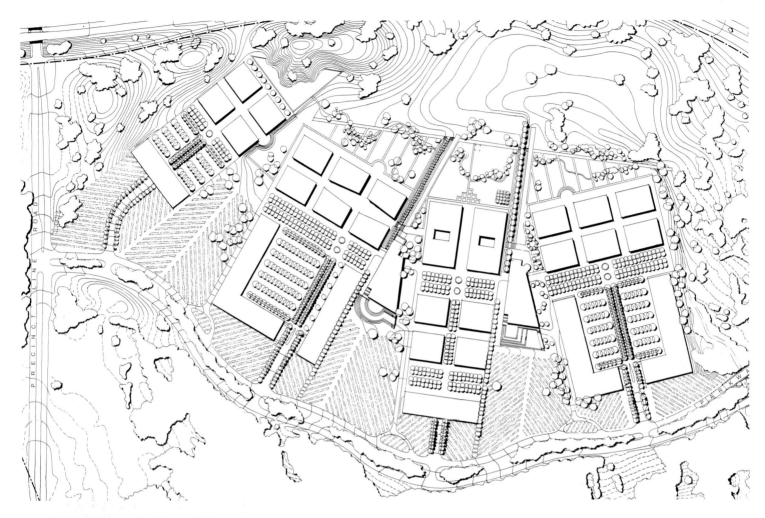

The ordered arrangement of the planter trees are reminiscent of orchards and take up the angular theme of the built structures.

Plan of the office area, revealing the strong landscape structure with the building groups tucked beneath the wooded ridge.

The landscape consultant, as part of a development team, undertook the environmental analysis, traffic and parking studies and the landscape design. The result to date is an open, largely unbuilt landscape that retains a strong contrast between the natural prairie and the man-made environment. Cars do not interrupt the distant views and all parking has been contained within the building compounds, 75 per cent within structures and 25 per cent in heavily shaded plazas.

The building compounds are reached by a four-lane, landscaped parkway, which follows the ridge line. From the parkway, the buildings rise above flowering meadows and orchards, their geometry modulated by the rolling terrain. Hedgerows of elm announce the entry to each compound, inspired by the idea of a villa or *hacienda* (a walled agricultural compound). The concept was one of sharp edges, separating the cultivated areas immediately surrounding the buildings from the rolling natural prairie landscape, with no anonymous, ambiguous zones.

The strong lines perceived in this structured landscape reflect Peter Walker's views on design objectivity. He feels that too many landscape architects fail because of the modesty of their goals: 'Sometimes they fail because they don't want to be objective. They want the work to become background.'

At Solana, the landscape embraces distinct images: a wildflower prairie, wooded uplands, 'agrarian' zones, a lawn parterre, a reflective stream, all contrasting with courtyards and plazas with formal planting and fountains. Emphasis is given to the visual gesture, suggesting movement in the landscape. In particular, hedgerows reach out over 200 metres (700 feet), cutting across the landscape into the prairie so that the objects of the 'garden' are related to the larger spatial object of the gesture. A walled court at the entry from the freeway

'Gestures' suggesting movement reach out, cutting across into the prairie, so that objects within the garden are related to the larger spatial object.

The meandering stream plays against the implied order of the sunlit lawns and sharp lines on the horizontal plane.

interchange suggests order in the agricultural landscape and the compartment landscapes have a similar order, like a piece of an orchard or vineyard.

A great parterre of lawn terraces and gardens of sculptural surprise provide a base for the buildings, integrating each compound into the larger physical order. Paths extend the geometry of the architecture into the landscape. But a shaded, meandering stream, flowing from a triangular lake through the prairie and parterres, plays against the implied order of the sunlit lawns and sharp lines on the horizontal plane.

The village centre is perceived as a series of continuously unfolding spaces; from arcades and parking plazas to gardens and buildings, where exterior and interior spaces overlap in a seemingly casual manner. Some of the village courtyards open out to the surrounding landscape; others are more cloistered. The office building complex is more compact and urban with lines in the landscape – paths, pools, canals, lawns – on a 'taut plane', emphasizing the horizontal dimension.

The various components of the Solana landscape structure contrive to become a massive statement of intent. Within the contrasting and often conflicting movements of environmentalism and post-modernism, Solana is a product of *modernism*. No one building is permitted to dominate as an object in space and the design team were particularly concerned that the design should express the history, regional character and the local landscape. At a distance, rolling prairie landscape is dominant, whereas, close to, the low clusters of buildings are urban in feel and relate spaciously to the larger site. The whole composition is a tribute to enlightened clients and to the powerfully motivated design team, who tugged and pulled at the venture until satisfied that the goals were being met and neither landscape nor architecture was being condemned to a background role.

Start on site: 1986
Handover: In progress
Size of site: 347 hectares (850 acres)

View looking towards the main entrance, with the interplay of colour and natural light. The simple, generous proportions of the space contrast with the quizzical workings of the Time Machine.

The view from above the main entrance of the Union Bank building shows the importance of water in pool and channel and the dominance of the Time Machine.

The administration building for the Union Bank of Switzerland is situated within one of Zurich's industrial zones. With the adjoining commercial buildings it composes a three-sided closed forecourt defined by an unsightly street location on Flurstrasse. First impressions of this project would suggest an unremarkable solution. What makes the scheme of considerable interest is the way in which the designers have risen through the challenge of the site and created for Zurich a composition to equal most modern city squares. The key factor in the site planning was the decision to set the main entrance back, but at the same time strongly to advertise its presence. The landscape architect responded with a bold geometric pattern emphasizing the axis of the entrance which is particularly successful when viewed from above in the surrounding buildings. Of equal importance has been the wish to provide a suitable recreational space for employees in an area somewhat devoid of alternatives.

The barren street has been improved with trees and the square interrupts the linear route by creating a strong directional axis. The diagonal lines focus on the entrance and this play on geometry is enhanced by the ribbed canopy at the entrance. By juxtaposing changes of level, each devoted to a different theme (water, plants and stone), the space offers distinct zones of activity, on the one hand, and contemplative calmness, on the other. The structured provision of water is particularly important in this. In front of the entrance is a 'water mirror', with a still surface reflecting the entrance canopy. Over waterfalls, stairs and along channels,

2.9 Recreation area, for Union Bank of Switzerland Administration Building

HEINER RODEL
Zurich, Switzerland

the water flows into the lowest two basins where the 'Time Machine' is installed. This is a spectacular and dominant sculpture. Described by the designers as a 'filigree iron structure', twelve metres (39 feet 4 inches) high, every hour one of twenty-four colourful polyester balls is released from the top of the Time Machine, dropping into the basin below. Time is thus shown as part of a wider process and not as an end in itself – perhaps a gentle reminder for the surrounding workforce. The steps and edges are constructed in a light-coloured granite which contrasts with the warmer, porphyry stone setts used in all other areas of pavement, even extending over the tramway into Flurstrasse.

Hard landscape accounts for 85 per cent of the budget and planting has a small but crucial part to play in the scheme. Acacias are used to emphasize the modular pattern and in time will add valued shade. In most urban squares open to the street, the small areas of lawn would disappear under a tide of dogs and soft-drink cans, but obviously not here in Switzerland. The designers have avoided a predictable response to this commission and succeed in catching the visitor or observer off balance by deliberately imposing the design on this space. The simple but strong lines, the wry humour of the Time Machine and the confident integration of art into landscape design, indicates that this town square outshines the surrounding buildings. But will it survive? Cars may encroach, grass wear thin and the Time Machine prove unreliable. The client will need to be vigilant to uphold this investment.

Section from entrance canopy to Flurstrasse, identifying the careful changes of level and the framework of acacia trees.

Start on site: January 1985
Handover: September 1986
Site area: 90 x 50 metres (295 x 164 feet)

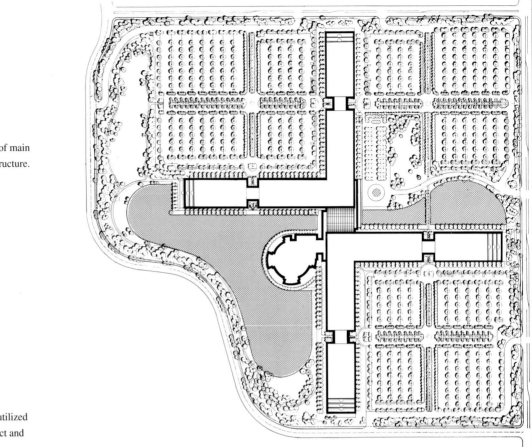

Plan of main
landscape structure.

Water has been utilized
to separate, reflect and
link features.

2.10

MPA DESIGN
Bishop Ranch Business Park, San
Ramon, California, USA

Pacific Bell Administration Center

This is a prestigious business park, constructed on a 'fast track' programme in accordance with client requirements. The administrative centre is formed of three- and four-storey 'L'-shaped buildings on a highly visible site in the San Ramon Valley. The whole complex includes 13.5 hectares (33 acres) of landscape framework, five hectares (12 acres) of lakes and parking for 4600 cars. MPA Design was retained as consultant to the architects, Skidmore, Owings & Merrill of San Francisco, and collaborated in producing the master plan, landscape development, parking, road and grading design for the whole site.

The business park is situated in the once important agricultural landscape of the San Ramon Valley, overlooking the attractive oak-covered Las Trampas Hills and Mount Diablo. The orchard-covered agricultural landscape has strongly influenced the landscape architect, who has incorporated repeating patterns of trees, particularly the California Coast live oak. The finely detailed, but massive commercial buildings, with strongly lined white concrete elevations, called for a landscape framework of major proportions and gentle touch, to balance the built form with an essentially spatial agrarian landscape. Additionally, the setting had to match the high-profile expectations of the client and at the same time adopt principles of energy-conscious design. One area in which this has had a major influence on the landscape design is through utilization of on-site well water.

The landscape philosophy within the master-plan design attempts to extend the structural lines of the built form out into the landscape, and in the opposite direction, draw in the character of the surrounding hills. With this approach, the landscape has been compartmentalized in both formal and informal ways to emphasize the variety of landscape expression. This contrast can be seen in the design of the lakes, planting, circulation and grading – formal where they are in close proximity to the buildings, soft and curving where they meet views of surrounding hills.

A constraint on development was the huge demand for on-site car parking in a State where unrestrained accessibility by private vehicle is an essential fact of life. The design team were at great pains to find an acceptable solution which did not destroy their bold concepts of architecture and landscape. Parking bays are flexibly designed to fit four 'standard' or five 'compact' vehicles. Recognizing changing ownership habits, the parking areas can be adjusted to take all compact vehicles. This modular system has reduced normal US parking area standards by 11 per cent on this site, and so released nearly two hectares (4½ acres) for recreational open space. The parking areas are also subdivided by a pattern of evergreen California live oak that spread to 15 metres (50 feet). Axial pedestrian walks, flanked by flowering trees and bordered with redwoods lead from parking lots to the buildings.

The most distinctive element in the landscape is the firm and bold way in which water has been utilized to separate, reflect, or link features of the whole masterplan. There are two lakes formed with both straight and curved lines, to correspond to the architecture of the new buildings and the surrounding flowing topography. For safety reasons, the lake edges are shallow (30 centimetres/11¾ inches) and gently shelve. A waterproof membrane, which guards against water seepage, is, in turn, protected by a 30-centimetre (11¾ inches) over-layer of heavy clay.

The cafeteria terrace
is shaded by a vine-
covered trellis.

Start on site: 1983
Handover: May 1987
Site area: 40 hectares
(99 acres)

The lakefront promenades are broad and close to the buildings and thus encourage use.

The lakefront promenades are broad and close to the buildings, thus encouraging use. Double rows of *Liquidamber* or crepe myrtle provide filtered shade and the seven-metre (23-foot)-wide walks have a striking concrete margin, which acts as a broad coping, overhanging the lake edge and throwing a strong shadow line. Features along the promenade include grassy park areas, vine-shaded cafeteria terraces and a dramatic, great arched trellis at the central plaza. Elsewhere, the lake boundaries are less formal, with grass or groundcover extending down to the water line. Broad recreation trails, surfaced in decomposed granite, wind their way through the wider landscape, sometimes at lake level, sometimes rising four metres (13 feet) above the water in among native hillside planting.

The significance given to the lakes within the design is highly conscious. They are seen by the design team to provide a sense of place, coolness, spaciousness and a backcloth of interest through changing reflections and movement. The strong presence of water has many practical and technical advantages. The lakes are fed from on-site wells and serve as reservoirs for landscape irrigation water as well as cooling water for the buildings' air-conditioning, thereby eliminating the need for cooling towers. In assessing the viability of investing in the construction of the lakes, the designers established that the water requirements to replace evaporation loss from the lakes was lower than that required for lawn and planted areas, thus reducing average water use over the site. The initial cost of installing the lakes was comparable to landscaped park areas, while future maintenance is lower than other landscape materials.

With the exception of key feature-planting areas, drought-resistant and other appropriate native plants have been selected. An additional conservation measure is the drip-feed irrigation of 45 per cent of the planted areas.

The Pacific Bell Administrative Center is the product of an efficient and demanding design process. There are of course many advantages here, including climate and adequate budget, as well as a fair weighting between architecture and landscape. But its success, including visual and commercial interest, must be assessed within the wider context of the business park as a whole. The water theme and planting structure really need to link all phases, without crushing separate creative expressions.

The strong horizontal
architectural bands
called for a landscape
framework of major
proportions.

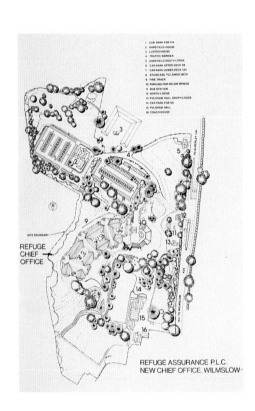

REFUGE ASSURANCE P.L.C.
NEW CHIEF OFFICE, WILMSLOW

Site layout.

The terrace staff area, with offices beyond, is located beside the natural river, with skilful landscaping designed to help the building sit unobtrusively in its parkland setting.

2.11 *Refuge Assurance PLC*

BUILDING DESIGN PARTNERSHIP
Wilmslow, Cheshire, UK

When one of the UK's major life and general insurance companies, Refuge Assurance, grew out of the imposing Victorian building in Manchester it had occupied for the previous 90 years, listed status precluded expansion within the existing building, so a decision was taken to start anew on a fresh site. That chosen was originally the mature and attractive parkland shared by seventeenth-century Fulshaw Hall and the Victorian Harefield House. Split by the A34 road with nearly 8 hectares (20 acres) to the east of the road and 4 hectares (10 acres) of pasture to the west, it lay in the heart of the Cheshire countryside.

The client wanted a building and landscape that would be traditional in appearance yet capable of projecting a modern image for the company. BDP, which was appointed to carry out design in all disciplines, saw a need to create a close relationship between the new landscape and the new building, as well as integrating new and old. Specific requirements were the relocation of the company war memorial within the gardens, the control of flooding problems and the provision of a pleasant environment for the staff. Preservation of natural features and mature trees, some within 10 metres (33 feet) of the proposed building, was seen as paramount.

The natural curve of the site influenced BDP's building design, which took the form of a series of pavilions tucked into the landscape – a three-storey construction with pitched roofs and materials selected to harmonize with its listed neighbours. Car parking for 410 cars was partially concealed by the careful use of levels in front of Harefield House to the south of the site. Spatial balance and visual interest was to be achieved by the use of open areas of grass and water, framed by ground modelling and planting contrasted with the more intricate detailing of features such as stepping stones, footpaths and intimate planting. In order to knit the existing traditional Victorian landscape of Fulshaw Hall with the modern landscape design of the new Refuge Headquarters, the lake was positioned to act both as a foil to the new building and as a harmonizing link between the two landscape styles. Similarly, local indigenous plant material was used alongside traditional ornamental and more exotic plant material.

The new site includes footpaths, new water courses, diverted streams, earth banking and bridges. Paving slabs have been laid to the lake edge, building surrounds and restaurant terraces; timber log edging (15 centimetres/6 inches in diameter) has been used for the lake, with timber decking to the river. The colour of all materials has been carefully selected to unify the site, such as grey boulders for the lake and large red boulders for the courtyard. The western end of the building surmounts a landscaped terrace facing the entrance from the A34. However, the layout of the site, curving away from the road towards Fulshaw Hall, allows for most of the new offices to be hidden from both the road and the older buildings. The war memorial placed next to the lake on the boundary between the existing gardens of Fulshaw Hall and the newly designed landscape acts as a historic link between the two. The use of a wide variety of plant material, much of it permanently labelled for educational purposes, incorporating semi-mature trees and shrubs and substantial herbaceous planting has contributed to the success of BDP's design. Sensitivity to building design and materials is, of course, important, but the combination of planting design and other landscape features is essential for the sympathetic integration of a large corporate building into mature Victorian gardens.

Landscaped banking with fountains (below *porte-cochère* entrance), housing dining room and services. The pavilions of the main building are beyond.

Start on site: 1985
Handover: 1988
Site area: 7.8 hectares (19 acres)

2.12 *North Carolina National Bank Plaza*

OFFICE OF DAN KILEY
Tampa, Florida, USA

Night-time illuminations in surrounding downtown Tampa are taken up by reflective surfaces in the plaza.

In considering the development of this important site as a new banking hall, the client, North Carolina National Bank (NCNB), was conscious both of its responsibilities to the immediate locality and also of the desirability of creating pleasant surroundings for customers and staff. The plaza occupies a wedge-shaped site next to the Hillsborough River in the heart of downtown Tampa. It is next to Tampa Museum and close to the exotic campus landscape of Tampa University which can be seen across the river. NCNB agreed with the City of Tampa to fund the construction of the plaza which is now owned and maintained by the city as a public park. NCNB owns only the land under the building's footprint.

Where some may have perceived the intense heat of downtown Tampa as a problem, to Dan Kiley, with his considerable experience, this proved an immediate source of inspiration. Water was deemed a vital component of the design in which he adopted the simple principles seen in the Moorish gardens of Spain and North Africa, where water channels are used not only to irrigate, but also to provide coolness.

Instead of being intimidated by the surrounding buildings of massive scale, the designer has drawn upon generally accepted design concepts to prepare a design for a town park of deceptive simplicity and appropriateness. The plaza is a geometric, chequered pattern of grass and pre-cast concrete shapes, interlaced with an elaborate system of canals and pools. The landscape takes on the proportions, geometry and material inspiration of the surrounding buildings. According to the designer, the design utilizes repetitions of architectural components and modules, inspired by the Golden Mean and the Fibonacci series of logarithmic patterns, to achieve its unusual unity and spatial clarity.

The lower plaza contains five large reflecting pools running parallel to a canal, 134 metres (439 feet 7½ inches) long, with a transparent glass lining. The six entrances to the underground car park which open beneath it are illuminated by the shimmering patterns made by the water flowing overhead. The water depth in the canal is only 10 centimetres (4½ inches). Nine water channels issue from the canal, flow across a grid of grass squares and pre-cast concrete walkways on the upper plaza and end in specially designed fountains interspersed among the shaded groves and open spaces.

Both the grass areas and the walkways on the upper plaza have a unifying modular design. The grass modules are composed of four, 1.7-metre (5 foot-6 inch) squares of lawn surrounded by pre-cast concrete pavers, 0.6 metres (2 feet) wide. The regularly spaced walkways on the upper plaza are lined with formal rows of *Sabal palmettos* (cabbage palm, the state tree of Florida). However, this rational geometry is overlaid with informally arranged groves of crepe myrtles laid over the grids. The selection of plant material was constrained by the city authorities – specifically, *Parkinsonias* were replaced with the crepe myrtles.

A secret garden for children, formed by a chequerboard of grass squares alternating with water squares, occupies one corner of the plaza. Its counterpart fronts the Tampa Museum at the other end of the plaza. Here, all the squares are planted with ground cover, separated by narrow water channels.

Bubbling fountain pools add vitality to the grid-like patterns in grass and paving, particularly when the water catches the sunlight.

Start on site: 1986
Handover: July 1988
Site area: 1.8 hectares (4.5 acres)

Viewed from above, the intricate geometric chequered pattern of grass and pre-cast concrete shapes can be seen clearly.

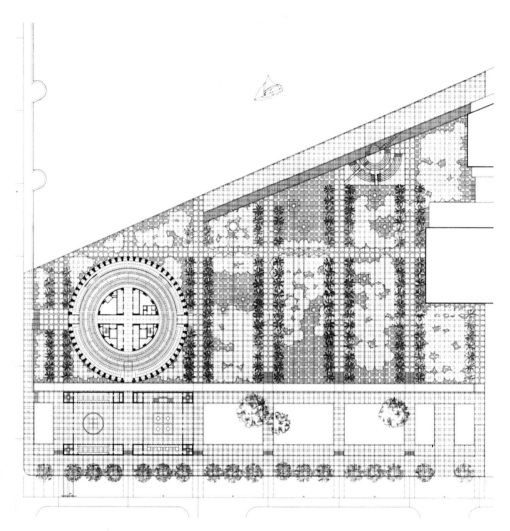

The carefully controlled introduction of trees and shrubs endorses the lines of the design grid.

This very popular local park is a year-round oasis of sunshine and deep shade, with the stimulus of fountains, pools, flowing canals and a clothing of lush vegetation, drawing nearby office workers at lunchtime. After dark, the plaza is transformed, with lighting pin-pointing features and the pools and canals dramatically reflecting illumination flooding out of adjacent buildings and embracing the city within its space. Despite the overall and surrounding ambient illumination, the lighting within the plaza is deliberately muted to enhance its geometry.

The project exudes confidence and demonstrates the strength in design when client, public authority and designer cooperate in the creative process. Here, there is no fear of a sophisticated and intricate adoption of water in many different forms within a public space. The overall scale of the development has been carefully brought down to suit human perception – even that of a child, who surely will find great delight in exploring the small, circular fountain pools. But, at the same time, the landscape structure keeps pace with the building structure. The modular approach successfully knits together the entire scheme and the lighting and reflective qualities in the water ensure that the whole composition comes alive by day and night. To achieve this harmony, there must have been accord between client, architect, structural engineer, civil engineer and landscape architect, with a client convinced of the benefits that would result. It is not just about funding, but also about an attitude of mind. The clean-cut lines of this design almost certainly result from a massive co-ordination role, which has successfully avoided the design principles being unhappily compromised.

Even in daylight, the
water surface reflects
the modular form of
surrounding buildings.

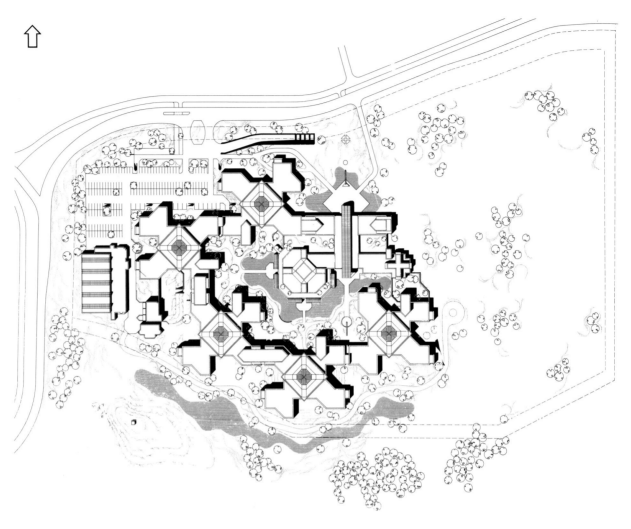

The relationship of buildings and water areas can be seen in the site plan.

2.13

GEORG PENKER
Cologne, Germany

Colonia Park

Colonia AG, one of Germany's most important insurance companies, planned the construction of a central administration park on the outskirts of Cologne to replace the thirty-six offices it occupied throughout the city. The site selected has a background of agriculture and foresty and a village history. The flat landscape was originally marshland and river landscape, with shallow valleys, elevations, and brooks flowing from the east to the Rhine. The client was concerned that the extensive construction should be integrated into the existing landscape, taking into account the need for ecological balance and also for a humane working climate. More practical considerations involved providing safety measures such as appropriate access roads for the fire brigade and extensive car parking facilities while disturbing the landscape as little as possible.

The designer planned to reduce the impact of the buildings by the planting of trees between the new structures and the surrounding forest landscape. The existing ecology was carefully studied to design naturalistic ground conditions and water areas, with the aid of computer systems. Planting was used, internally and externally, to create a unified effect and to mask the apparent size of the buildings, to recreate a 'village' environment.

The external landscape falls into three areas. The main entrance forecourt, in the shape of a square, is planted with groups of mature trees and nestles in an extensive water area, which is much admired. The central design feature of the large inner courtyard is a structured water landscape, part architectural and part organic. Lush planted roof gardens produce a jungle-like atmosphere. Spacious restaurant terraces offer a chance to relax in this green oasis. South of the office block lies a natural-looking water area more than 300 metres (984 feet 4 inches) in length, which functions as an ecological balance. It has a variety of marshland zones and wet hollows and is home to a variety of flora and fauna. The area is accessible via a carefully integrated system of public footpaths. Art is also a feature of the design. A piece by Runke – 'Concept Art' – links the main entrance with the inner courtyard and a stone sculpture by Rückriem has been placed on a tree-covered hill.

Penker has achieved the integration of Colonia's administrative buildings into an as yet unrestored Rhine lea, through the creation of water areas, moist biotopes and the planting of large trees. This has been aided by the adaptation of local planting and the encouragement of fauna and flora. Both visitors and employees have responded with enthusiasm to Colonia Park and use it extensively.

Planting detail along
the footpath.

Start on site: 1982
Handover: 1984
Site area: 5 hectares (12 acres)

A view looking west over the new pond from the centre of the courtyard.

A view looking east, showing the clusters of waterside vegetation, the plant room and new buildings beyond.

Harston Mill was built in the mid-nineteenth century on the banks of the River Rhee in Cambridgeshire. As a result of a diversion of the river to reduce the risk of flooding, the mill fell into disuse forty years ago and had been neglected ever since. In 1984, the client, Prime Computer, bought the mill in order to build a group of plant, office and research and development facilities, centred around the old mill and mill race. The consultant architect involved landscape architects in the project, recognizing the sensitivity of the landscape setting and the high expectations and interests of the client.

Of immediate concern was the riverside setting and the relationship with the old mill pond. The latter has been retained, but the core of the development is located around an open courtyard on the opposite, south side of the restored mill, which is now used for recreational and training purposes. The close proximity of the mill pond and defunct mill race inspired the landscape architect to create a new pond on the south side. The mill race, which runs through the building, connecting the two ponds, has been retained as a permanent sculpture. An overflow fronts the mill race. Preben Jakobsen sees the new water feature as a counterpoint to the larger, old mill pond, and it also forms a focal point at the heart of the development. The stylized new pond is constructed as a series of terraces with a total difference of level of over one metre (39 inches) from top to bottom. A sluggish flow has at times created an awkward problem with algae growth, but this has now been solved by introducing oxygenating plants and a filtration pump.

2.14

PREBEN JAKOBSEN, JAKOBSEN
LANDSCAPE ARCHITECTS
Cambridge, UK

Harston Mill

The clean lines of the landscape treatment are reflected in the new, blue-glazed building at the entrance area.

The firm lines of the covered way are matched by the colour and form of bamboos and other striking foliage plants.

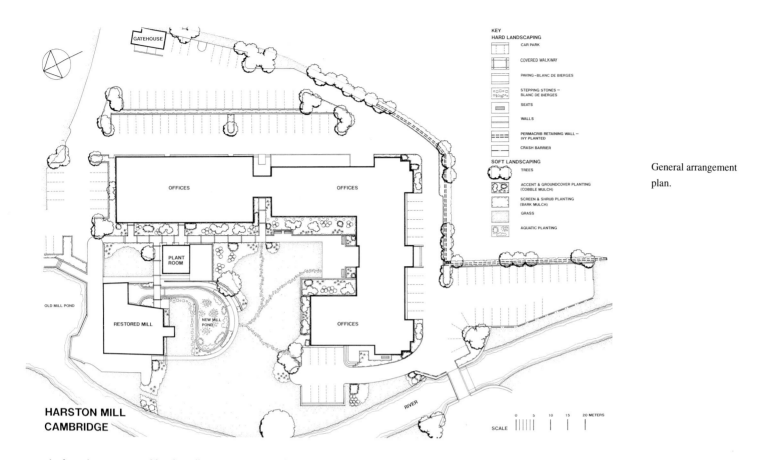

KEY
HARD LANDSCAPING

CAR PARK

COVERED WALKWAY

PAVING ~ BLANC DE BIERGES

STEPPING STONES ~
BLANC DE BIERGES

SEATS

WALLS

PERMACRIB RETAINING WALL ~
IVY PLANTED

CRASH BARRIER

SOFT LANDSCAPING

TREES

ACCENT & GROUNDCOVER PLANTING
(COBBLE MULCH)

SCREEN & SHRUB PLANTING
(BARK MULCH)

GRASS

AQUATIC PLANTING

General arrangement
plan.

GATEHOUSE

OFFICES

OFFICES

PLANT
ROOM

OLD MILL POND

RESTORED MILL

NEW MILL
POND

OFFICES

RIVER

HARSTON MILL
CAMBRIDGE

SCALE   0   5   10   15   20 METERS

In fact the new pond is virtually over the site of an earlier one which had silted up and been filled in later, so that excavation was relatively easy. The pond has a butyl membrane liner and the walls are constructed in concrete block with edging in Staffordshire Blue engineering brick to link with the traditional materials of the mill. Initially the designer wanted a large reflection pond to fill the courtyard, but this was rejected on cost grounds. As it happens, the reflections found in the pond are more subtle, especially with the attention given to plants which provide a different and new dimension to what would otherwise be a hard industrial landscape.

Cream-buff concrete setts were chosen for the main paving to link with the yellow stock bricks of the mill building. This theme has been carried into the main entrance area where tall bamboos and fissured slate boulders feature strongly. The Staffordshire Blues, also found in the mill, have been used for edging, including the pond, and for retaining walls.

Plants that emphasize the character of the watery setting have been selected, notably alder, birch, bamboo and a collection of unusual willows, including 'Corkscrew', and 'Coyote'. The pool contains various aquatic plants, such as water lilies, iris, and submerged oxygenating plants. The margins of the pond are stocked with appropriate plants, including elegant grasses such as *Miscanthus*. The water theme is signalled clearly in the wide use of waterworn pebbles which sometimes give the buildings the appearance of being surrounded by a dry riverbed. Elsewhere, ivy and vines have been used to create an effective and dense covering, while olive and dark green foliaged shrubs complement the new glazed blue steel buildings.

The scheme has proved popular with the client, who also occupies the site. The landscape architect found support in the original client's interest in ecological and aesthetic values. With a project which had a highly visual historical core, there was always a danger of producing a pastiche of traditional elements. The architect and landscape architect have avoided this and have interjected new elements which complement the old, and have brought a fresh appeal to Harston Mill. This is particularly evident in the careful but striking plant compositions. However, this balance will only continue if the scheme is correctly maintained.

The main route through
the courtyard runs
beneath an unusual
covered way.

Start on site: 1986
Handover: 1989
Site area: 9771 square metres
(105,177 square feet)

2.15

The Broadmoor Park

ROBERT DANIELSON, DANIELSON
AND ASSOCIATES
San Francisco, California, USA

Situated in central San Francisco, the Broadmoor is a four-storey retirement hotel with no outdoor space for the use of its residents. The owner (and client) was able to acquire a small plot adjacent to the hotel in order to provide a private garden for his elderly guests. Since their average age was 85 years, the main priorities were to create a restful and safe environment, protecting himself from the liability risk which is an integral part of providing services for the elderly. Nevertheless, design quality was, from the start, an important consideration for the client.

Before starting work on the site in 1985, Robert Danielson, the landscape architect retained by the client, carried out a survey of the residents. There were both married and single people, who were often quite independent, with interests and routines of their own. Not surprisingly, in view of their age, activities tended to be of a sedentary nature, with watching TV in their own rooms heading the list. The landscape architect first produced a model to illustrate his design concepts to the client. Although refinements to the landscape design were made, the final working drawings, completed in conjunction with the architect and structural engineer, were very close to the original model.

The 9 x 39.6 metre (30 x 130 foot) site is 2.1 metres (7 feet) below the level of the hotel foyer and slopes a further 3 metres (10 feet) downhill away from the hotel. Danielson's novel solution was to elevate the park to an average height of 3.3 metres (11 feet) above the external pavement and to the same level as the foyer. Pedestrian ramps connect all three levels of the garden, allowing residents easy access from the hotel and preventing casual access from the street outside. (The hotel intends to use the space below the park for much-needed new offices.)

The design theme lies in the creation of a series of circular shapes that effectively break up the long rectilinear site into more intimate areas. These extend past the property line to overhang parts of the street. This adds width and is also intended to reflect the traditional curved bay windows found in the architecture of the area. Danielson wanted the circular spaces to be as flexible as possible to allow for such amenities as:

- *a circuit for health and leisure walking including ramps with handrails to make walking and exercising easier.*
- *secluded spots for sitting in the sun, reading, observing the streetscape and the two pieces of garden sculpture.*
- *seating for intimate or group conversation.*
- *tables and umbrellas for outdoor meals in good weather.*

Although only 5 per cent of the cost went on soft landscape, the garden aims for a colourful and fragrant planting scheme, which includes rhododendrons, camellias, star jasmine and roses. There are also fruit trees, such as crabapple and varieties of citrus. The intention is to have at least one species in full colour at any time. Since the completion of the garden in 1986, the landscape architect visits the site not less than once a week to direct the

Handrails are an important safety feature in this development.

Start on site: 1985
Handover: 1986
Site area: 9.1 x 39.6 metres (30 x 130 feet)

A view of the park and
its overhanging planting
from the street.

Below The circular
shapes in the design
break up the space
into more intimate
areas.

Site plan with the
hotel entrance on the
left, showing the
circular theme.

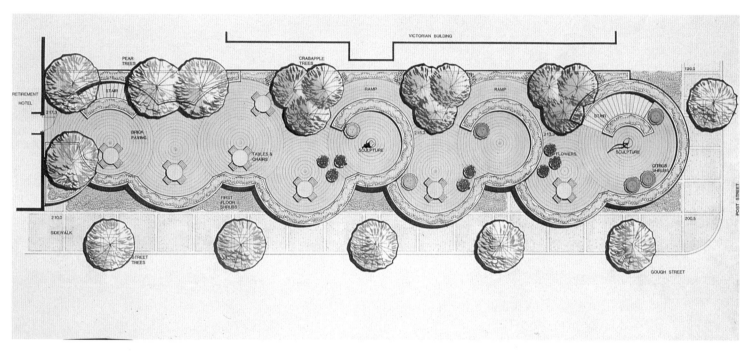

horticultural maintenance programme. Since the park is in effect a roof garden, the design team has taken advantage of the latest technology to ensure long-term efficiency of maintenance for the planting areas. Materials include a special soil media mixture, polypropylene woven-cloth filter and a honeycomb-shaped, polyethylene drainage system connecting to storm drains. Planters and planter walls are of pre-cast concrete, paving of thin brick setts and railings of stainless steel.

In spite of the unpromising nature of the site, through imaginative design the landscape architect has achieved a park which offers privacy and safety from external dangers, together with fresh air and an attractive garden for otherwise house-bound elderly people. The green planting overhanging the street from the circular bays also enhances the street below. The Broadmoor Park is much appreciated by the existing guests and this improvement to the quality of the hotel's life is underlined by its importance to the hotel's sales programme in attracting new residents.

Aerial view of Useppe
Island, showing the
Gardens of North Point
in the foreground.

The trellis-type railing
and strong off-set line
of the footpath works
well, slotted into this
mature vegetation.

2.16 *The Gardens of North Point*

PETER B. BURNER, BURNER
AND CO. INC.
Useppa Island, Florida, USA

The octagonal gazebos
are a key element of the
composition and points
of focus in the linear
promenade.

Useppa Island was inhabited by the now extinct Calusa Indians over a long period, who used it as a tribal meeting point amid plentiful shell-fishing grounds. Some five thousand years ago they created the island's shell ridge, surrounded by ceremonial and burial mounds. With a lively history of piracy and smuggling, Useppa Island had long been viewed as an attractive and romantic island, though this century has seen a gradual transition in its occupation.

The island's owners and occupiers have deliberately restricted access to it, which is only possible by boat or seaplane, and there are no roads. Development is carefully controlled to conserve the island's historical and architectural style. Peter B. Burner was commissioned to design the Gardens of North Point, which cater for both visitors and residents. The landscape architect was required to coordinate a sensitive programme for several different clients. In addition, there was the logistical challenge of bringing all materials and equipment to the island by barge, including a crane to lift in the largest coconut and queen palms.

The design brief for the Gardens of North Point was to secure privacy for residents in a very restricted area, while creating a series of public and semi-public spaces. Established uses needed to be changed and the density of occupation increased for both residents and visitors, without destroying the unusual atmosphere of the island. In this the designer was helped substantially by clients who wished to enhance the very special landscape qualities. Another major concern was to protect the ceremonial and burial mounds. A striking element of the design is the timber decks and gazebos. A special consideration was raising the structures to meet local flood zone requirements so the decks are elevated using piled construction, thus utilizing the cooling, ventilating breezes and allowing for the movement of flood water in tropical storms. Pressure-treated southern yellow pine is used for the gazebos' frames, while softer Alaskan yellow cedar, which is splinter resistant, forms the planking for the decks. The designer has carefully selected materials to coordinate the gazebos, railings, seats and paving within their new functions, as well as reflecting the inherited conditions on the island. Constructed with arches, lattice work, traditional tin roofs and stained white, the octagonal gazebos are designed to orientate to the different sunset positions throughout the year – important in such a beneficial climate. The designer set out to echo the vernacular architecture and protect key features such as the 'Pink Promenade' which had evolved out of the shell ridge back in the 1920s.

Although unusual conditions prevail in this scheme, it does demonstrate how a designer can respond to precise physical conditions and attentive clients. It would have been all too easy to over-design and attempt to integrate competing demands or lose sight of the subtle balance between public access and private occupations within a very restricted area.

The design has created
both public and more
private spaces for
relaxation.

Start on site: 1984
Handover: 1988
Site area: Approximately
40 hectares (99 acres)

133

2.17 *Riverwoods Office Park*

ENVIRONMENTAL DESIGN
PARTNERSHIP
Beford View, Johannesburg,
South Africa

This project was a speculative office development by the AECI Pension Fund, who anticipated that the available office space would be let in separate units. To attract appropriate tenants, the client recognized the advantages of maximizing and strengthening the natural features to create an environment of high quality and maturity. In fact the whole office complex was let before completion and handover.

Riverwoods lies in a parkland setting: the site slopes steeply to a river on the east boundary and is characterized by large specimen trees. The configuration of four buildings creates a large central courtyard. This focus of attention on one point of the development contrasts with the design philosophy for the more open area adjacent to the river, where building is restricted to a 50-year floodlevel mark. The brief from the client required maximum floor area for the offices, but without damaging the character of the existing natural features. In particular, this meant conserving the excellent specimen trees and enhancing the landscape zone adjacent to the river.

The courtyard arrangement was developed in partnership with the architects and this also helped to keep as many vehicles as possible in underground parking. The buildings are placed on the site forming an enclosed courtyard, with the main vehicle entrance to the site on an axis with the pedestrian avenue into the courtyard. As a focal point, the courtyard is treated with particular care and the landscape composition springs from here. It is the setting for formal water features designed to illustrate many moods of water. After a series of cascades, fountains and waterfalls, water runs smoothly through channels and also reflects the surroundings in the deep, still pools. The sloping site has significantly aided this diverse use of water.

The walls associated with the water features were constructed in facing brick to match the adjacent buildings and each water area has its own separate, pumped circulatory system. Brick has also been used extensively for the paving that crosses and surrounds the very dominant pools and channels, creating an area of highly formalized design, intentionally reminiscent of historic mediterranean villa gardens, though expressed through a different idiom.

The configuration of the three buildings creates a large central courtyard, which has become the setting for formal water features illustrating the many moods evoked by water.

Utilizing the natural slope of the site, the designer has cleverly introduced a series of cascades, fountains and waterfalls.

Start on site: 1989
Handover: 1990
Site area: 5 hectares (12 acres)

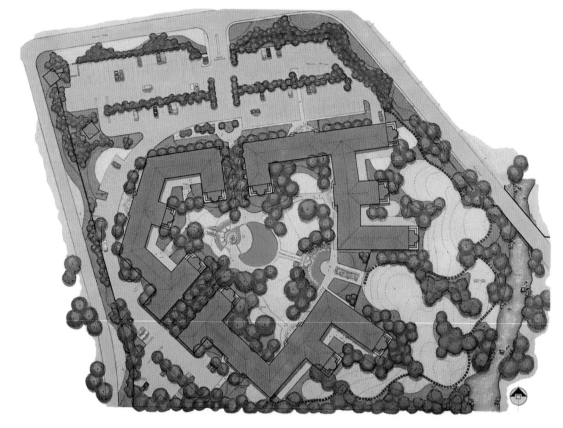

Opposite The geometric patterns in paving layout and the intricate way water flows around and across the footpaths are intentionally reminiscent of historic Mediterranean villa gardens.

KEY

LAWN
GROUNDCOVER
SHRUB
LARGE SHRUB
TREE
PAVING
FOOTPATH
PROPOSED CONTOUR
RETAINING WALL

Brick has been used extensively, creating an area of highly formalized design. In time the edges will be softened by the growth of vegetation.

There were a number of constraints preventing optimal use of the site. The position of the trees meant that, in certain cases, building positions had to be modified. But the two major constraints were the overhead electrical transmission lines and the river flood levels, which effectively prevented building development on large areas of the site. Height restrictions beneath the transmission lines meant that this area was given over to parking and vehicular access. No trees could be planted here, but taller-growing shrub species ensure effective screening and partial shade throughout the year.

The water-related theme within the courtyard also serves to link with the landscape adjoining the river. From the courtyard, balconies and terraces, views of the river emphasize this link, but the planting gradually changes from the controlled composition of the courtyard to a free-flowing natural woodland character beside the river, with grassy glades. Although no buildings encroach within the zone of the 50-year floodlevel, lesser floods have necessitated gabion protection and relatively low-key planting, as it is likely to be washed away. In contrast to the flood danger, the whole scheme is supplied with automatic irrigation utilizing borehole water and storage tanks.

Throughout the developed world, tenants and occupants of offices are increasingly concerned about their work conditions and, in the case of the employer, the image of the company. This has been translated in many countries into a conscious investment in the surrounding landscape, not just as a sop to local planning or building regulations. Riverwoods Office Park is an instance of how this commercial-based philosophy has resulted in a coherent landscape strategy of equal merit to the architecture. After all, the pension-fund client would wish to secure its initial investment for long-term benefit. The landscape designers were able to work with the cooperation of the architects and a generous budget to maximize the possibilities of this project. The effort has been wisely concentrated (in the courtyard area) and consistency achieved in implementation. Both clients and tenants appear to appreciate the scheme and it is significant that the consultants have been retained to supervise a yearly landscape- and irrigation-maintenance programme.

The residential plaza takes advantage of spectacular views towards the main valley of Caracas and Avila Mountain.

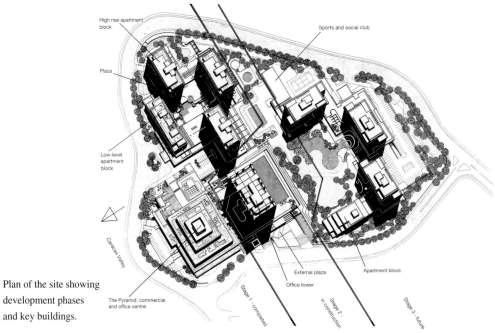

Plan of the site showing development phases and key buildings.

2.18 *Prado Humboldt Complex*

JOHN STODDART AND FERNANDO
TABORA PENA
Caracas, Venezuela

Preliminary design for this complex began in 1978 and development was divided into three phases. The first phase comprised a small but prestigious office building and commercial centre called the Pyramid, together with three high-rise apartment blocks, which, with a lower apartment block, form a space that has become a plaza. The second phase was for a high, 35-storey office tower, while the third was for three additional, 20-storey apartment blocks and a residents' club with connecting sports area and pool. The first stage has been completed, the second is in construction and the third lies in the future.

The southern boundary of the site is formed by a street of slum housing and, in order to succeed, the complex must upgrade the whole area and be sufficiently attractive for inhabitants of the city to want to live there. Stoddart and Tobora were called in by the architect Federico Beckhoff at the beginning of the design process.

The Pyramid was the first building to be completed and includes a shopping centre on its lower floor. The offices constituting the rest of the building are of fixed area and allow considerable space for a garden. The landscape team designed these upper level gardens as intimate patio-like spaces where users may sit out on the terraces surrounded by tropical plants. Each patio has a small weir fountain to add coolness, as well as visual and aural interest. They also take advantage of a spectacular view toward the main valley of Caracas, with Avila Mountain in the background.

Special attention was given to the relationship of the building to its site. The main access is flanked by a large lake incorporating another weir which recirculates the water. The design structure is geometric and all elements, such as curbs, stairways, waterfalls, benches and planters are in fair-faced concrete without an applied finish.

The architect's design produced a split level in the garages underneath the first group of apartment blocks to be constructed. The landscape designers took advantage of what could have been a problem by using the different levels to create a more interesting civic space than is usually found over the structural slabs of garages. The resulting plaza is also on two levels, which have been integrated by two lateral concrete staircases rising between large-scale, concrete planting boxes. The edge of the higher slab of the garage has been broken up by introducing a circular fountain on top of a large supporting cylinder standing in a lower pond to receive the falling water from the fountain. The actual parking environment is screened by a metal grille. Again, all planting is over structural slabs but uses small trees and palms and tropical foliage plants to create the effect of a quiet internal garden. An overall floor design in two separated colours of pebblestone creates unity and strict attention has been paid to detailing and obtaining a high standard of concrete finishes.

Unfortunately, problems have arisen in maintenance of soft landscaping. However, the garden areas are appreciated by the apartments' owners and other users. Hard landscape areas, on the other hand, have been well kept and show no signs of deterioration, such as worn surfaces. With the apparent emergence of Venezuela from its economic difficulties, the last phase of development seems set to begin. It is to be hoped that when the Prado Humboldt Complex is finally completed the landscape designers will have achieved their aim of revitalizing a slum district.

Planting detail of the area in front of the main façade of the Pyramid Building.

Start on site: 1979
Handover: In progress
Site area: 10.4 hectares (25¾ acres)

139

New Parliament House,
Canberra (see pages
176-181)

3 Civic & Educational

Farnborough College of Technology (see pages 172-175)

Paving, edging and
pillar detailing.

Paving and lawn in the
dramatic approach to
the University building.

3.1 *Courtyard of the Catholic University School of Biotechnology*

ANDRESEN AND CASTEL-BRANCO
ARQUITECTURA
Oporto, Portugal

The pool is a key feature in the design, capturing reflections and adding to the meditative atmosphere.

A conceptual sketch of the site.

Andresen and Castel-Branco (ACB) started work on the landscape for a courtyard at the School of Biotechnology, part of the Catholic University in Oporto, in 1987. The challenge was to provide a setting for research workers and students at the cutting-edge of biotechnology that would both stimulate and refresh the mind. The client – the University – was particularly sensitive to the need for green landscape in this space and also concerned about future maintenance costs. Above all, the landscape designers were asked to respond to the imposing architecture of the building designed by Joao Adao da Fonseca.

The designers quickly realized that the pavement layout would have to be the key to the whole design and that it should follow a geometric pattern. Keeping in mind Leonardo da Vinci's words that 'every part is disposed to unite the whole that it may thereby escape from its incompleteness,' they set about applying the golden-section proportions to their plan. After much trial and error, they succeeded in reconciling the classical model with the existing space.

The most innovative contribution to the design, according to the designers, was the use of the tradition of the cloister. In analyzing the site – a courtyard enclosed by the building façades – the analogy of a cloister emerged: a quiet retreat for the contemplation and development of ideas could still be relevant in a new secular context. In order to reproduce a scholarly ambience the designers studied all the local examples of cloister designs of which there are many in and around Oporto, in all architectural styles from the thirteenth century onwards. From this they recognized the need for green surfaces (to reduce pavement reflection), water, sunshine and shade.

The courtyard is effectively designed as a modern cloister surrounded by imposing pink façades and functions as a focal point visually, an academic meeting place and as a passageway. Access to the courtyard is via a circular staircase located on the axis that

descends from an elevated gallery facing the main façade, which is reflected in ornamental pools. From the staircase, a clear view of the whole courtyard is obtained. Pavement in a pattern of black-and-white squares gives unity to the design and contains four lawns.

The role of water is crucial to the ambience of the courtyard. A fountain situated in an intimate spot in the south-west corner feeds a canaletto that runs into a small square pool, which in turn has an underpass to the large reflective pools. Another fountain in the form of a slate square rising from the water is situated in the opposite, north-west corner. Rising from the water, a series of decomposing squares scatters to meet the squared pavement. Slate is used for curbs, fountains and specially designed lamps, and there are marble-clad concrete benches. Pavements and staircase are in '*calcada portuguesa*' built with limestone and basalt cubes.

Plant materials are of white or near-white hue: two structural *Magnolia soulangeana*, centrally located, are the only vertical elements, while peripheral shrubs are camellias and azaleas. Drainage and automatic irrigation systems have been installed. The ratio of 20:1 in the costs of hard to soft landscape reflects the preponderance of hard landscape materials used, which helps to achieve the low maintenance costs required by the client as well as supporting a high carrying capacity.

The weaving together of the key elements of plant materials, water and paving has produced an inviting meeting place enhanced by the contribution of colour, in this case restricted with great visual effect to pink, black, white and green. This academic courtyard was seen by its landscape designers as a unique opportunity for cooperation and agreement between client, architect and landscape architect to achieve the solution to a contemporary challenge.

The circular stone staircase.

Start on site: 1987
Handover: 1988
Site area: 2700 square metres (29,063 square feet)

The redesign
incorporated floral beds
and theme gardens
found in the original
garden design.

3.2 Enid A. Haupt Garden

SASAKI ASSOCIATES INC.
Smithsonian Institution, Washington D.C.

This public garden occupies a site of great significance and concern to American citizens, bounded by the Smithsonian Institution's 1849 Victorian Arts and Industries Building, the Freer Gallery and Independence Avenue. The Washington Memorial, White House and the Capitol are all within a short walk. The commission for a garden on such a sensitive site arose out of the decision to build a new Gallery of Asian and Near Eastern Art and the National Museum of African Art beneath the existing garden. In the inevitable upheaval, the original garden by Dan Kiley was destroyed and the brief to Sasaki Associates involved a redesign of the embroderie parterre adapted from the 1887 Centennial floral beds; theme gardens related to the gallery and museum, to include water features and outdoor exhibition space, and a formal entry into the garden from Independence Avenue.

Although the brief was very specific with precise requirements and few unknown factors, the delicacy of any development proposals on such a site taxed the resources of the designers to the full. The landscape architect was retained through the office of the architect, who in turn worked with the client body of the Federal Government. Sometimes the General Services Administration had difficulty in agreeing with the Smithsonian Institution, particularly on design matters. With many other advisory organizations interested in this project, the designers had to work hard to maintain coherence and protect the style of the scheme. The main requirements of replacing a valued garden and meeting the constructional and technical conditions of subterranean buildings proved a major challenge. Particular factors influencing the design were loading restrictions, drainage requirements and the need to prevent water penetration. Soil depth was strictly controlled, with only 50 centimetres (19⅝ inches) beneath the parterres, which coincided with the maximum structural span beneath, whereas the trees are located over building columns, walls and beams.

The wider views and circulation of the main garden are deliberately contrasted with two thematic, small 'gardens of repose and reflection'. A fountain garden provides a link with the National Museum of African Art, while an oriental-style garden is located beside the Gallery of Asian and Near Eastern Art. An intimate scale and character has been achieved, using a wide choice of plants, carefully selected to provide maximum interest throughout the seasons. The client has shown a willingness to replant throughout the year, especially the parterres.

The traditional nature of the overall composition is appropriate for this unique site, but it will take continued watchfulness to prevent intrusions being made. The client seems proud of the result and describes the Enid Haupt Garden as 'a living horticultural exhibition that transforms more than four acres into an elegant park ...with plants cascading in profusion'. Perhaps the greatest measure of its success is that it looks as if it has been there for the last hundred years.

The archway provides an intriguing 'key-hole' view midway along a lengthy footpath.

Start on site: 1983
Handover: 1987
Site area: 1.7 hectares
(4¼ acres)

147

3.3 *New Canadian Chancery*

CORNELIA HAHN OBERLANDER
Washington DC, USA

Spirit Canoe, a sculpture by Bill Reid, is sited in a pool, whose waves add movement and sound to the courtyard.

Situated at the junction of Pennsylvania and Constitution Avenues, opposite the East Wing of the National Gallery of Art, the new Canadian Chancery in Washington DC occupies an imposing position. In addition, it enjoys commanding views to and from the Capitol, John Marshall Place Park and the judiciary buildings. Canada's representative, consular and administrative facilities were previously housed in three separate buildings. In the new building they were to be combined under one roof. A team of architects, engineers and landscape architects was thus presented with a splendid site on which to display its combined skills. Underlying the whole design was the concept of the important relationship between Canada and the US, which the Chancery was to symbolize.

Oberlander drew on both classical and natural sources for her inspiration in planning the landscape: from Hadrian's Villa, with its clipped topiary and rose-filled gardens; the Hanging Gardens of Babylon, and also from Canada's rugged mountain ledges. The client was concerned that the scheme should measure up aesthetically, to Washington's existing civic architecture and, at the same time, reflect Canada's essential spirit. On a practical level, the requirement was for office space, reception areas, and public entrances for library, art gallery and theatre. The landscape designer was faced with stringent local building restrictions on Pennsylvania Avenue, which limited the choice of trees and plant material. In addition, she had to contend with budgetary restrictions, since only 0.25 per cent of building cost was allocated for soft landscape.

The U-shaped Chancery building occupies two-thirds of the available site. Oberlander made the most of the limited space and resources by making planter boxes central to her design. Entering the paved courtyard, accessible from Pennsylvania Avenue and providing 30 x 60 metres (98 feet 5 inches x 196 feet 8 inches) of outdoor space, the visitor is first greeted by a pool containing a sculpture by Bill Reid. It is called *Spirit Canoe* and is filled with mythological creatures, half-human, half-animal. Waves in the pool splash against the canoe, contributing movement and sound to the courtyard and adding to a cool, open-air effect. The success of this dramatic feature is a striking example of successful cooperation between landscape architect, artist and architect.

Immediately afterwards, the visitor experiences a spectacular view of gardens apparently tumbling down the face of the building itself. It is created by planter boxes filled with groundcover azaleas, cascading memorial roses and clipped hawthorns (1.5 metre/5 feet on centre and with 1.5-metre/5-foot trunks) and placed to coincide with the spacing of the window mullions. Apart from the greenery, the selection of plant material shows a predominance of red and white, Canada's national colours:

Trees *Quercus coccinea* (scarlet oak), *Quercus rubra* (red oak), *Juniperus virginiana* (eastern red cedar).
Shrubs *Crataegus crus-galli inermis* (thornless cockspur hawthorn), Azalea 'Gumpo White', Azalea 'Delaware Valley White', *Rosa wichuraiana* (memorial rose), *Ilex crenata 'Conveca'* (boxleaf holly).

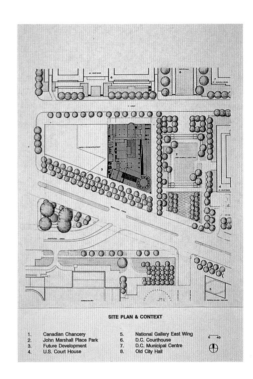

Site plan showing the Canadian Chancery (rendering by Elisabeth Whitelaw).

Start on site: 1985
Handover: 1989
Site area: 30 x 60 metres (98 x 196 feet)

The gardens appear to
tumble down the face
of the building.

A close-up of planter
boxes with clipped
hawthorns (*Crataegus
crus-galli inermis*) on
1.5-metre (5-foot)
centres with *Azalea
'Gumpo White'* and
memorial rose.

View through the
columns to the
cascading gardens.

Easement and entrance gate located between the Chancery and John Marshall Place Park. The strip is planted with red oaks (*Quercus rubra*) and Azaleas (*Azalea 'Delaware Valley White'*).

The plant material selected reflects Canada's national colours - red and white.

There were many technical points to be taken into consideration by the landscape designer. Having located suitable plant material in sufficient quantities from various nurseries, a support system had to be developed which would allow the plants to grow in confined planter boxes using a lightweight growing medium and suitable drainage methods. A low-water-consumption irrigation system was employed and slow-release, non-toxic fertilizers were specified. Full supervision of the landscape contractor during installation and subsequent maintenance periods has been provided for. There were also a human element to take into account: specifying safety devices for workers maintaining planter boxes on the higher levels. All of these problems have been satisfactorily resolved.

The ingenuity and imagination shown by Oberlander have produced a scheme which both complements and enhances the dignity of the architectural composition. The use of planter boxes makes up for the scarcity of space available and provides green garden areas for those working inside the building, as well as a superb vista from the entrance courtyard. This in turn takes full advantage of the landscape of John Marshall Park, which sweeps up to the courtyard providing much-needed verdure for the Chancery workers and links with the external landscape. The soft landscape input may have been small in financial terms but not in impact, and the new Canadian Chancery is an example of what can be achieved when a landscape designer works successfully as part of a multi-disciplinary team. It also shows that successful landscape design is unrelated to the amount of space available; a sympathetic response by the designer is the main requirement.

The strong diagonal cross axis framed by trees creates an important spatial structure.

Low evergreen clipped hedges and geometric granite-sett paths define plot areas and ensure that the individual graves do not disrupt the overall landscape structure.

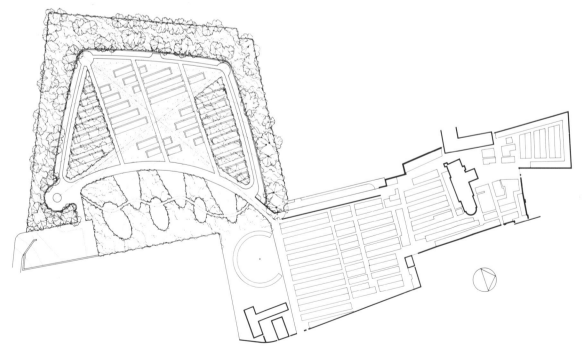

3.4 *Greve Kirkegårds (churchyard)*

ANDREAS BRUN
Greve Kommune, Udvidelse, Denmark

Scandinavia has established an enviable reputation for designing institutional landscapes, such as those surrounding schools and hospitals. Into this category falls landscape associated with religion. Christian churches worldwide have traditionally incorporated graveyards for burial adjacent to the church or cemeteries further away, perhaps with a chapel of rest. Inevitably, some quite extraordinary and extensive cemeteries have developed in cities, which are often poor examples of spirituality or even coherent design and management. In the twentieth century, demands upon available land, an increasing inability to maintain the upkeep of the intricate grave-covered churchyards and the changing practice in favour of cremation, have all combined to focus attention on the appearance and function of land surrounding churches.

The churchyard within Greve kommune (village) is indicative of a change of direction which has attracted a new and positive approach to landscaping around churches. Greve lies in the flat, highly productive and relatively featureless agricultural landscape of Zealand, in which the settlements and surrounding vegetation stand out. The brief to the landscape architect was to extend the churchyard into a defined area adjacent to the existing one and into the wooded rectory gardens on the west side. The churchyard has grown steadily since the 1950s, with graves packed in back-to-back, so a major replanning was undertaken in the early 1980s with the guidance of the landscape architect. The parish authorities envisaged a park-like graveyard, but Andreas Bruun imagined a garden of moods, symbols and mystery, to reconnect the spirituality of the place with the Bronze Age barrows found in the wider Danish landscape.

The expansion area only joins the old churchyard by a few metres common boundary at its north-east corner. This provides an important point of entry, looking south-west over ground that rises three metres (10 feet) and framed within a carefully protected diagonal cross axis. Today the new churchyard holds three types of graves; two for burial and one for urns.

The main structures of the landscape in sections, details and selection of plants, were monitored and revised to ensure a dynamic relationship between symbols and the requirements of the whole composition, in order to create, in the words of the designer, a place of beauty and some mystery.

From beyond the village boundary, a generous belt of perimeter planting softens this edge, and yet clearly defines the village. This planting also effectively encloses and shelters the new churchyard. The boundary definition is emphasized by the low granite boulder wall which also provides a resting place for urns or cineraria after cremation.

The designer has attempted to come to terms with the fundamental dichotomy between the wishes of the individual and their family, and the long-term policy of the parish authorities and the community to maintain a manageable and acceptable appearance.

The curved enclosing wall constructed out of large granite boulders, with ivy trailing from the top, also provides a refuge for cineraria after cremation.

Start on site: 1983
Handover: 1984
Site area: 10,000 square metres (107,642 square feet)

3.5 New Victoria Theatre

CHRIS BAINES
Newcastle-under-Lyme, UK

When the Victoria Theatre, Stoke-on-Trent, moved into its new octagonal, purpose-built home in 1986, it also moved into an old vicarage garden. Some of the mature trees on the site dated back to the late eighteenth century and their protection was a priority from the beginning. Chris Baines, landscape consultant for the theatre, decided in 1982 that there was little of ecological value in the neglected garden, but that its potential for wildlife was considerable. His brief was to landscape the 0.8-hectare (2-acre) site for this theatre-in-the-round and to incorporate parking for cars and coaches, outdoor rehearsal and performance spaces, and environmental-education facilities for groups of local schoolchildren.

Chris Baines is known for his innovative work in introducing the idea of wildlife gardening to the general public, particularly through television. This, and his involvement in community landscape schemes, came into play here. Local volunteers carried out a wildlife survey of the site and this information was combined with the practical problems of car parking and circulation to work out the details of the scheme. The landscape was designed to maximize the value of existing mature trees, to be planted almost entirely with native wild flowers and to be managed both for wildlife and educational use. Perhaps the most important factor was that the landscape was to be created largely by local volunteers, especially children. A major problem was to build the theatre without damaging the character of the existing landscape. The solution was to define conservation zones around which the contractors erected fencing and to which only the surveyor was granted access.

The siting of the theatre building as near to the road as possible allowed for maximum space at the rear. Unsafe trees were removed, but, generally speaking, the mature trees around the site give an impression both from inside and out that the theatre is surrounded by trees. The parking areas were turned into meadowlands by using fibre-reinforced grass and meadow turf. Hedgebanks of second-hand stone planted with field maple, guelder rose and blackthorn, built by volunteer coal miners, divide the parking bays and add to the natural effect of the landscape. This provides a pleasant outlook for the theatre staff and visiting classes during the daytime when the car parks are usually empty. Initial drainage problems in the car parks have been overcome; the only disappointment is the necessarily less secluded appearance of the coach park. Brick paving has been used for the main entrance approach and a paved terrace behind the theatre acts as circulation space for audiences and as an outdoor classroom for school children during the day.

The car park is screened by hedge banks constructed from secondhand stone and planted with field maple, guelder rose and blackthorn.

The proximity of the planting to the building and the incorporation of existing trees in the scheme can clearly be seen here.

Start on site: 1986
Handover: 1988
Site area: 0.8 hectares (2 acres)

Wild flowers, in the foreground here, are planted in the approach to the building.

Detail of hard landscape in the terraced area behind the theatre, which is used as an open air classroom during the day.

Another group of volunteers, a club for young ornithologists, constructed a small pond, which not only provides water for birds, but attracts amphibians. Most of the plants were grown and donated by local gardeners and, with the use of recycled materials and volunteer labour, costs have been kept to a minimum. This is one of the advantages of Baines' innovative approach: it does not require vast sums of money, which are anyway rarely available for this kind of project, and it engenders a sense of community ownership that can only be good for the future of the theatre.

The most important factor in the entire scheme is the massive involvement of local people and the continuing educational use of the site. Peter Cheeseman, director of the New Victoria Theatre, has been enthusiastically involved from the signing of the lease in 1981. He fully appreciates the need for a long-term commitment to the management of the site and the importance to the theatre of the fullest use of all facilities. The theatre has its own conservation officer, whose duties include direction of garden maintenance and teaching: over 3000 children of all ages take advantage of the environmental education service offered.

Chris Baines has created a landscape which can be shared and enjoyed by theatre staff, actors, theatregoers and schoolchildren. He has also provided the entire community with a project it can justly regard as its own and in which it can take pride and pleasure for many years to come.

A pre-cast concrete pergola, with the climber *Quisqualis indica* in the early stages of clothing the structure, will provide vital shade and contrast to the glare of the hard surfaces.

Part of the North Garden Court. The geometry of the raised beds is inspired by traditional Arabic motifs. Plants are all desert varieties, particularly *Bougainvillea spectabilis* and *Aptenia cordifolia*.

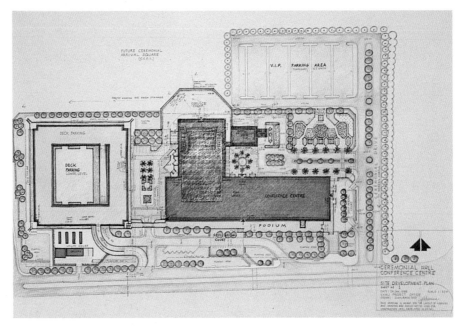

160

3.6

JOGINDR JUDGE KHURANA
Jeddah, Saudi Arabia

Ceremonial Hall and Conference Centre, King Abdulaziz University

This scheme exemplifies the challenges of creating a landscape composition within the specific climatic and social conditions in Saudi Arabia. The project is within the overall campus development for the university and the facilities are designed to serve both the university and, on occasions, the wider city of Jeddah. The landscape architect benefited from being involved in the project design team from the earliest stage and the Ceremonial Hall and Conference Centre is the first project within the university to have a completed and integral landscape framework. The design had to take into account the special conditions prevailing in the country. The social requirements separating men and women in public necessitated dual entrances, courtyards and other facilities. Exceptional provision also had to be made for visits by the royal family and other notables.

In pure landscape terms, the impact of climate is all-pervading. In the stifling heat of Jeddah, the provision of shade is essential and movement of air desirable. The ground conditions are harsh, with acute saline soil and a severe shortage of water for irrigation. Plants have been selected that are either native species or have adapted to the taxing local conditions. Treated sewage effluent is the only source for irrigation water, topped-up occasionally with portable water, especially during the hot summer months when there is a smaller population on campus. An average monthly demand for the supply of irrigation water was assessed as 5000 cubic metres (176,572 cubic feet).

The approaches and entrances to this enormous building complex have both symbolic and practical significance. Vehicle access is encouraged right up to the curtillage of the building to enable visitors and students to step from their air-conditioned, chauffeur-driven limousines, without a long, debilitating walk in the heat from a distant car park. The entrance courts also double-up as access points for pedestrians. Each entrance is emphasized by architectural and landscape detailing, in particular, by introducing a variety of different fountains. Similarly, planting design recognizes the separate functions of the external space and species have been selected accordingly. The two most important arrival courts have been planted with date palms (*Phoenix dactilifera*) 8 metres (26 feet 3 inches) high. By way of contrast, the North Garden is a splash of colour and cheerfulness to offset the somewhat severe appearance of the building, but the climatic and irrigation constraints limit the range of planting possibilities. Grass has been avoided altogether and succulents and tolerant groundcovers provide an alternative carpet.

It is inappropriate to compare this design solution with any scheme outside Saudi Arabia. The stringent physical, social and administrative conditions severely restrict the freedom of the landscape designer. Expensive materials such as granite, cut Carrara marble and glazed tiles have been effectively used to enhance the composition and the introduction of plants carefully considered and applied. One hopes that the design draws strength from the culture, rather than constraint from the climate. Competent schemes such as this may encourage others and be the forerunners of a new era of landscape design in the Islamic countries of the Middle East.

Fountain and water jet with the Royal Pavilion entrance area in the background. Water conservation demands that this feature is intermittently working.

Start on site:
Handover: April 1989
Site area: 5.8 hectares
(14⅓ acres)

161

A view of the striking
architecture and the
way this has been taken
up and manipulated in
landscape form.

3.7

EDA COLLABORATIVE INC.
AND PARENT, LATREILLE
ASSOCIÉS LTD.
Ottawa/Hull, Quebec, Canada

Canadian Museum of Civilization

The brief for this project was to house the precious cultural artefacts of the Canadian nation within a setting befitting its heritage that also looked to the future. The interpretation by the architect Douglas Cardinal was to create a museum in a park, utilizing many symbols from the Canadian environment. The landscape designers, EDA Collaborative Inc., worked directly for the architectural consortium, whose client was the Canadian Museums Construction Corporation, a Crown corporation of the Government of Canada, set up specifically to manage and build the museum. The site is in an important riverside location (previously used for car parking and as a construction site), looking across the Ottawa River to Parliament Hill, at the heart of Canada's capital city.

The landscape designers were considerably influenced by the unique curvilinear form of the museum and by the wish to create a new approach to museum experience. In particular, the concept of a museum in a park was the basis for creating an environment for outdoor activities and events to complement the experience of national and international visitors within the museum. The building mass has been split into two parts to form a central space and emphasize the view axis, which links two parts of the national capital; the City of Hull in Quebec and Ottawa in Ontario. The architect had a strong respect for the landscape context and its ability to symbolize the integration of national symbols. The museum within the park mirrors the emergence of the North American continent with its form sculpted by the winds, rivers and glaciers. The architect evoked the metaphor of a melting Canadian glacier to describe the form of the buildings and this concept has been extended into the landscape, flowing down towards the Ottawa River. This synthesis is described briefly in the promotion literature for the museum: 'A stroll around the grounds reveals constantly changing perspectives – a glass wall captures pictures from the landscape, a stone wall coils like a snail shell, while at night the copper vaults and domes float on cushions of light.' A recreational bikeway and walkway links the park with the city, thus integrating this dominant, focal river-front site with the local, open space.

The landscape design introduced a series of zones, from the natural soft edges along the river, through curved terraces, water features, ponds, waterfalls and fountains, which step upward through a central axis to the entrance plaza, which is the deck over hidden car parking. Looking back, there are evocative views of the Parliament Buildings as a symbolic image of the Canadian nation.

The low seat-walls of limestone match the building walls which, by this coordination, are extended sensitively into the surrounds. Also, the special pre-cast pavers use limestone aggregates in modular curved shapes to complement the soft colour and curves of the building. Major earth mounding and site grading with 'buffer' planting separates and screens the service and delivery areas. The framework tree planting recreates part of the original evergreen forest which was part of the Ottawa river valley.

The design exploits the site's impressive views of Parliament Hill.

Start on site: 1985
Handover: 1989
Site area: 10 hectares (25 acres)

One of the stronger areas of planting, colourfully setting off the elevations of limestone texture and wash.

The complexity of the building and the large number of individuals and organizations with an interest in its development necessitated sophisticated methods of coordination and presentation. For example, the landscape project management team and the client in Ottawa were linked by on-line electronic communication, and specialist computer applications were developed to help landscape architects and architects to work together on the curvilinear geometry and forms.

Behind the enthusiasm of the designers, one senses that the creative process was difficult and often frustrating. Numerous groups were involved in the consultative and approval stages and each member of the client groups, including various agencies and departments, had very high expectations for a quality landscape, but no budget to offer. Only limited sums for landscape works were allocated in the original budget for this very prominent site. In addition, changes in political priorities during the period of the project also challenged the determination of the design team to see through the crucial conceptual elements and structure. The fact that this has largely been achieved is very creditable.

The budgetary constraints which, at first appearance, may have compromised the external design, have to an extent been turned to advantage. With a consciousness that 'visitor fatigue' quickly sets in within a conventional internal museum, great play is made on the ability of the landscape framework to host outdoor experiences and displays. User groups are encouraged to provide elements which were considered within the programme, but beyond the landscape budget. In fact the whole site, including the buildings, is used by the government for more functions than those offered by a traditional museum, including outdoor receptions and special events.

The architectural and landscape statement is powerful and, despite some uncertainty on the way, is apparently now well received. But the landscape composition is incomplete and will continue to need a firm hand to see that the integrity of the initial investment is not lost by inadequacies in later thinking. In the words of the architect Douglas Cardinal, 'Canadians with their roots in several different cultures are evolving a new culture'. This project ably portrays the dynamics and vitality of Canadian society.

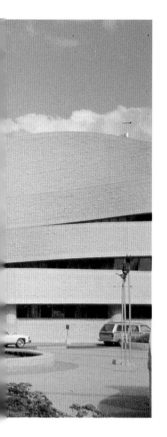

Like glacial water, the fountains and pools fall towards the Ottawa River. The shadow of Parliament Hill looms over the whole scheme and contrasts with the Museum.

The metaphor of the glacier can be seen in the broken rocks and sparse planting, allowing the whole vista to become a symbol of the wider Canadian landscape.

View of City Hall
showing the rock
formations and tree
planting.

Blocks of stone at the
pool and fountain.

3.8 *City Hall, Public Park*

GEORG PENKER

Hagen, Germany

When the city of Hagen held a competition for the building of a new city hall in the mid-1970s, it was Georg Penker's landscape proposals that decided the winning entry. The client, Hagen Town Council, wanted a strong and attractive identity for the park surrounding the city hall. Complete integration of architecture and landscape entailing full cooperation in external and internal design between landscape designer and architect was the key. The selected site was a former quarry on a piece of high ground at one end of the city, with imposing rock faces up to 40 metres (131 feet 4 inches) high. All the other entries located the building directly in front of the rock face; the winning team sited it at the end of the ridge overlooking the city, allowing the full height of the face to be seen.

Penker's basic idea was to emphasize the existing landscape, making rock the decisive design element, both as a material and as the rock face itself. In order to reinforce the idea of a 'rock park', all other structures were kept in the background. The rock theme was to provide the linking concept between the internal and external spaces. Initially, this idea took a lot of selling, as an image of the traditional town park, complete with lawns, flowerbeds, trees and shrubs, was deeply embedded in the minds of the city's representatives. Fortunately, they were open to persuasion and accepted this innovative scheme.

Excavation for the basement floors of the new city hall involved blasting out the solid rock. Originally, it was intended that small pieces should be blasted out that could be used as road-base material, but, after further persuasion, the designers were able to obtain an agreement for the excavation of 3- to 4-metre (10- to 13-foot) cubes of rock. These were to form part of the characteristic landscape treatment. The city hall is linked to a hotel by a large flight of steps broken up by these blocks of stone. They also act as a backdrop for a specially designed fountain. Together, these features form a dramatic entrance to the building from the city.

The area of the park located close to the rock face is characterized by near-natural rock and scree vegetation. In order to encourage the development of limestone grassland flora, all planting areas were covered in a 30-centimetre (11¾-inch) layer of quarry waste. The few paths are also designed as rocky footpaths and covered with a surface of quarry waste. Car parking is divided into small areas of rocky landscape and carefully integrated into the surrounding park. Night-time illumination of the rock face provides a particularly attractive feature. A deliberate decision was taken not to create any specially designated zones, such as play areas. The intention was to encourage children and citizens to spontaneous and imaginative use of all of the park's spaces and this seems to have happened. In particular, the area in front of the rock face has proved suitable for open-air concerts. What is innovative about this scheme is the scenic integration of the external spaces of a former quarry into a civic park. Instead of a possibly rather bland, traditional style of park, the people of Hagen may now enjoy a contemporary space with the drama of the rock.

Detail of the large flight of steps linking the City Hall to the hotel, broken up by blocks of stone.

Start on site: 1981
Handover: 1983
Site area: 3.5 hectares (9 acres)

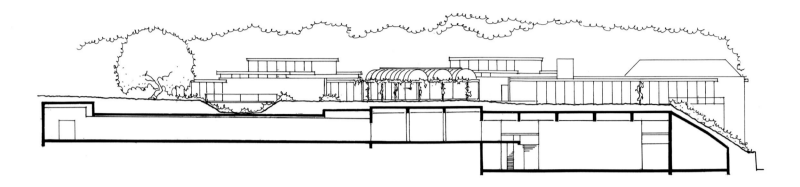

Plan view of the whole of the Museum of Modern Art with the hidden harbour to the left (west) and the Sound to the right (east).

An approach through the majestic beech trees is enlivened by the dappled shade falling on the gently curving granite-sett path.

The house and park at Louisiana date from the middle of the nineteenth century, with the park developed very much in the English landscape style. However, the site was originally fortification for a hidden inland harbour built during the Napoleonic wars between England and France, which ended in 1815. These bastions and embankments have influenced the effective collaboration between architectural and landscape design at Louisiana. The Museum of Modern Art first opened to the public in 1958 and has been steadily extended in phases during the intervening years, with the new graphics wing being the latest and perhaps final part of this composition of art, landscape and architecture. It is an impressive and intriguing fact that the client, Knud Jensen, and the designers have worked together on this project since the mid-1950s (the landscape practice since 1964), and this clearly shows in the continuity of design philosophy, although each phase has created its own demands and solutions. The design approach to the new graphics wing has followed that of the earlier phases, with the client contributing greatly to the design process. The resulting interplay of ideas between designers and clients demonstrates a rare confidence in form and function.

Louisiana is also known as the hidden museum, and the latest phase lives up to that name. The new graphics wing has been placed entirely below ground to avoid blocking out the stunning views over the sound towards Sweden. The gallery connects the earlier winged museum extensions, thus completing a circular tour, described by the designers as 'a little voyage of discovery'. At each end of the gallery the visitor can emerge into the wider world. The greenhouse in the south wing and the interchange point at the north encourage visitors to pause before striking out in a new direction. These are pivotal points in the relationship between the architecture and the landscape.

The major rooms in the new gallery are of such a size that, had they not been firmly anchored into and below the landform, their mass would significantly have altered the careful balance between architecture and landscape within the whole museum. The various phases of development have thus gradually taken over the park but not overwhelmed it. Interiors have been sunk ever deeper to avoid dominating the park and the older trees.

The success of the landscape design associated with the new graphics wing is in its apparent simplicity. A grass carpet has been pulled over the building mass, preserving the critical views, but also drawing architecture and landscape together. A grass plateau was created by a two-metre (6-foot 6-inch) retaining wall from a rough slope that ran down to the foreshore and ended in a steep drop. With the slopes, this forms a simple backcloth, encouraging relaxation, play or theatre. The terraces and steps provide unobtrusive resting places, particularly the granite steps. The visitor is encouraged to explore the park, and the careful placing of sculpture within quiet enclosed gardens, or dramatically viewed against the ever-changing sea and sky, adds a real sense of surprise.

Start on site: September 1989
Handover: June 1990
Site area: 30,000 square metres (322,928 square feet)

168

3.9 *New Graphics Wing, Louisiana Museum of Modern Art*

LEA NØRGAARD AND VIBEKE HOLSCHER
Humlebaek, North Zealand, Denmark

The grass roof to the new graphic wing offers a spectacular setting for sculpture. The museum rightly prides itself on presenting sculpture in advantageous settings.

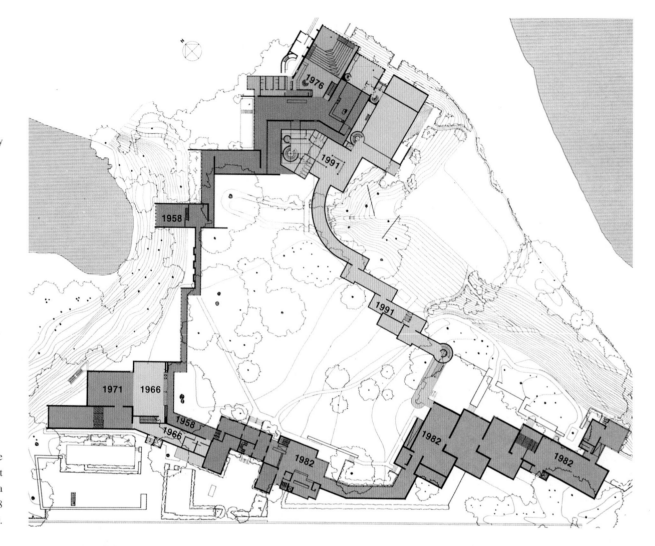

Opposite The glass bay with the grassed roof above, giving spacious views over the Sound.

Plan showing the various development stages at Louisiana between 1958 and 1990.

The new graphics wing emerges out of the tightly knit landform. The winter garden and the terraces in front of the cafeteria and concert hall can be glimpsed above.

The landscape architects have worked carefully with the palette of materials laid down over the past thirty years. White walls and red clinker-brick floors draw internal and external spaces together, while granite flags, steps and small setts extend the coordinated pavings away from the building. Ground cover of ivy, vinca, pachysandra and ferns continue earlier planting, and the rare but mature collection of trees within the park has been augmented by new planting. In particular, the beech, so pervasive in North Zealand, forms a graceful framework, and care has been taken to extend this for the future. Twining and self-clinging plants are encouraged where the building dares to rise above the turf and specialist plants have been introduced into the quite separate zones found in the winter garden, glass bay and conservatory in the south wing.

The landscape composition is largely one of restraint and straightforward principles, which can easily be overlooked in the stimulating environment of this museum. That need not detract from the achievement of the overall design.

It would have been so easy to damage the delicate interrelationships or overwhelm the subtleties of the total composition, but the various phases have led on to enhance this composition within the park setting. The landscape architects have been retained to advise and supervise the maintenance programme and this should help to ensure that the high standard of design is protected in the future. The new gallery is indeed a worthy successor to the early enthusiasm and innovation at Louisiana. The masterly stroke of rolling the lawn over the gallery enhances the visitor experience, and certainly improves the unusual visual contact between the park and the seascape of the sound.

170

The dwarf tubular steel fence, set in curvilinear patterns within a sunken garden, adds a striking element in a tranquil composition in which all the various elements work comfortably together.

3.10 *Farnborough College of Technology*

PREBEN JAKOBSEN, JAKOBSEN
LANDSCAPE ARCHITECTS
Farnborough, Hampshire, UK

Hampshire County Council is one of the more enlightened educational authorities in the United Kingdom and has an enviable reputation in recent years for school and college design. It has given particular emphasis to the learning environment and this has been translated into the building programme in areas such as energy conservation and landscape design. The brief for the landscape architect for this project had to meet the prime objectives of uniting both existing and new landscape in a coherent overall scheme, of providing a design of environmental quality in keeping with the architecture, and of establishing a dynamic image suited to a forward-looking college.

The site area is flat, acidic heathland with a number of mature trees, notably oak, scots pine and holly. Part of the site has a parkland landscape and of particular note are the twin rows of mature deodar cedars which form an impressive avenue at the centre of the site.

The scheme was based on several courtyards, with a spine mall and several lesser malls, crossing the spine. This fitted with the client's preference to see order and elegance in the architecture and site planning of an educational environment. The architecture is a relatively high-tech, grid-based design in which all the subsystems of structure, envelope, mechanical, interiors and external landscape are fully integrated.

The circulation is perceived as a network of pedestrian ways passing through the site. The grid acts as a neutral support for changing social and educational demands to which the facilities may be put. Working with this order, Preben Jakobsen emphasizes the spatial structure and aims to bring relief to the virtually flat site by reducing levels to create sunken gardens and raising levels elsewhere. He sees the landscape design process at Farnborough as essentially land art.

This interpretation would have been given greater credence if his ambition to introduce an earth sculpture adjacent to the main highway, on the boundary of the site, had been successful. The intention was to convert a subsoil disposal problem into an earth sculpture symbolizing a humanistic and dynamic life force, with a continuous curvilinear arris line, rising rapidly to five metres (16 feet 5 inches) at one point. The artistic merit was lost on the local authority planners (with completely different responsibilities to the client body) who deemed it to be construction and insisted that it be removed.

The landscape architect has attempted to affirm connections with nature in other ways. He feels that centres of education should be highly landscaped in order to draw attention to the qualities and potential of the surrounding natural world. The placement of free-standing boulders reminiscent of standing stones in Northern European and Japanese cultures particularly stresses this connection. The boulders also appear at corners and junctions, helping to protect plants from robust students. This is another subtheme in which the practical and aesthetic appreciation of landscape are combined.

The mature deodar cedars form a major element in the courtyard design.

Start on site: 1984
Handover: 1988
Site area: 3.25 hectares (8 acres)

173

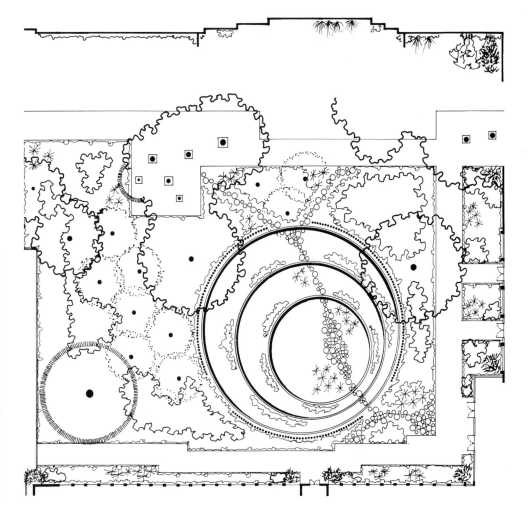

The Refectory
Courtyard, with
luscious foliage against
the fully glazed
building elevation.

The external landscape is divided into courtyards and gardens. Most striking is the cedar courtyard, where nine mature specimen deodar cedars have been carefully protected and form a major element in the courtyard design. Due to the new, lowered floor-levels of the adjacent building, it was necessary to form a rectangular raised plateau for the cedars. The surface pattern under the dark-stemmed trees has been articulated by a series of circular stepping stones and groups of carefully selected craggy, vertical slate boulders which contrast with large smooth granite stones on a bed of amber-coloured marine aggregate.

As a contrast, the refectory courtyard has a theme of green organic sculpture formed from stylized, peat-filled columns of wire mesh planted with ivy. The planting towers vary in height and size and incorporate, an internal irrigation system. Distinctive plants are used, including bamboo, parasol pine and the blue-grey willow-pattern pine.

The new college building is mainly glazed and can best be likened to a conservatory. The cold-house conservatory regime has the enormous advantage to a landscape designer of being a suitable environment for a wide range of temperate duality plants – plants which can be used both inside and outside. Many temperate plants are on the borderline of outdoor hardiness in Britain and the conditions of the main malls at Farnborough have proved an exciting location for temperate plants. The malls are naturally ventilated with shading introduced on the south-facing elevations. Smoke vents open in warm weather to allow outside air to circulate.

From the beginning, an exuberant jungle-like plantscape was envisaged, using many bamboos and colourful climbers to soften and interact with the building fabric. Plants from all over the world have been introduced and the European Bamboo Society now lists the college as a location for checking bamboo varieties. Plants are introduced direct into the open

ground, dug deeper in internal situations and watered by means of a subterranean, automatic irrigation system.

Although the sensitive touch of a knowledgeable plantsman can clearly be seen in this design, the hard landscape has also been the product of careful scrutiny and proper coordination. In particular, frost-proof blue paviors link external and internal circulation spaces and they have also been used to form drainage channels. The column bases have been filled with aggregate in polyester resin, to match the amber aggregates used as ground cover in the courtyards.

In such a complex scheme in which planting plays a major part, effective maintenance is crucial to ensure a thriving and healthy environment. The optimum growing conditions have meant not only a phenomenal growth rate, but also the opportunity for rapid spread of plant disease and pests, which need to be kept under constant control.

Farnborough College of Technology can be considered a firm and aesthetically satisfying design, where the skills of landscape architect, architect and service engineers have been able to work well together. The seams are not too obvious. The landscape architect advised on maintenance over the first three years of occupation and produced a maintenance manual for the client. The designers recognized that changing educational requirements might put unforeseen demands upon the organizational and physical structure. The network of communication routes can be altered or the grid adapted. But one feels that the landscape which so influences the atmosphere of this place would suffer irreparable damage if too many incremental extensions or physical adjustments were necessary. Is the landscape flexible enough to cope with future demands? An impossible question to answer, but it may be vulnerable to change.

A jungle-like plantscape was envisaged in the glazed malls that criss-cross the building. Supplied by automatic irrigation, the plants are fully monitored for pest and disease control.

The 'green' rooftops merge with the planting beyond.

View from Lake Burley Griffin. The effect of the building and its tower is of a spaceship reaching into the sky.

3.11 *New Parliament House*

PETER G. ROLLAND AND
ASSOCIATES
Canberra, Australia

In 1979, the Australian Government launched a two-stage international design competition for a new Parliament House in Canberra, to house all legislative and executive facilities and take Canberra into the twenty-first century. The landscape programme was to include a wide range of services for a staff of 3500 and 2 million visitors annually, including roads, parking, circulation and recreational facilities.

Peter Rolland of Rolland/Towers led the landscape team, chosen as part of the competition-winning design group out of 329 entries from 29 countries. The team comprised an architect, engineers and landscape architects, who worked closely together from concept to execution to ensure the integrity of the design. The landscape architect was responsible for the design, development and coordination of all surface elements and works external to the building. This included plazas, roadways, lawns and gardens over extensive underground facilities, such as a loading dock, parking and major public rooms. Integration of the complex architectural and engineering technicalities was essential. Since major portions of the building complex were underground, the landscape designer had, in effect, responsibility for 85 per cent of the 33-hectare (81½-acre) site. The work involved included layout, grading, planting, irrigation, design of fountain and pool (in conjunction with technical consultants), pavings and design features, such as lighting, and the location of art works.

The original competition for a new Australian capital held in 1912 was won by the architect Walter Burley Griffin, who had worked with Frank Lloyd Wright and was sensitive to the importance of landscape in the overall design. Using the topography of the Molongolo Valley as his main design influence, Griffin arranged the important design elements in a formal geometric order that successfully merged the built form with the natural landscape. Capital Hill was a focal point both architecturally and symbolically. The designers of the new Parliament House were similarly concerned to balance the need to build on Capital Hill with its impact on the natural landscape. They therefore decided that built form and land form should be treated as equally essential elements, and that only by merging them completely could a suitably monumental yet natural result be achieved.

From all major areas of the city of Canberra, a series of avenues converge on Capital Hill, formally connecting the city with its Parliament. Capital Circle encloses a circular site within which is Parliament Drive, the main access road into which all the avenues flow. This drive forms an inner square separating the site into two distinct landscape areas. The peripheral areas within Capital Circle and outside Parliament Drive contain dense plantings of Australian native trees and shrubs. Care will need to be taken that they do not, in time, obscure the building. The central loading dock is located here and its elevations were lowered so that its roof would function as a series of stepped formal gardens from Parliament Drive, with truck access kept at a discreet distance well below the sloping terrain. 'Rooms' have been carved out of the native woody bosques to allow for various recreation needs. Meandering paths also provide a relaxing contrast to the formal area immediately surrounding Parliament House.

Courtyard showing path detailing and reflecting pool.

Start on site: May 1988
Handover: May 1989
Site area: 33 hectares (81½ acres)

NEW PARLIAMENT HOUSE CANBERRA
DESIGN DEVELOPMENT
LANDSCAPE PLAN

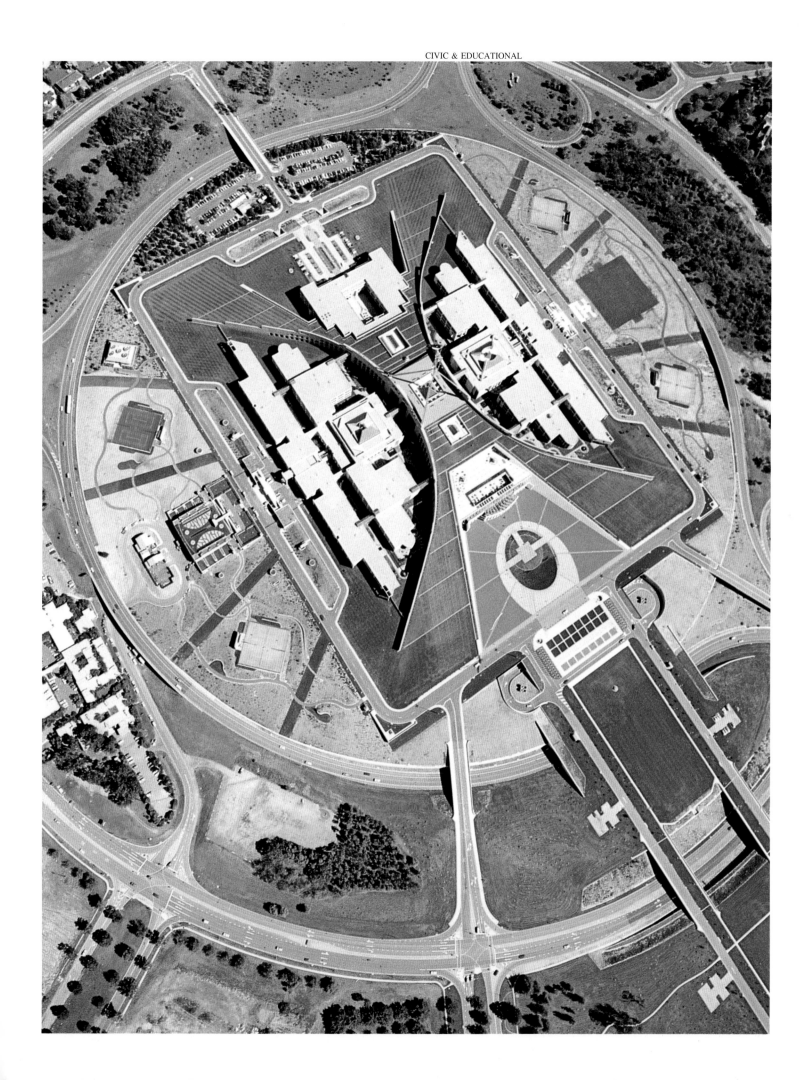

Hard landscape in the great verandah and forecourts.

Within the area created by Parliament Drive, a park-like setting, with groups of eucalyptus set in clipped lawns, offers views of the building. Entry areas to the House, Senate and Executive Wings are defined by patterns of granite paving, fountains and more formal planting. Grass ramps, which appear to flow over the roof, are traversed by a series of granite bands, increasing in frequency as the ramps get higher and culminating in an observation terrace at the summit below the flag.

The main focal point for all visitors is the forecourt. Its broad expanse is accentuated by the inclined planes of the perimeter walls and, with its ground surface designed with a progression of different paving materials, creates a sense of reception. To this end, the progression works subtly from Parliament Drive up to the Great Verandah, as well as inward towards the central fountain. Colours, patterns and textures of water, granite and gravel are designed to provide tactile finishes and suggest the vastness of Australia's desert interior.

The courtyards of the House and Senate are formed by the open areas between the curved walls and the office wings. A pattern of grass-jointed paving is flanked by elegant lawns, shrub beds and water features. The courtyards are linked by a continuous winding granite path and punctuated by carefully sited small sculptures. The large central courtyards are designed for major gatherings while the smaller more intimate areas are for quiet strolling or relaxation.

One vital aspect of this scheme, as far as landscape architecture is concerned, has been the raising of public consciousness of the landscape profession. In particular, the landscape architect was seen to have responsibility for establishing site engineering criteria and for his ability to bring together natural and manmade landscapes. Indeed, after the usual public scepticism that tends to greet vast government projects the world over, the Australian public became very involved in the scheme. For example, at one point when cost-cutting measures threatened the entire landscape budget, local schoolchildren left small potted plants on the project's doorstep. Most importantly, perhaps, the nation has been shown a design standard that successfully integrates rather than segregates the varying elements of landscape and architecture, which can only be to the good of both professions and to Australia.

Previous page Aerial view of the site, showing geometric shapes within the circular layout.

Opposite View down onto a courtyard, showing grass and paving detail, formal planting and curving pathway.

The University square
has become a focus for
celebration and
creates a new sense of
place.

3.12 *University Square*

GUTTORM GUTTORMSGAARD
AND BJARNE AASEN
The University of Tromsø, Norway

In early 1988, five artists were invited, in a limited competition, to submit ideas for the form and shape of the whole of the University Square around which are located the main buildings of Tromsø University. A year later, Professor Guttormsgaard's proposal for a labyrinth, with a central feature of a hot-water spring, was accepted as the winning scheme and implementation began soon after. There has been little change since then from the ideas submitted for the competition. Professor Aasen, a member of the competition jury, was asked by the University of Tromsø to collaborate in the implementation of the scheme.

Tromsø is the most northerly university in the world, on latitude 70 degrees North, and, for a period of exactly two months from 21 November, the polar night sets in and the sun never rises above the horizon. But the dark snowy winters give way to light summers with the unrivalled beauty of the midnight sun. For staff, students and the local population, surrounding natural elements and the forces of nature are very evident and a real part of everyday existence. It is both appropriate and practical that the designer turned to this recurring theme. A labyrinthine snake surrounds and guards a symbolic, warm, luminous source in the centre. The idea of the labyrinth pattern here stems from Arctic folklore which is one of the youngest labyrinth cultures in the world. The labyrinths were probably formed as a magical symbol to protect communities against external forces.

Even in the snow the essential pattern can still be seen with exposed boulders placed carefully to follow it.

Start on site: 1989
Handover: 1991
Site area: 3000 square metres
(32,292 square feet)

Illumination streams into the winter twilight, an image of the polar sky overhead.

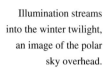

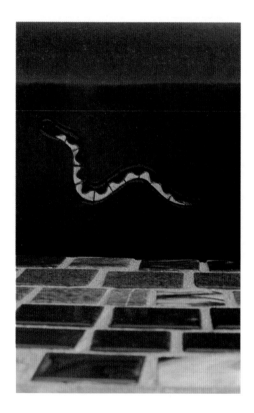

A labyrinthine snake symbol and polished, locally occuring stones.

It was very important to all concerned that this design for the University Square should be constructed by people from northern Norway, using local skills and materials. Specially selected stones in all sizes, from gravel and natural occurring shingle, to errant boulders ground by ice or shaped by water, have been joined with cut, honed and polished stones and placed in intricate patterns within the overall labyrinth. The centrally placed basin conjures up the immediacy of earth and sky. From within the polished, mirror finish, hot water creates frost 'smoke' in winter and in summer is suggestive of warmer climates further south. Illumination from a light source at the bottom of the basin streams out into the darkness from 4000 holes, to symbolize the star-studded northern polar sky. Aware that for many weeks of the year the ground is frozen and snow-covered, the designer has installed underground heating to melt the snow and ensure that the central feature is always visible and active, even in the depths of winter.

Vegetation has little place in this composition, corresponding to the Arctic character of the surrounding area. But small Arctic birch have been collected from nearby and spruce and pine brought in from nurseries in northern Norway.

It is expected that, in the near future, sculptures by the Lapp artist Anne Lise Josefsen will be added to this unusual landscape design. The whole project has been made possible through the cooperation of Tromsø University and the Norwegian Fund for Art in State Buildings.

The designer has turned the apparent adversity of the severe climate into a powerful, positive force, forging a highly symbolic and fascinating statement out of what might otherwise have been an alienating experience. Reliance on local crafts, labour, and materials has, one feels, reflected many of the values in this community. Although a deterministic design, it would appear to offer room for expansion and adaption if the enthusiasm is there! In its own way, the labyrinth theme responds to the local atmosphere and creates a vivid sense of place – highly appropriate to a university.

The central basin has a polished mirror finish over which hot water flows, giving a sense of vitality even in the depths of the long winter.

The central theme of this project is the labyrinthine snake pattern stemming from Arctic folklore.

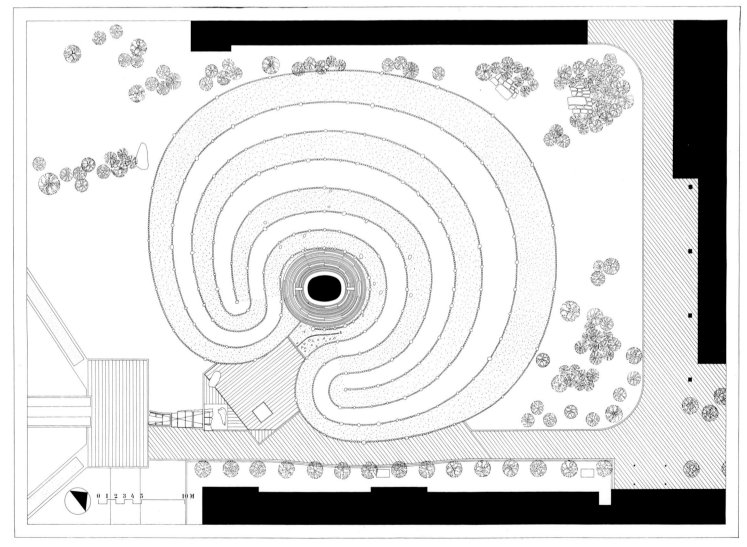

Franconia Notch (see
pages 196-201)

4 Landscape Planning & Management

Stockley Park (see pages 218-223)

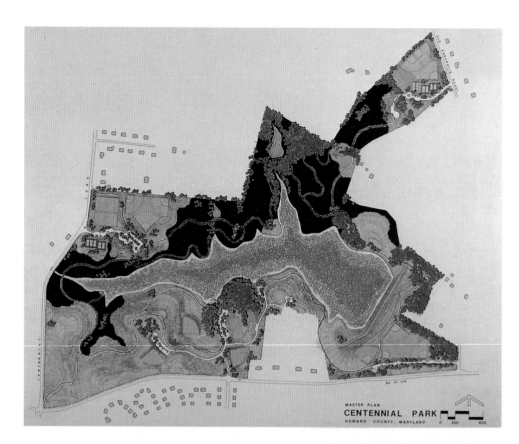

This aerial sketch of the proposed park illustrates the high percentage of land dedicated to meadows, old fields and succession woodlands.

The headquarters building, the largest of the park's family of structures and shelters, provides concessions and restroom facilities as well as a park rangers' office.

4.1 Centennial Park and Reservoir

JOHN C HALL, LDR
INTERNATIONAL INC.
Howard County, Maryland, USA

Howard County, in the State of Maryland, has a predominantly rural history, but, trapped between the major urban centres of Washington DC and Baltimore, it has come under increasing development pressure in recent decades. Public officials have also become increasingly concerned with flood control and the protection of the Patuxent River watershed. Several sites for small reservoirs were identified by the United States Department of Agriculture Soil Conservation Service and the proposed site of the Centennial Park and Reservoir was seen to meet both the flood protection requirements and the anticipated recreational needs of Howard County's expanding population. Support for the flood control project increased significantly after Hurricane Agnes sent a 1.5-metre (5-foot)-high wave through a recently completed local town centre.

Land assembly by the local authority commenced in 1967 to safeguard the basin and critical adjacent land areas, which were already attracting the attention of major developers. LDR International Inc. was appointed in 1975 to prepare a masterplan for the whole site area. The initial brief identified the requirement for a flood relief reservoir and an undefined combination of active and passive recreational facilities. The proposals that were eventually accepted and implemented only became apparent during the design process.

The master plan for the Centennial Park and Reservoir predicted that the resource would in time become surrounded by suburban development, which has in fact happened. The master plan not only identified the importance of the valley and water-supply feeder streams, but also the wider conservation value of established meadows, old fields, woodland margins and sustainable woodland. Protection of these zones within the overall landscape framework was only achieved by resisting pressure for commercial development.

Whereas the surrounding rural land has been built upon, the plan has safeguarded a cross-section of the local vegetation communities, wildlife habitats and topography. Visitors to the park are free to roam at will and discover the diversity of this conserved countryside. As the master plan progressed, special attention has been given to stressing the natural resource and protecting its essential components. The result is a mature and respected park, rather than a purely functional engineering solution to a flood-control problem.

The reservoir features varying depths and edge treatments to provide suitable shoreline and submerged habitats for fish, turtles and birds. Shoreline stabilization techniques utilized indigenous vegetation; trees felled during lake construction were used to create shallow bars for fish spawning. The many islands invite quiet exploration by canoe, while providing refuge and nesting sites for waterfowl. Use and access by people is encouraged, but with a careful eye to appropriate nature conservation. Active recreational uses are not given preferential treatment and are limited to the margins of the park adjacent to residential development. Community involvement in the planning process and in the management of Centennial Park attempts to reduce areas of conflict as well as encouraging support and understanding in the balance necessary between recreation, conservation and flood control interests.

Centennial Reservoir features varying depths and edge treatments to provide suitable shoreline and submerged habitats for fish, turtles and birds.

Start on site: 1980
Handover: 1987
Site area: 133 hectares (328 acres)

An aerial view of the lake site: the diverse nature of the planning objectives demanded a multidisciplinary approach.

Footbridges and varying vantage points increase visitors' enjoyment, while protecting sensitive habitats from excessive pedestrian traffic.

The landscape consultant has been responsible for preparation of the master plan, design development and contract documents for all phases of the park programme over a twelve-year period. The landscape plan, which was part of the original master plan, also guides the annual landscape maintenance programme. Undoubtedly, the multi-disciplinary team approach has contributed to the success of this project: engineering consultants provided lake design; civil, mechanical and electrical engineering services and specialized consultants were retained to advise on shoreline stabilization, habitat protection and establishment, as well as creating fish-spawning beds.

When the planning for Centennial Park began, the land was not under immediate threat, but subsequent development pressures in Howard County have proved the value of investing in this substantial landscape plan. The designer provided the vision and the client offered the necessary stewardship. The resource has become more precious and appreciated by nearby residents and visitors as time has gone on. It demonstrates the benefit of creativity on a large scale over a long period of time.

Centennial Park and Reservoir is used for educational programmes and experimental resource management. It appears to have achieved recognition and respect in a relatively short period. This must in part have been achieved by the careful attention to detail and community support in the planning stage, as well as the continuing commitment through public funds.

Site plan showing
planting areas.

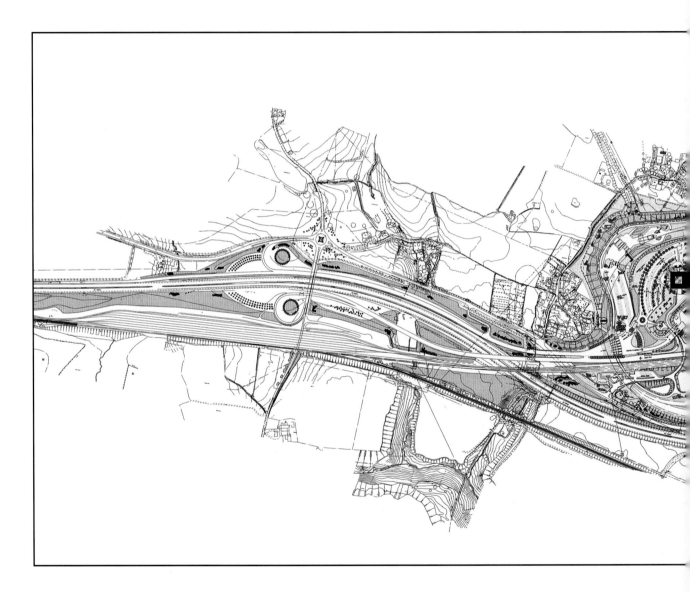

4.2 *Channel Tunnel, UK Terminal*

BUILDING DESIGN PARTNERSHIP
Folkestone, Kent, UK

Start on site: 1986
Handover: 1992
Site area: Approximately 100 hectares
(247 acres)

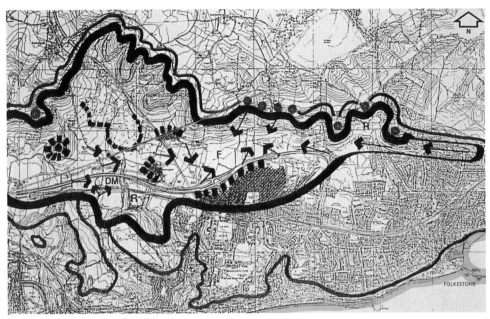

VISUAL BARRIERS WITHIN VALLEY
Road embankments woods, buildings

VIEWS FROM ROADS

AREAS WITH VIEWS OF THE
HIGHEST MAST LIGHTING

AREAS WITH VIEWS OF THE SITE

HOUSING AREAS WITH VIEWS OF THE SITE

IMPORTANT VIEWS FROM NORTH DOWNS

F   FOLKESTONE SITE

DM   B R DOLLANDS MOOR SITE

R   RETENTION LAGOON

H   HOLYWELL COOMBE SITE

The terminal site lies in
an Area of Outstanding
Natural Beauty.

This has been one of the largest construction projects in the world in recent years. The requirement to accommodate responsibly enormous quantities of spoil from the Channel Tunnel excavations, while at the same time developing prestigious terminal facilities, including roads, car parking and surrounds to reception buildings, has challenged the design team. It is a high profile project on the outskirts of Folkestone, on a critical development path, with many factors governing overall progress.

In landscape terms, it has proved a particularly sensitive project. The site falls within the statutory and advisory controls of an Area of Outstanding Natural Beauty and, under the European Community directive governing such work, a comprehensive Environmental Assessment was required from the landscape consultant. As part of the consultative and advisory process, the landscape programme and proposals had to be considered by Parliamentary Select Committees in order to obtain approvals.

The brief to the landscape consultant was simply to integrate the terminal into its surroundings and meet the demands of the planning authorities and operators (Eurotunnel) in the most cost-effective way.

The landscape strategy set out to satisfy many criteria. As well as announcing the terminal as a project of national importance to travellers, the design aims to be a highlight of the journey. The setting has to be of appropriate scale and quality for an Area of Outstanding Natural Beauty, as well as for surrounding residential areas. An important design intention was to consider carefully the impact on these areas; new planting had to relate to the scale of existing planting and the strategy was conceived to promote and protect nature conservation interests.

The successful integration of the engineering and building works has in part been achieved through the early involvement of landscape architects in the preparation of the environmental assessment and the site planning. Existing resources have been sensibly husbanded; topsoil and turf have been transplanted to recreate the vegetation in parts of the site which will now be left undisturbed, and oak transplants have been grown from seed collected from the site before development. Within the terminal, planting has been graded to create a transition from the surrounding native woodlands to a more formal central landscape. Planted bunds protect nearby villages and the new road system is integrated into the landscape by large-scale planting. Where possible, the effect of the structural landscape proposals has been accelerated by advance planting in order to achieve greater impact at the time the terminal is opened. This has involved a careful programme of pre-ordering at the supplying nursery.

Landscape design has been at the centre of this massive architectural and engineering construction project. It has been perceived at all levels of interest and responsibility within the client organization and government as welding together the functional requirements of the project and also as a means of integrating with the surrounding countryside and urban fringe. No project of this size and complexity can avoid leaving a huge mark on the landscape. The landscape architects have attempted to convert the problems of integration and scale into an opportunity for a comprehensive landscape design. Substantial resources have been dedicated to this, but at the time of writing it is still too early to measure truly the success. But one can commend the visionary scale of the landscape proposals in a landscape design and planning exercise of great political and physical sensitivity.

The landscaping plan aims to integrate the new terminal with the surrounding countryside and urban fringe.

FILL SLOPE PLANTING

MEDIAN · TRAVEL LANE · SHOULDER · CURB · PLANTING LIMIT · EXISTING GRADE
3' · 12' · 9' · 21' · 30'

The 'Old Man' viewing area, showing boulders used to stabilize the lake edge and screening of roadway and interpretive displays.

Top Conceptual plan of north-bound Profile Lake viewing area. The secondary viewing area shown needed careful siting because of landslide hazards.

Franconia Notch State Park is set in the White Mountains National Forest, whose scenic attractions, including Appalachian Trail hiking and cycle routes, draw two million visitors each year. Its most famous feature, a natural profile known as The Old Man of the Mountain, has been New Hampshire's state symbol since 1945.

In 1971, a decision was taken to construct a 17.7-kilometre (11-mile) segment of Interstate 93 on the park's narrow valley floor. This led to a bitter and lengthy debate between state and federal highway engineers, park representatives, legislators and environmentalists as to how the work should be carried out. The New Hampshire Department of Transportation was looking for design solutions which could accommodate the demands of the diverse interest groups and meet highway engineering, environmental and recreational objectives. Overcoming such problems as a harsh climate, landslide hazards, lack of topsoil and a limited growing season seemed quite straightforward by comparison.

The fundamental challenge for Johnson, Johnson and Roy (JJR), whose proposals were given the go-ahead in 1982, was to reconcile potentially conflicting uses within the confines of the valley floor which, at its narrowest point, is only 76.2 metres (250 feet) wide. A major priority was, therefore, the consultation process between designers, park planners, transportation engineers and the state as client. Innovative design solutions were essential, a prime objective being to minimize evidence of environmental disturbance and to design new facilities that blended with the scenic context. Persuading the US Congress to authorize modification to interstate highway design standards was a major breakthrough. It enabled JJR to use two- and three-lane parkway segments within Franconia Notch and to create the only two-lane interstate highway in the country. This overcame many environmental objections, although the new road alignment made it necessary to relocate and replace many park facilities, such as the visitor centre and trails.

4.3 *Franconia Notch State Park and Parkway*

JOHNSON JOHNSON AND ROY INC.
White Mountains National Forest,
New Hampshire, USA

An interpretive trail located near Profile Lake.

The original proposal for the roadway to occupy the centre of the narrow valley floor inevitably restricted the potential for recreational use. JJR's landscape architects proposed instead to locate the roadway at the edge of the valley, ensuring that its alignment followed the natural terrain, preserved important visual relationships and protected special features and environmentally sensitive areas. With the need to reconcile road development with the natural setting, emphasis was placed on construction techniques, materials and colours which would blend with the environment.

Driving north on Interstate 93 offers views of the White Mountains, the largest public space in New England, with Cannon Mountain, a major ski resort, in the distance. In the upper region of the Notch, steep mountainsides delineate the valley edge. The protection of these views, the screening of development and the major changes in grade all had to be taken into account in the design. JJR worked with the consulting transportation engineers in aligning the new interstate roadway and identifying appropriate shoulder design treatments. Careful on-site supervision of grading operations, re-use of boulders, use of native granite for curbs, central reservations and retaining walls, together with a special aggregate in the roadway's bituminous paving helped to ensure that the new features were integrated into the existing landscape.

Looking north on Interstate 93 with Cannon Mountain in the distance. Critical design issues in this segment were the screening of contiguous development and responding to major changes in grade. Pedestrian underpasses link parking to visitor destinations such as Layfayette Campground. Top right is a major rock-climbing area.

Start on site: 1982
Handover: 1988
Site area: 17.7-kilometre (11-mile) segment of Interstate highway; inter-valley *circa* 1.6 km (1 mile) long; width of valley 76-396 metres (250-1300 feet)

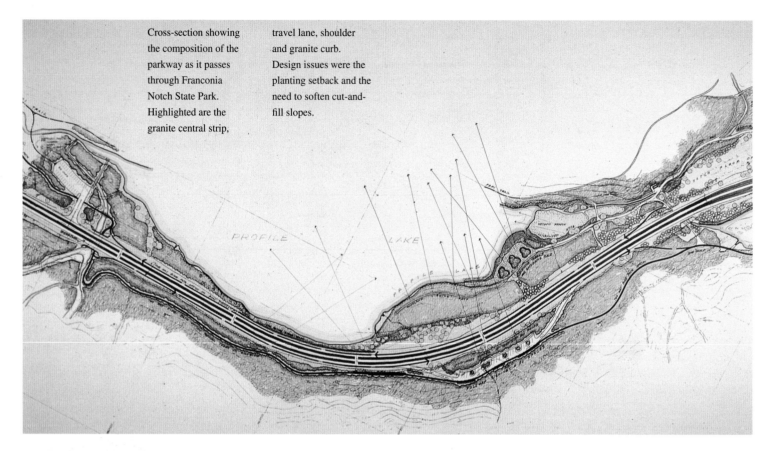

Cross-section showing the composition of the parkway as it passes through Franconia Notch State Park. Highlighted are the granite central strip, travel lane, shoulder and granite curb. Design issues were the planting setback and the need to soften cut-and-fill slopes.

Changes to interstate highway design standards enabled JJR to use two-lane parkway segments.

The bicycle path at Echo Lake follows the edge of the interstate parkway with views to Cannon Mountain.

Many park features, including a major campsite, required pedestrian underpasses to link parking safely to visitor destinations. The new visitor centre and car park also had to be located. This enabled a creek to be returned to its original alignment and the surrounding area to be restored to meadow. The disturbed areas were successfully replanted with a selection of indigenous trees, grasses and wild flowers to merge with the undisturbed areas. The site of the new centre, architecturally in keeping with historic tourist buildings in the Franconia Notch region, was chosen to be sympathetic to its surroundings.

A series of interpretive trails was designed to lead visitors through sensitive portions of the park, minimizing their impact on the area. A particular problem arose at the interpretive centre at Profile Lake, which offers views of The Old Man of the Mountain. Because of heavy over-use of the viewing area, the lake edge had to be stabilized with large boulders, creating a hard-surface area with interpretive displays carefully screened from the new roadway alignment.

Cycling has always been popular within Franconia Notch, but the new parkway prohibits cycling on the road shoulder. JJR has compensated by creating a bicycle path as an independent feature sited to give maximum access to the park's scenic areas. In winter it doubles as a cross-country ski-trail.

Landscape architects are often required to find solutions to conflicting user demands through imaginative design. In this case, JJR's ability to interact with diverse user groups throughout the process proved successful. Sensitivity to recreational, environmental and aesthetic values ensured that the potentially negative impacts of the new roadway were reduced. Completed in 1988, the public response is highly favourable. In particular, the environmental protection groups have been very supportive of the new road, which they say has improved both the park and highway in ways that the 'locals' and vested interests had not believed possible. It would be encouraging to think that this scheme could set a precedent and that state departments world-wide would be willing to accept a landscape solution to future highway problems.

4.4 *Landscape plan for a Linear Park*

MARISA MAFFIOLI
River Stura, Turin, Italy

In parts, the urban fringe marches right up to the banks of the river and requires a different approach in renovation.

The brief for this project was to create a major landscape for the lower reaches of the River Stura, addressing issues which should be considered through design and management. The River Stura is a tributary of the great River Po, the most important river basin in northern Italy. The confluence of the two rivers occurs just to the north of Turin and the Stura flows through the city on its way to meet the Po.

Semi-naturalized vegetation on the urban fringe, along the banks of the Stura.

In times past, the banks of the River Stura were areas of high scenic quality, with crops, pasture and woodland. As this area of northern Italy was industrialized, the land along the banks of the Stura became seriously despoiled and polluted. In recent decades, as the city continued a spiral of economic growth, Turin has largely turned its back on the huge asset of the River Stura flowing along its edge.

Over ten years ago, the local political and planning authority commissioned a study of the River Stura landscape in the context of the overall plan for the river system within the whole metropolitan area of Turin. Progress in implementing the plan has been slow. But, over the years, there has been a gradual awakening of interest and concern. The growth of the Green Movement, and protests at the inadequate open space provision within Turin, have fortuitously blended with a new attitude in big business, particularly the car manufacturer, Fiat, which has substantial industrial interests in the city and in this area. The result has been to establish a new urgency and realism in the project, with the development in 1991 of a specific new master plan.

Start on site: 1985
Handover: In progress
Site area: 1300 hectares
(3,212 acres)

203

Top In earlier times, the River Stura was a natural and defensive barrier for the city of Turin. Later, two great areas close to the river were transformed into pleasure gardens.

For a long time this area has been considered a suitable setting for a regional park.

The main priorities within the project were, firstly, to interpret the existing landscape structure, which runs along the northern urban edge of Turin, particularly where it meets with the River Po, and in its historical context. Secondly, the aim was to draw together public and private sector interests to cooperate in revitalizing the riverscape. This approach requires that the sensitive issues of land-use changes, building control and land reclamation, be considered within the general objective to improve the River Stura landscape.

The project has been divided into two major stages; the first (Part A) is a landscape-planning proposal which attempts to reorganize the open space along the river frontage. This will be a zone of natural vegetation interspersed with sports facilities and gardens. It is designed to be implemented in sections and handed over to the city.

This first stage has been further subdivided into two sections. Section A1 has been badly neglected, but is a very important area at the confluence of the Stura and Po. The fertile plain is designated for nature conservation with wooded hills on the far bank of the Po forming an attractive backdrop. This crucial landscape area will be protected, but restricted access will be permitted with emphasis given to the fine views. Section A2 is the one part of the study area (upstream from A1) in which work on *both* banks of the River Stura can be considered in what is predominantly a residential area. A new pedestrian bridge has been proposed to link the landscape of the two banks, breaking at a mid-stream island to give unexpected views of Turin and the river. Wedges of landscape improvement are now being pushed out from the linear river landscape into the adjacent residential and industrial areas.

The second major stage (Part B) involves action on only one bank, but this is a significant environmental improvement and restoration programme. On the opposite bank there is an important municipal rubbish tip which is only partially filled. The area within the Part B stage contains many problems, including large quantities of waste from the industrial districts, which now cover most of this area. As a result, an extensive restoration programme is planned but it will take many years to implement. A new riverside park is proposed and a management plan is being set up.

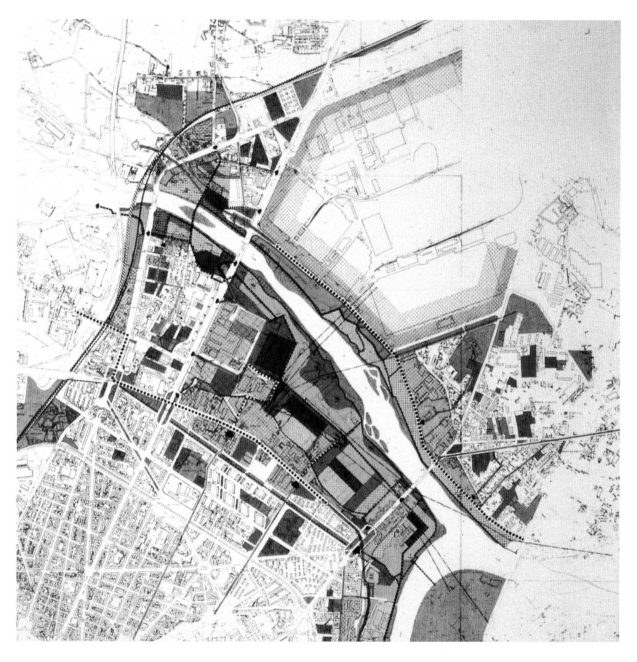

Diagram showing the green strategy within and surrounding Turin. A linear river park is proposed along the lower reaches of the Stura and along the River Po.

The project is an interesting example of landscape design being considered at various levels and by different agencies influencing the process of change and management. At one end of the spectrum, the proposals are assessed within a regional master plan to promote riverside protection and natural resource management. At the other it is as an enabling framework to encourage voluntary groups to participate in neighbourhood projects.

The citizens of Turin are now becoming aware of the values associated with the rivers, and it will not be a very long time before the process of degradation is finally stopped and reversed. In the meantime, the measures taken for habitat creation, pollution control and protection of scenic quality, are beginning to reestablish the generous proportions of this rural and urban landscape. It is a strategy which recognizes a limited ability to solve problems quickly, but one which plans each opportunity within a broader, coherent framework.

Planning permission was granted on condition the landscape proposals showed how the generating station could be integrated into the surrounding landscape.

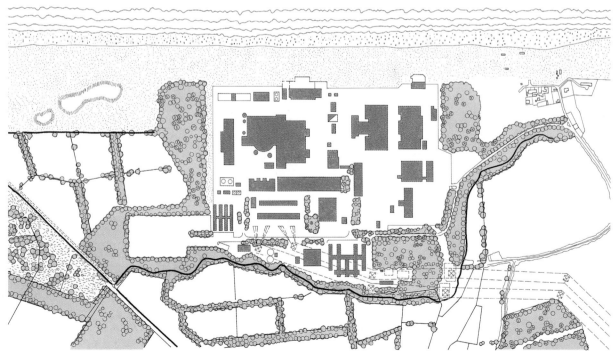

 pine trees mainly corsican but some scots & maritime

 deciduous trees: common alder ash, birch & willow in low ground: grey alder; ash, birch wild cherry, sweet chestnut, oak, grey poplar, sycamore on high ground

 thicket: blackthorn, bramble, elder gorse, hawthorn, wild rose pussy willow

 reedmarsh: existing

 dune grassland new areas pre-dominantly fescue with flowering plants provided by U.E.A. consultants, & marram grass close to shingle

 shingle: with sea holly, seakale sea pea and horned poppy provided by U.E.A consultants

4.5

PETER YOUNGMAN
Leiston, Suffolk, UK

Sizewell B Power Station

Peter Youngman's consultancy with the Central Electricity Generating Board (CEGB) and, later, Nuclear Electric, started with Sizewell A Station in 1957. Sizewell B was the subject of the largest public planning inquiry to date in Great Britain. It lasted for three years from start to publication of the inspector's report in 1981. The scheme was not submitted for formal planning approval until July 1991. Throughout these complicated procedures, landscape has maintained a high profile. Planning permission for Sizewell B Station required the local authority to approve a landscape plan showing the means of integrating the generating station with the surrounding landscape and include: planting on site; the management of existing and newly planted areas; earth moving and soil disposal measures, and a programme of implementation related to site development. Nuclear Electric was also required to deposit for approval details of planting schemes for each area covered by the plan before any landscape work could be started within that area. Delay has occurred in submitting a definitive plan for the whole site because of uncertainty over the future of the proposed Sizewell C.

Two undertakings of particular interest were given to the local authorities during the public inquiry: the integration of the CEGB land with the surrounding landscape and provision for offsite planting and its management, and for the further management of existing offsite woodlands. To this end, Youngman prepared a management and maintenance report for Nuclear Electric for the area under discussion. There were many other constraints, such as public right of access to the beach and foreshore, and designated areas: Heritage Coast, Area of Outstanding Natural Beauty, Environmentally Sensitive Area, Site of Special Scientific Interest. Only the highest standards of management and maintenance will reassure the public and conservation groups' concern that what is termed 'overriding national interest' does not destroy the delicate fabric of the area. In order to plan this massive campaign, areas of woodland for retention, sites and areas for new planting had to be identified; a description prepared of the scope, management and planting proposals for each of the above sites, and an indication of the preferred agency for implementation given. Ecological surveys of the area were carried out prior to 1984, with particular attention to wetland habitats and bird life.

Planning ahead is essential, since, even if no new stations appear, it has been estimated that Sizewell B will need its site landscape maintained until AD2140. For example, the management must retain the woodlands as a feature of the landscape. This will entail a regular regime of inconspicuous felling and replanting, since few of the existing trees will survive that long. Timber production is planned to recover operational costs. Educational projects, such as Nature Trails, will also require maintenance and agricultural ones must enhance the long-term fertility of the soil and avoid pollution of groundwater. Although there are many unknown quantities, Youngman's vision in preparing both landscape proposals, and latterly the necessarily futuristic management document, is impressive. Yet it also takes in detailed plans and specifications for contract maintenance of building sites, outlines agreements with landowners and farm tenants, as well as the management of the varied landscape types within the site and its surrounding area. What is shown clearly is the vital nature of long-term management if any landscape scheme is to remain viable.

Existing landscape conservation is a priority in this scheme.

Start on site: 1980
Handover: In progress
Site area: 90 hectares (222 acres)

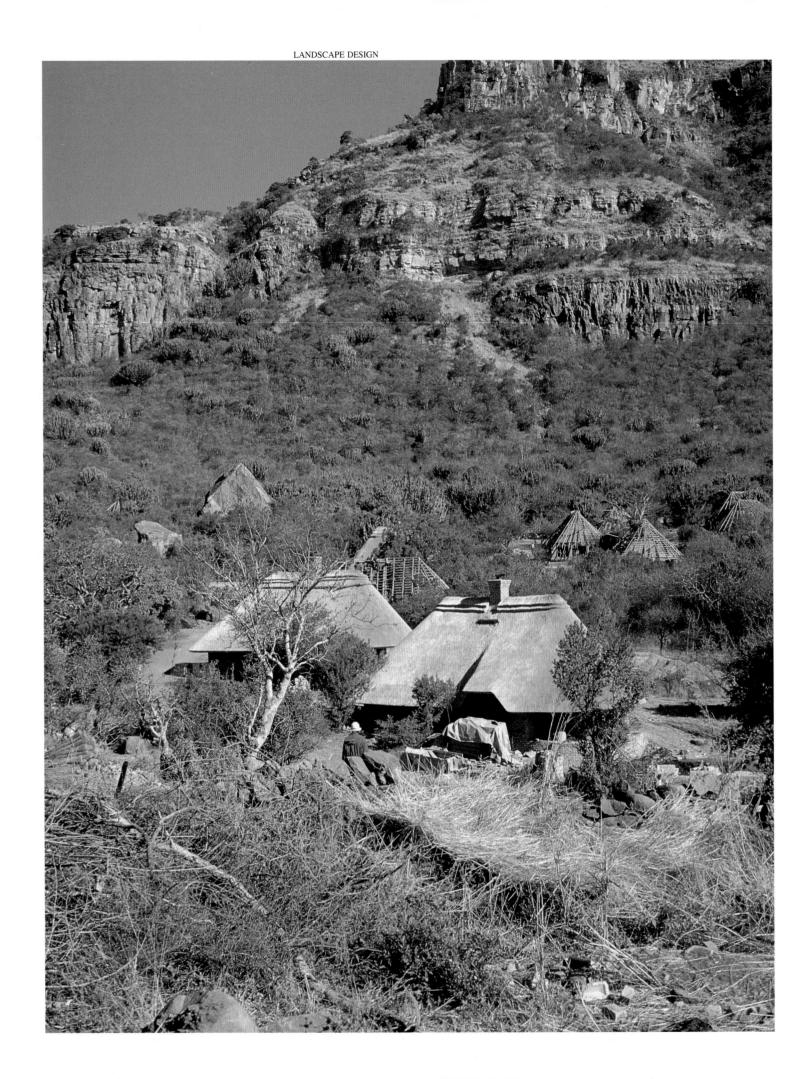

4.6 *Ntshondwe Camp*

ENVIRONMENTAL DESIGN PARTNERSHIP INC.
Itala Game Reserve,
Natal, South Africa

The camp is perched above the general level of the area, at the base of steeply rising cliffs. This photograph was taken during construction.

Itala Game Reserve in Northern Natal was established in 1973 and is administered by the Natal Parks Board, which has a policy to extend the boundaries of the reserve when opportunity permits. The primary responsibility of the board is to conserve species and habitat and to allow 'natural, physical and ecological processes' to operate without interference. A secondary responsibility is to permit educational, research and recreational use, providing it does not interfere with the primary responsibility. In the early 1980s, government funds for the administration of the reserves became harder to secure and there was also a growth of interest in the character of wilderness areas. Responding to these changing circumstances, the Natal Parks Board commissioned a detailed study within the Itala Game Reserve. Ntshondwe Camp was the result and is the first such development by the board.

The brief specified overnight and conference accommodation for 200 people, a conference centre, administration, restaurant/bar, interpretation facilities, shop and staff accommodation. All this was to be set within a very sensitive landscape under the aegis of a client (the Park Board) that had little direct experience of such development but a refined policy of resource management and conservation. The management plan for the Itala Game Reserve defined four zones of compatible use and only activities relating to the policies for each zone are permitted. The four basic zones are intensive use, limited use, wilderness and special zones. An intensive use zone is an area characterized by a substantially modified environment which is considered compatible with the siting of camps. The area of Ntshondwe Camp has been modified by agriculture throughout this century, including the presence of old kraals and vegetation clearance.

In 1985 work commenced on the feasibility plan and by 1989 the client was sufficiently convinced to allow work on site to begin. The landscape architect consultant (EDP) was appointed to coordinate the project with a consulting team of architects, engineers and quantity surveyors. EDP was responsible for site planning, setting out the infrastructure including services, buildings and the lake, as well as supervising the Natal Park Board Horticultural Branch in the landscape construction programme. The pre-construction phase included a feasibility study, environmental assessment statement and monitoring of conditions. This was in order to determine the 'carrying capacity' for the proposed camp, and for the preparation of a development framework. This led on to a coordination role for the landscape architect in the detailed design and implementation, and the rehabilitation of the natural vegetation.

The camp is perched above the general level of the area at the base of steeply rising cliffs. The camp site is a bowl protected by the surrounding hills and cliffs, so largely screened from distant view, except to the north and west where extensive vistas reveal the wider reserve and land beyond. The intention has been to minimize the physical and visual impact of the camp but, at the same time, allow the development to relate to its surroundings rather than be seen as an unfortunate intrusion.

A fine view over the development, illustrating the way in which the settlement sits snuggly adjacent to the lake beneath the surrounding hills.

Start on site: 1989
Handover: Phased handover completed in April 1991
Site area: Ntshondwe Camp: 20 hectares (49½ acres)
Itala Game Reserve: 35,000 hectares (86,484 acres)

ITALA GAME RESERVE
TSHONDWE HUTTED CAMP
Master Plan

The dished nature of the camp lies within the protection of surrounding hills and cliffs.

The camp was sub-divided into day use and overnight zones, separated by a physical barrier carefully formed of massive granite boulders from the site and large indigenous trees, some of which were transplanted. The configuration of the buildings also allowed for a dramatic gateway between these zones. Constructed in an existing low-lying area, the lake assists site management by restricting pedestrian movement through sensitive habitats. The lake also forms a focus for the development, especially as game now use it as a water hole. It has been stocked with fish and baby crocodile will be introduced at a later stage. The lake covers an area of 0.5 hectares (0.0 acres) and has been designed with a very irregular margin, retained by a curved earthdam, lined with Bentonite and, in part, extensively planted with grasses and bush. The edge has a shallow profile to encourage plant establishment, but shelves steeply to discourage the spread of reeds.

The hutted camp comprises 41 self-contained chalets, conference units, a conference centre for 120 people and other specialist facilities appropriate to this use within a sensitive setting. The development has been deliberately broken up into smaller built units, which hug the lower slopes of the hills where there is good vegetation cover and also where the majority of the large granite boulders are found. Some of the chalets are hidden in dense vegetation while others are more exposed in open areas to provide for different tastes. Construction is in textured rockface brick with pitched thatch roofs.

The roads have been designed to be as narrow as possible with varied vertical and horizontal alignment to reduce traffic speed. Car parking is adjacent to the access road, so minimizing the impact on the camp. There is a network of footpaths within the camp, but no formal paths lead into the bush. Road and footpath are treated with a special brick paver to blend with the building construction.

Particular care has been given to conservation of the flora. Specified zones were protected during construction and plant material endemic within the reserve was used in the replanting programme. Some was propagated from cuttings by the client's horticultural branch, but other stock was purchased through normal commercial channels. Large specimen trees for key locations were lifted from the reserve and indigenous grass sward establishment was encouraged through seed collection, or turf transplant. Wherever possible, the bush has been reinstated to its original nature. Planting was done at random, to reflect the bush characteristics and, where there are dead trees, these have also been left to provide roosting and nesting points for birds.

View across the artificial lake area of the camp, with the bush stretching into the distance.

Entrance to the reception building, showing one of the more formal areas of landscape treatment.

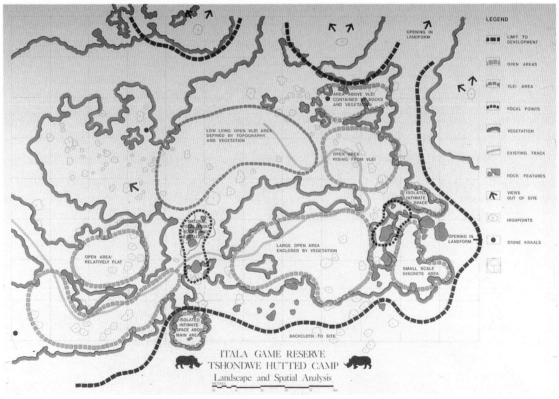

ITALA GAME RESERVE
TSHONDWE HUTTED CAMP
Landscape and Spatial Analysis

Even in the very short time since construction started in 1989, the initial fears of the client in launching into a new commercial venture within highly sensitive surrounds would appear to have been largely groundless. The viability of the scheme seems to have been proven, with 90 per cent occupancy within the first nine months of operation. This has been achieved despite little formal marketing, with users particularly appreciating the uncluttered and open nature of the camp. In fact, unlike in other parks, the game is free to move through the camp, and a rhino that roamed the site before the development has returned and is frequently seen grazing within the camp. Porcupine and warthog have also returned to forage on the newly landscaped areas.

The landscape architect has succeeded in meeting a challenging brief through persuasion, an apparently crucial coordinating role and a clear understanding of what was both possible and desirable. EDP particularly stresses the high level of cooperation between client, consultant and contractor. This client needed to be encouraged to look at new possibilities in the context of established values and interests. The fact that the Park Board did so is apparent in the high acceptance level in both human and wild game visitors.

It was significant that this project was assessed within an overall management plan for the Itala Game Reserve. Ntshondwe Camp gives the appearance of successfully reconciling intense human use with the wilderness dream, all within a controlled landscape plan. This formula could be relevant in many parallel situations throughout the world, but it is essential that the landscape architect is given a fair brief and has the ability and confidence to protect the key landscape values.

The timber deck close to the lake allows visitors to view the unspoilt surroundings without significantly interfering with the game who now use the lake as a water hole.

213

A legacy of the
Olympic programme
will be an expanded
network of parks within
Barcelona.

4.7 The Olympic Games, Summer 1992

HOLSA
Barcelona, Spain

This is by far the most ambitious project to be considered in this book. Barcelona has acquired an enviable reputation for urban renewal in recent years, but siting the 1992 Olympics within the city provided the impetus for a huge programme of revitalization. The transformation takes many forms and the landscape resource is only part of the whole. It would be wrong to consider the landscape of Barcelona within the orderly progression of a conventional master plan; it would seem that the urgency of the Olympic development programme, coupled with specific requirements, has resulted in a series of unrelated landscape opportunities. To attempt to understand these, one should first look at the overall programme which is changing the face of much of Barcelona.

Barcelona Holding Olympic SA (HOLSA) was set up after the city was successful in its bid to hold the 1992 Olympics and is charged with implementing the necessary major infrastructure for the Games as well as achieving various refurbishment objectives for the long-term interests of Barcelona. HOLSA is responsible to the national government of Spain and the city council of Barcelona. The overall programme of work falls into three sectors: (1) the urban recovery of a run-down sector (Poble Nou); (2) the extension and completion of an ambitious road programme throughout the city, and (3) the rehabilitation of four specific zones (Montjuic, Vall d'Hebron, the Diagonal and Estacio del Nord-Glories) with a concerted development programme for sports culture and open spaces.

Poble Nou was a zone of obsolete industrial and commercial plants divided from the city by 4 kilometres (2½ miles) of railway track which cut Barcelona off from the sea. With the removal of the track and construction of the new Glories underground railway, the area has been transformed into 50 hectares (123 acres) of prime land, incorporating the Olympic village site, reuniting the city with its seafront. A new coast road, planned as a road-park highway, has improved access to the original marine promenade. Four kilometres (2½ miles) of beach have been recreated and linear sea parks established, along with many other smaller green spaces. A flamboyant style of architecture and civil engineering together herald a new beginning for this part of the city, although little effort has been made to secure a comfortable fit. Because of this the landscape has an important role in establishing the development.

The massive redevelopment programme includes the construction of 2000 apartments for 15,000 athletes, two 44 storey blocks – one a hotel and the other commercial – an exhibition hall and a major new yacht harbour. For the first time since 1956 (Melbourne) the sailing Olympics will be held at the same venue as the rest of the Games, within the host city. This has meant that the major investment has gone into the new yachting harbour which encloses 7 hectares (17 acres) of sea and 6 hectares (15 acres) of wharf for recreation and storage. However, the shoreline of Barcelona is once again accessible for leisure and relaxation.

Following a period of disruption, the modern view of the city confirms the grand scale of development which requires a bold landscape response.

Start on site: Mid-1980s
Handover: Spring 1992

215

The programme of work includes the completion of an ambitious road network which still shows raw edges.

The Vall d'Hebron park has benefited from the presence of dominant sculptures. This is *Matches* by Claes Oldenburg and Coosje van Bruggen.

The **Montjuic area** is the site of the major sports facilities comprising the Olympic Ring, entrance to which is obtained via the Plaza d'Europa constructed over a reservoir of 60,000 cubic metres (2.1 million cubic feet), which supplies water to Barcelona. The focal point within this area is the stadium from the 1929 Barcelona Exposition which has been refurbished for the 1992 Barcelona Olympics, and will host the opening and closing ceremonies. The newly commissioned Sant Jordi Sports Hall has a carefully curved roofline to reflect the gentle folds of the dominant Montjuic Mountains and this theme is reiterated in the lines of the surrounding green spaces. As a result of the Olympics, Montjuic will benefit from three new urban squares and the Parc del Migolia, which has yet to show its true worth, although it has splendid views of the plain and Barcelona coastline. The terraced area of the **Vall d'Hebron** rehabilitation is situated at the foot of the Callserola hill and represents 82 hectares (202 acres) of urban development of which 10.7 hectares (26 acres) has been designated for sports facilities associated with the Olympics including the velodrome, multi-purpose sports hall and sports fields. Five hundred apartments are also being built here for the Olympic press corps and 27 hectares (67 acres) has been designated for parks, the whole creating a new urban geography which will remain for the use of the city after the Olympics.

The **Diagonal Area** forms the junction of three municipal authorities and is the focus for further sports facilities including athletics tracks, which will initially be used in the summer Olympics. The development of the area is focused on the organization of a new longitudinal axis suitable for walking, horse-riding, cycling and driving. In **Estacio del Nord**, the construction of the ring-road system and the removal of the railway track which served the now defunct Nord railway, has opened up an area – the Glories Plaza – which will eventually house important cultural centres as well as the Nord Park, the old station itself being home to various public services. Barcelona is determined that the expensive infrastructure associated with holding the 1992 Olympics will be fully utilized by the city in later years. The inevitable disruption to the city has been used to evaluate future requirements, including green space strategy. Much has been done in the last decade to provide both the centre and suburbs with new parks but the municipal authorities hope that the momentum generated by the Olympics will increase open-space provision from 400 to 750 hectares (988 to 1729 acres). This is a bold objective and Barcelona will do well to examine earlier Olympic cities where, too often, the initial investment has not been adequately managed and is often subsequently underused. It is still too early to test the long-term landscape strategy arising out of the substantial development in Barcelona associated with the Olympics, but their ambitious plans could provide the city with an enviable landscape framework for many years to come.

Illuminated views at dusk of the Plaza Del Anillo Olimpico, emphasizing the bold lines and axial strength of this space.

4.8

EDE GRIFFITHS PARTNERSHIP
Heathrow, London, UK

Stockley Business Park

'The designated Greenbelt to the west of London near Heathrow Airport is in reality not so much "green" as composed of a mixture of land uses ranging from reservoirs, gravel workings, down-at-heel agriculture, car dumps, abandoned development, abandoned tips, motorway corridors and interchanges, and of course, landfill sites.' Thus wrote the landscape architect for this project, Bernard Ede in 1990. He went on to describe the site he was investigating as an area which had been excavated from the mid-eighteenth century for brick earth and gravel for building works in central London. The site was then backfilled with domestic and industrial waste before being clay capped and poorly grazed. Severe underground fires broke out and groundwater polluted by waste materials seeped out into the Grand Union Canal on the site's southern boundary. In short, this was a severely degraded landscape which had become an embarrassment and a danger. What was required was a visionary approach to this problem and fortunately, the public local authority, the London Borough of Hillingdon, responded positively to the approach from the client developer.

Stockley Park is a major reclamation project to transform the worked-out land into an international business park and public parkland with a championship golf course, sports fields and equestrian facilities, just a short distance away from Heathrow Airport. The key to the whole operation was the agreement to release a proportion of the site from statutory Greenbelt land-use designation so that it could be developed as a business park, in exchange for the developer guaranteeing reclamation of the whole site. This included provision of extensive infrastructure in accordance with a very detailed set of planning conditions and to a high specification.

The concept of a business park in which the work place is located in countryside environs is now well established in many countries. It appeals both to employees through the opportunity to work in pleasant surroundings, and to employers who can achieve an enhanced image for the company with maximum control, away from the expense of city locations. But to succeed, a business park has to do this in a competitive market. At Stockley Park, the challenge was doubly hard, as the locational advantage was offset by the difficult site conditions and the sensitivity of trying to develop within the London Metropolitan Greenbelt.

The client's brief stressed the importance of excellence in the *total* environment, both internally and externally. The client recognized the sensitivity of UK Greenbelt protection and the need to maintain the integrity of the Greenbelt wherever possible. But at the same time, a massive land-reclamation programme was necessary to provide both the quality environment essential for the success of the business park and also to encourage the local authority into partnership.

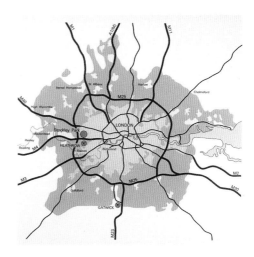

Location plan showing the relationship to London, the M25 motorway and designated Green Belt.

The landscape has been structured with a series of stepped lakes. The structure is strengthened by 'green walls', often blocks of hornbeams.

Start on site: 1985
Handover: Phased; in progress
Site area: 160 hectares (395 acres)

219

The readily available supply of water has encouraged the designers to explore its many different characteristics, including formal displays and cascades.

Planting has become quickly established and prevents the buildings from dominating their surroundings.

Opposite As part of the landscape structure, water threads through the scheme in canals and small lakes.

Reclaiming the backfilled site involved the movement of 4.6 million cubic metres (16.2 million cubic feet) of rubbish, clay and gravel to establish platforms for pavilion-type buildings within the business park area, while a new landform was created in the public park zone, including a hill 30 metres (98 feet) high. A striking but simple landscape structure has been formed, combining the new landform with water, in a series of stepped lakes separated by weirs and a stream, which provide two valley-like open spaces for amenities. The structure is strengthened by 'green walls', often formal blocks of hornbeam which have been designed to create outdoor rooms to enclose car parks, and sheltered, water-orientated gardens or large spaces. A lime tree avenue winds through the development, acting as a linear building control.

The buildings, individually and collectively, have been drawn into the landscape strategy and with rare exceptions, do not dominate their surroundings. This is, in part, a tribute to the integrating role given to landscape design at all levels and at all scales in the project development. The landscape architect was fully involved in all stages, from master planning, through to detailed design and construction. Architects, landscape architects and engineers have worked very closely together to solve some difficult site problems. Of particular significance have been innovative 'soil-construction' techniques to create a growing medium to overcome problems of methane generation, which have also prevented the need to import large quantities of top soil.

The functional water and storm-water control system has been turned into a major environmental asset rather than perceived as an engineering problem. The readily available supply of run-off from buildings and car parks has encouraged the landscape architect to explore many different characteristics of water – still, flowing, cascades, fountains and more natural marshes. The selection of plants for Stockley Park has been carefully specified to establish native trees, shrubs, wetland and wildflower species within the broader parkland, whereas in the business park the palette of native species has been reinforced with water and ornamental species.

The landscape has been conceived as a source of discipline and order into the development process. The various components are firm and designed for impact – a contrast between enclosure and openness, formal vistas, or lines of trees and hedges linking separate building compartments. The 'naturalistic' patterns of the public park contrast with the geometric character of the business park.

Site plan, showing use of water.

STOCKLEY PARK ↑
LANDSCAPE MASTER PLAN

Great care has been taken in the plant composition as seen here in the water margins.

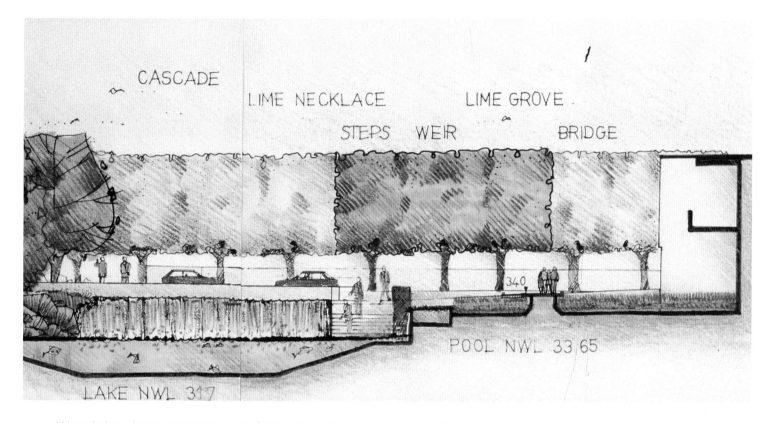

Section emphasizing the importance given to plant walls in the spatial structure.

Although the scheme represents a significant advance in landscape design, it has not been without its problems. Although the local authority has fully cooperated in this privately funded project, it has produced extensive requirements which have had to be met within a tight timetable and with an exacting client. As the project has progressed, the fluctuations in volumes of spoil have demanded rapidly recalculated land forms. Inevitably, conflicts between land use and circulation have arisen, such as in the reconciliation of the golf course, footpaths and bridleways.

The client, who has a track record of environmentally aware urban developments, proved equal to the task of keeping this unusual greenfields comprehensive project on course. The determination to see it through and justify the £19 million expenditure on landscape engineering and amenity work has been vindicated. The quality of landscape and architectural design is high and well respected, both by tenants and by the constant stream of visitors. This commitment has attracted wide interest and the scheme has received many citations and awards in its short history, including the Best Urban Planning Project in Europe Award in 1991.

It is still early days to view the whole project and to examine the long-term management. But the level of site maintenance is impressive and the client would appear to be firmly committed to a management regime to safeguard its investment interests. It has been an enabling project where there have been many winners and few losers. The transformation of despoiled Greenbelt into a site of broad-based land use must give encouragement, although the balance between commercial exploitation and public accountability is a very delicate matter in such a designated landscape.

Ede Griffiths Partnership has been retained to give specific guidance on the management of Stockley Park. This is particularly important in the more complex areas such as the forestry and aquatic zones. Information covering the various landscape zones is currently being put on computer data record to improve monitoring and future management. Although the landscape architect has a continuing responsibility, the client has also established an on-site team to implement essential maintenance within the guidance given by the landscape architect.

The visitor centre and
bog landscape was
designed to be in
keeping with the
character of Glenveagh
Castle and Gardens,
shown here.

4.9 Visitor Centre, Glenveagh National Park

ANTHONY AND BARBARA O'NEILL
Glenveagh, Co. Donegal, Eire

Glenveagh, 'The Glen of the Birch', is one of the most outstanding stretches of natural landscape in Ireland. In 1975, the Irish Government confirmed a policy to conserve representative areas of the country's natural landscape. Kilarney National Park was the first, but Glenveagh (along with two others) was designated soon after and 10,000 hectares (24,710 acres) of granite upland covered with blanket bog were given formal protection. A further 3200 hectares (7907 acres) are conserved within An Taisce, the Irish National Trust property which abuts the National Park.

The park was created along a narrow, deeply cut valley shaped during the ice ages, with a public road touching one end. Little human activity has ever touched or changed this isolated valley, and its natural cover over the millennia has ranged from dense woodland to the present upland blanket bog, which provides grazing for a large herd of red deer. The park contains the famous Glenveagh Gardens, which are situated in the centre, about four kilometres (2½ miles) along the valley adjoining Lough Veagh.

A zoning plan and master plan were prepared for the park, designating various degrees of use and protection. At an early stage, the remoteness of the central area was recognized including Glenveagh Castle and Gardens and it was decided that visitor cars or buses would have no access to this area or to the wilderness beyond. Traffic would be halted on the periphery of the park, where a visitor centre would be built near the public road. Visitors could then either walk or cycle the six kilometres (3¾ miles), or use a minibus service to the Castle Garden zone, from which point they could disperse.

The landscape architect consultants were involved from the very early days, working with many government agencies on the preparation of the master and zoning plans for the park. Close cooperation with the local authority – Donegal County Council – meant that the park and a large buffer zone were incorporated into the county development plan. By the time the consultants were commissioned to design the visitor centre, agreement had been reached on most major issues, including an important by-pass road. Two government departments were directly involved in the preparation of the brief; the National Parks Section of the Office of Public Works required an interpretive centre and an administrative and maintenance building with parking for cars and buses. The overall development had to be as undisruptive and unobtrusive as possible. Secondly, Bordd Failte (The National Tourist Board) wanted a facility to serve as a focal point for the series of holiday villages along the Donegal Coast and help extend the tourist season.

The various options for development were very carefully scrutinized, as this project was seen as a model for other national parks. The maintenance building is a self-contained facility to serve a range of projects within and outside the national park. For the visitor centre, a prime requirement was for display and interpretation of local flora, fauna and specialist habitats, with associated theme gardens. An auditorium for 90 persons (two coachloads) and a suitably sized restaurant were also included. The landscape of the existing blanket bog had to be retained and the visitor centre be in keeping with the character of Glenveagh Gardens.

The dramatic view across the lake is deliberately hidden until visitors have walked from the Visitor Centre to the lake margin.

Start on site: 1983
Handover: 1986
Site area: 1130 square metres (12,163 feet)

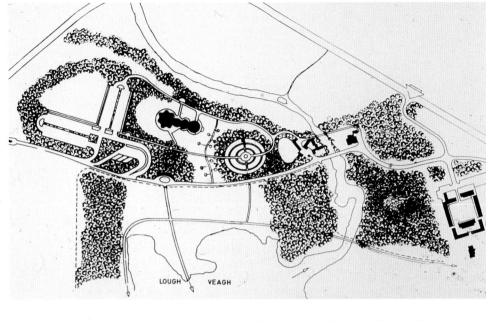

The buildings are surrounded with a peat-sod retaining 'ha-ha' wall, which, in time, will soften and merge with the surrounding vegetation.

The visitor centre comprises a series of circular spaces, with interpretive and theatre rooms at one end, entrance and toilets in the centre and the restaurant at the other end. The interpretive rooms and theatre are lowered two metres (6 feet 6 inches) into the bog, as far as the underlying layer of gravel. The buildings are enclosed with a peat-sodded retaining 'ha-ha' wall, planted on top with *Rhododendron fastnosum 'Grandiflora'*, which also acts as a backdrop for small, theme gardens linked to the internal displays. The restaurant takes advantage of the sloping ground and protrudes from the excavations, allowing panoramic views.

All the domed roofs were covered with 50 centimetres (19⅝ inches) of peat soil. This had been carefully stored during construction for respreading to encourage the re-establishment of plants indigenous to the bog or moorland habitat. The reward here and in the re-spread soils surrounding the visitor centre has been a rich carpet of wild flowers, heather and other plants, including thousands of small birch, alder, and holly.

Externally, the simple circular form of the building pods has been carefully protected and protrusions eliminated. This purity of form may have presented problems for the architect in designing the interior of the building. One critic has suggested that fewer but larger forms would have been less demanding of detailed ingenuity and more satisfying in spatial serenity (*Irish Architect*, Feb-March 1987). But even photographs taken within a short time of practical completion show how well this composition responds to its awe-inspiring setting. In time, even the heavy overhanging concrete fascias will be softened by the plant growth from above and below. However, the fragile habitats and the demands placed upon the theme gardens will require continued vigilance and management. Happily, the example of using indigenous plant material has already encouraged the local county planning board to designate the buffer zone around the national park as a special amenity area, where vegetation will receive attention and protection. The landscape consultants have been retained to advise on this policy.

The design responds firmly to the unique requirements and sensitivities of the immediate environment. Integration of *any* built form in this location and the implied intensification of use, raises fears of a clash between tourism and conservation. Crucially, the brief was set by authorities representing both interests and the landscape architects have had experience in creating policies for the wider landscape within and beyond the national park. This experience has helped the landscape architects achieve support from parties with very different points of view, for example, in getting agreement and understanding on a policy to restrict vehicle access and in adopting a concept which channelled visitors through the centre before even revealing the dramatic views across the lake. Glenveagh is very conscious of its sense of place and should not be considered as a straightforward blueprint for other situations.

Elevational view of the Visitor Centre, demonstrating its low-cluster profile.

The evocative wildness and remoteness of Glenveagh demanded positive planning to avoid damage.

Further Reference

BIOGRAPHIES OF DESIGNERS

BJORNE AASEN was educated at the Norwegian Institute of Agriculture from 1960-63, where he later taught from 1976-85. He was also Professor of the Architecture Department at the University of Tronheim. In 1985 he formed a collaboration with 13.3 Landskapsarkitekter with whom he still works, in charge of projects such as the plaza and park for the Kreditkassen Headquarters in Oslo and the university plaza at Tromsø University.

AI LANDSCAPE PLANNING CO. LTD. The architect and landscape architect firm, AI, was founded in 1973 and today has offices in Tokyo, Okinawa and Tokai. The practice involves itself in all areas of the design process from investigations, planning and design to construction and supervision and is active mainly in the fields of city parks, green areas and specialist gardens.

ANDRESEN AND CASTEL BRANCO ARQUITECTURA PAISAGISTA Andresen and Castel Branco was founded in 1989 by Maria Cristina de Fonseca Ataide Castel Branco and Maria Teresa Lencastre de Melo Breiner Andresen who both studied at the University of Massachusetts and have Masters in Landscape Architecture. Ms Castel Branco undertook consultancy work and many landscape projects within Portugal before going into partnership. She also teaches at the Instituto Superior de Agronomia and the Universidate Complutense de Madrid, as well as publishing texts on her work at home and abroad. She has received many awards for her schemes, notably the Andrea Palladio Premio Internazionale de Architettura in 1989 for the School of

Biotechnology in Oporto. Maria Andresen has taught at the Artistic Cooperative as well as at the Lisbon, Aveiro, Oporto and Madrid Complutense Universities. Before going into private practice she worked in government planning and landscape departments. Ms Andresen has published her work in Portugal and abroad and attended numerous national and international conferences.

PROF. CHRIS BAINES is a landscape architect who trained as a horticulturist. He taught Landscape Design and Management at the City of Birmingham Polytechnic for fifteen years. Previously working in the landscape contracting industry and in international landscape consultancy, he now works principally as a television presenter and writer and an environmental adviser to industry and local government. Prof. Baines is one of the UK's leading environmental campaigners and a frequent contributor to conferences around the world. He has a particular professional interest in community-based educational projects and in creative nature conservation.

KARL BAUER studied architecture at the University of Karlsruhe and later became teaching assistant to the Chair of Garden and Landscape Architecture. In 1978 he formed his own independent landscape architectural business with an emphasis on open-space planning in redevelopment areas, roofdeck planting, historical gardens, pedestrian zones, city planning and urban design.

BCP – BRIAN CLOUSTON AND PARTNERS Brian Clouston and Partners Hong Kong Ltd. (Clouston) is a design company offering professional services in the fields of environmental planning and landscape architecture. Founded in 1978 it began operations in Hong Kong as a branch of the Clouston Group, a UK company established in 1965. Commissions have been undertaken for a wide range of clients, including government departments, development corporations, industrial and commercial organizations, health, water and transport authorities, property developers, tourist and recreation organizations, as well as architects, engineers and private individuals. The practice provides professional services throughout Asia in environmental planning and design, from feasibility studies through detailed design, implementation and subsequent management advice. The firm has been engaged on nearly 300 projects in Hong Kong, including planning and environmental impact studies, major public park and open space developments, highway, housing and recreation landscape schemes and large-scale land restoration projects for clients in both the public and private sectors.

BDP – BUILDING DESIGN PARTNERSHIP is one of the larger landscape practices in the UK. With offices throughout the country it undertakes both small and large schemes from the feasibility, planning and design stages through to implementation, aftercare and long-term management and has worked in all the major market sectors on a variety of projects for public, commercial and corporate clients.

BOFFA MISKELL PARTNERS was established in 1973 in Christchurch, New Zealand by Frank Boffa, Don Miskell becoming a partner in 1984, and now has offices in Auckland, Wellington, Christchurch and Queenstown. They employ the full-time expertise of urban designers and ecology consultants, as well as maintaining established working relationships with regional and town planners, engineers and architects. A subsidiary company, Geographics, offers computer mapping, digital-terrain modelling and visual simulation services. Boffa Miskell's main areas of practice are urban design, environmental planning, recreation and open space design, utility, service and energy projects, as well as regional, district, maritime and conservation planning, and they have won national acclaim for their designs.

ANDREAS BRUN is a Danish landscape architect who graduated from the Royal Vetinary and Agricultural University, Copenhagen in 1959. He completed his studies in Paris at the Ecole Nationale Superieure D'Horticulture Versailles and has been in private practice since 1961. From 1970-79 he was an IFLA delegate of the Association of Danish Landscape Architects.

BURNER AND COMPANY Peter Burner, President and founding member of Burner and Company, received a Bachelor of Landscape Architecture degree from the University of Florida in Gainesville and today holds a Professional Membership certificate from the American Society of Landscape Architects. The firm offers a full land-planning, site-planning and landscape-architecture service and has undertaken a wide variety of recreational, institutional, commercial, municipal and multifamily projects throughout Florida. They have been the recipient of numerous ASLA (Florida Chapter) awards for their work on schemes such as Useppa Island and the Sanibel Residence. In 1986 and 1989 they were given ASLA National Merit Awards for the Safety Harbor Club and Seawatch of Boca Grande respectively.

MICHEL AND CLAIRE CORAJOUD have been working together since 1979 when they founded their own landscape architecture practice. Michel Corajoud trained at the Ecole Nationale Superieure des Arts Décoratifs de Paris after which he worked for the Atelier d'Urbanisme et d'Architecture. Major projects have included the New Town of Kourou in Guyana and various parks and housing projects on the outskirts of Paris. He has published many texts both in France and abroad and attends conferences worldwide. Claire Corajoud studied at the Ecole Nationale Superieure du Paysage de Versailles. Before going into partnership she was a member of the landscape architectural group 'Carre Vert' where she undertook a number of housing schemes as well as the new town of Marne la Vallée. She has published widely and is a visiting lecturer at the ENSP. Since 1980 the Corajouds have been working on major public schemes such as the Parc Sausset and the town planning of the international city of Lyon.

DANIELSON AND ASSOCIATES is a California-based practice providing professional landscape architectural and planning services for clients in both the public and private sectors. The principal, Robert Danielson, founded the firm in 1985 after acquiring the staff and office space at Baronian and Danielson, the firm he co-formed and was principal of, for twenty-eight years. Recent projects include work at the Sacramento Metropolitan Airport Second Terminal, Broadmoor Park, San Francisco and the Lincoln Plaza, Sacramento. Robert Danielson was an instructor and professor at the University of California for fourteen years in the Department of Environmental Horticulture.

DENTON CORKER MARSHALL PTY LTD. The Denton Corker Marshall Group was founded in 1972 and now has offices in Sydney, Melbourne, Canberra, London, Hong Kong, Beijing, Tokyo, Singapore and Jakarta. The firm provides consulting services in architecture, landscape architecture, planning, interior design and project management to private individuals, companies, developers and government bodies. The firm has completed projects of every scale from residential work to professional project management in major urban redevelopments. The DCM group has gained a reputation for its high level of design and planning skills and has been successful in a substantial number of design competitions, several of international importance.

EDA COLLABORATIVE INC. was founded in 1978 and today is a professional consulting practice of landscape architects, urban designers and environmental planners with domestic and international experience, with offices in both Edmonton and Toronto. The firm has won over twenty planning and design awards, including the Canadian Society of Landscape Architects National Citation Award for the Canadian Museum of Civilization in Hull, Quebec. EDA's area of expertise lies in large-scale public commissions and numbers among its clients many government bodies, Canadian cities and universities. Before co-founding EDA, the principal, Ron Tatisciore, worked for HLC Consultants, New York and Project Planning Association, Toronto, Ontario and London where he has responsibility for the Middle Eastern schemes. He is visiting lecturer and design critic at several universities in Canada and has published many texts on his work.

EDE GRIFFITHS PARTNERSHIP was formed in 1987 by Bernard Ede and Roger Griffiths who had previously worked together for the Milton Keynes Development Corporation. Today the Partnership comprises twenty-three personnel in two offices in Warminster, Wiltshire and Rugby, Warwickshire. Each office is run by either Bernard Ede or Roger Griffiths, undertaking major business and recreational parks throughout the UK. A partner is involved in every project in their respective offices and is in direct contact with all aspects of the work undertaken. Major schemes include Folkestone Harbour Redevelopment, Kent; Alexandra Park and Palace landscape master plan and the award-winning Stockley Park project. Bernard Ede, responsible for Stockley Park, was educated at Nottingham and Newcastle Universities, qualifying as Landscape Architect in 1974, and, previous to founding EDP, had had his own practice since 1982.

ENVIRONMENT DESIGN INSTITUTE was formed in 1968 and is active in the areas of landscape architecture, architecture, town planning and play structures, employing today a staff of fifty. Mitsura Senda, principal and founding member, was educated at the Tokyo Institute of Technology and received a PhD in Engineering and Planning. He lectures widely within Japan and is Professor at the Waseda and Ryukyu Universities and the Nagoya Institute of Technology. Major works undertaken for EDI are the Yokohama City Irifune Park, Hamamatsu Science Museum, Yamata Yacht Club, Toyama Prefectural Canal Park and Toyama Prefectural Fugan Canal, all of which received national design awards. In 1988, the Tokyo design magazine, *Process Architecture*, devoted an entire issue to EDI, 'Environment Design: Strategies of Senda and the Environment Design Institute'.

ENVIRONMENTAL DESIGN PARTNERSHIP
was formed in South Africa in 1981 when Gareth and Sarah Singleton moved there to represent a British firm of landscape architects. EDP now has four directors, all of whom are British, employing twenty-two people, making it one of the largest environmental service teams in Southern Africa. Projects have been undertaken throughout the African States from offices based in Johannesburg, Durban, Botswana, Namibia and Swaziland. The workload is extremely varied, with the main disciplines of operation being resource and environmental planning, tourism and recreation planning, landscape architecture and urban design. Over 400 commissions have been undertaken, including the development of tourism accommodation facilities in sensitive areas. Several urban design projects have also been completed including a university campus, a government office enclave and a new central business district for a major city.

JOHN GRISSIM AND ASSOCIATES, INC.
was established over twenty-five years ago and offers a variety of services, including site and campus planning, recreational facilities, urban redevelopment, commercial and industrial projects, and has completed schemes throughout the United States. Clients include Forbes Cohen Properties, Ford Motor Land Development, Sea World, Albert Kahn Associates, Inc. and the City of Farmington Hills, Michigan.

gRUPO DE dISEÑO uRBANO The Mexico-City based grupo de diseño urbano was founded in 1977 by Mario Schjetnan and Jose Luis Perez, since which time the practice has become internationally recognized for its creative and innovative work in landscape architecture, architecture and urban design in both the public and private sectors. The emphasis of gdu's work is towards large-scale public projects among which figure the Centro Cultural Mexiquense, and the master plan, architecture and landscape architecture for the Museum of Arts and Crafts and the Museum of Modern Art, Mexico City. The practice has been the recipient of many major awards and in 1989 it was given the President's Award for Excellence from the American Society of Landscape Architects for the Parque Tezozomac.

GUTTORM GUTTORMSGAARD is an artist and at present is Professor at the Academy of Fine Arts, Oslo, specializing in graphics and book design.

GEORGE HARGREAVES was educated at the University of Georgia School of Environmental Design and at the Harvard University Graduate School of Design, receiving a Bachelor of Landscape Architecture, Magna Cum Laude, 1976 and a Master of Landscape with Distinction in 1979. He worked initially for the Cheshire Design Group in England before joining the SWA Group in Sausalito, California and forming his own company, Hargreaves Associates. George Hargreaves is an Adjunct Professor at Harvard University Graduate School of Design and is visiting professor/critic at many institutions across America. He has sat on international panels and in 1988 was the Chairman of the American Society of Landscape Architects' Professional Awards of Excellence. He has also published and exhibited his own works widely.

HEADS CO. LTD. was founded in 1967 as Otsuka Landscape Gardening Design Office Ltd., changing to its present name in 1969. Today it employs forty-seven personnel and has offices in Osaka, Tokyo and New York. The company's activities cover a broad spectrum, including surveying, designing and supervising the landscaping of institutional,

recreational and industrial complexes. The company is also involved in the survey, research and design of large-scale projects such as land development and comprehensive urban planning. Heads Co. is a member of the Japan Landscape Consultants Association, the Parks and Open Spaces Association of Japan and the Japanese Institute of Landscape Architects. In 1981 he was awarded the Institute's Prize for the design of Hanashiro Park in Senboku New Town, Japan.

JAKOBSEN LANDSCAPE ARCHITECTS
Based in Cheltenham, UK, Jakobsen Landscape Architects was founded in 1969 by Preben Jakobsen and his architect wife Margaret and is today a medium-sized professional consultancy offering landscape services throughout the UK and abroad. Clients range from large national and international concerns to private individuals, and emphasis is placed on quality and attention to detail. Recent projects include exterior and interior landscaping for government agencies, financial institutions, industrial companies, health and local authorities, plus modern and historic gardens. Preben Jakobsen is a Danish landscape architect who studied at the Royal Botanic Gardens, Kew and the Royal Academy of Fine Arts, Copenhagen before spending eight years with Eric Lyons, being responsible for most of the landscaping of the 'Span' housing schemes during the 1960s. He has been the recipient of many Civic Trust awards and also notably the BALI Award of Merit for Interior Landscaping in 1988 for his design achievements at Farnborough College. He lectures extensively both at home and abroad.

JOHNSON JOHNSON AND ROY INC. JJR was established in 1961. Early work with the University of Michigan leading to numerous other campus assignments gave the firm early national recognition in that field. They place great emphasis on planning and work in the areas of urban design, parks and recreation, historic preservation and commercial and industrial site design. Today the firm has offices in Dallas and Ann Arbor and employs sixty professional landscape architects, planners, scientists and engineers.

KEIKAN SEKKAI CO. LTD. is a planning and design firm founded in 1986, the principals being Tadashi Kubo, Yoshishige Fujita and Tooru Mijakoda. It has offices in Osaka, Tokyo and Singapore, providing environmental design, landscape architectural and engineering services for both the public and private sectors. Its work is known internationally.

JOGINDAR JUDGE KHURANA trained at the Delhi School of Planning and Architecture and the Harvard Graduate School of Design, USA, where he received respectively a BA in Architecture and a Masters Degree in Landscape Architecture and Urban Planning. Before moving to Saudi Arabia, he worked in Canada for over fifteen years, including three years in his own Toronto-based firm UDEP. He has retained an interest in Canada where he is a member of the Canadian Society of Landscape Architects and the Canadian Institute of Planners. Judge Khurana has been on the Faculty of Engineering, School of Environmental Design, Department of Landscape Architecture, King Abdulaziz University (KAU), Jeddah, Saudi Arabia as a Professor of Landscape Architecture and Urban Design since 1982. Over those years, he has been carrying on both the academic duties in the Department and the professional project activities related mostly to the development of the existing and the proposed New Man's KAU Campuses.

DANIEL URBAN KILEY trained at the Harvard Graduate School of Design and is the Senior Principal of the Office of Dan Kiley which he founded in 1940. The firm has offices in sixteen states and offers a full range of master and site planning, including landscape, horticultural and architectural services, as well as project administration for clients who include corporations, universities, museums, government agencies and private individuals. Major projects have been undertaken for the US Air Force Academy, Dulles Airport, the John F. Kennedy Library and the North Court at the Lincoln Center. The firm has worked actively in sixteen foreign countries and thirty-seven states in the US and today it is considered to be one of America's leading landscape architectural practices. Dan Kiley is the recipient of many awards and honours, the most recent being

the 1989 American Academy in Rome 'Year of the Landscape' celebration and the 1989 Brandeis University Citation in architecture. He also sits on several advisory committees and has lectured throughout the US and abroad, at most major American universities, for the State Governor's Conferences, the Smithsonian Institute, the Graham Foundation, the MOMA in New York City and the AIA and ASLA.

BÜRO KNOLL consists of thirty professionals with landscape offices in Sindelfingen, Heilbronn, Berlin and Dresden. Their work ranges from landscape planning to site design and they have won competitions for and built two Landesgartenschaus (State garden festivals) and will be responsible for the 1997 garden show in Mosbach, Germany. Robin Winogrand, who was responsible for the Enz Garden, graduated from the University of Wisconsin in 1979 with a BA in Environmental Design before taking a Master of Landscape Architecture at the Louisiana State University. Since 1989 she has been Artist in Residence at the Staatliche Akademie der Bildenden Kunst in Stuttgart, Germany. Robin Winogrand has worked for several American landscape architecture practices and presently acts in a professional capacity for Büro Knoll, Planungsgruppe Landschaftarchitecktur and the University of Stuttgart, School of Architecture.

BERND KRÜGER AND HUBERT MÖHRLE, FREIE LANDSCHAFTSARCHITEKTEN Bernd Krüger and Hubert Möhrle formed their Stuttgart-based partnership in 1987. They see themselves primarily as 'open-air architects' and believe that each design should be fresh, individual and fully sensitive to the environment.

LATITUDE NORD Laurence Vacherot and Gilles Vexlard, joint directors of the Paris-based Latitude Nord, both trained at the Ecole Nationale Superieure d'Horticulture de Versailles. They work primarily on urban projects, sometimes in an advisory capacity, but are often involved directly in long-term schemes which include town planning, leisure and sports facilities, and the development of historic sites, for example the medieval village of Valbonne. This diversity of scope has led

them to employ a team of specialists in areas such as ecology, lighting effects and agronomy.

LDR INTERNATIONAL INC. was founded in 1969 and since that date has become both nationally and internationally recognized for its work in more than fifty cities throughout the USA and Europe, gaining numerous major accolades, including twelve awards from the American Society of Landscape Architects. Based in Columbia, Maryland and London, LDR provides planning, urban design, landscape architecture and graphic design services to a wide spectrum of public- and private-sector clients, including Mobil Land Development Corporation and the Marriott Corporation.

DEREK LOVEJOY AND PARTNERS With offices in London, Leicester, Manchester, Christchurch, Bristol and Edinburgh, Derek Lovejoy and Partners was founded in 1969 by Derek Lovejoy and is now established as a leading environmental design group with experience in over thirty countries. In addition to a large permanent staff with skills in a wide range of disciplines, close links are maintained with specialist experts and research organizations to enable the practice to undertake all aspects of environmental design. The practice has won eight international competitions for architecture and landscape architecture, notably in 1970 for the Cergy Pontoise Park in Paris, and in 1972 for La Corneuve Regional Park, also in Paris. They have been the recipient of numerous national design awards such as the 1991 BALI prize for the RMC International Headquarters and competition prizes, such as first prize in 1990 for the masterplan of Parque de Salburua Victoria-Gasties, Spain.

MARISA MAFFIOLI is a self-taught landscape architect who trained both in Italy and France. She was employed by the Turin Municipality and Piedmonte Region as their consultant and has worked extensively on landscape projects connected to the river system in the Turin metropolitan area. At present she is a researcher in the field of urban landscape planning and design at the University of Turin in the Dipartimento di Agronomia Selvicoltura e Gestione del Territorio.

MPA DESIGN is a landscape and urban design practice based in San Francisco, employing twenty professionals. It was established in 1969 as Michael Painter and Associates and since then has successfully completed over 400 master-planning and landscape-design projects throughout the US and abroad. Michael Painter was educated at the University of California at Berkeley and the Harvard Graduate School of Design where he obtained a MLA in Urban Design in 1966. Since founding MPA he has been awarded many regional and national design awards and is a frequent lecturer and panellist at Harvard University and the College of Environmental Design, Berkeley. He has also been chairman of the American Society of Landscape Architects.

LEA NORGAARD AND VIBEKE HOLSHER LANDSCAPE ARCHITECTS

The architectural firm Edith and Ole Norgaard was established in 1954. The company today is led by Lea Norgaard, architect, and Vibeke Holsher, landscape architect, under the name of Lea Norgaard and Vibeke Holsher Landscape Architects. Work emphasis is on large-scale public commissions, education and research institutions, administration, industrial and cultural buildings, planning and urban renewal. Major schemes include work for IBM in Brussels and Lundote, the Louisiana Museum of Modern Art, Humlebaek and the planning and redevelopment of an old gravel-mining site into a regional park and recreation area, 'Hedeeland', south-west of Copenhagen.

CORNELIA OBERLANDER trained at Smith College, Northampton, Massachusetts and Harvard University Graduate School of Design, where she received a Bachelor of Landscape Architecture. Over the past forty years she has worked on a wide range of projects with internationally acclaimed architects and public agencies in Canada and the US. She began her career working for architects Louis I. Kahn, Oscar Stonerov and landscape architect Dan Kiley. Since 1974 she has worked with Arthur Erickson Architects as Landscape Architect; projects include the Museum of Anthropology, Vancouver and the Canadian Chancery, Washington, for which she was awarded the

National Landscape Award. Since 1983 work has continued in association with Moshe Safdie Architects on the National Gallery of Canada and in 1990 the team of Harman, Henriquez and Oberlander won the Peace-Keeping Monument Competition in Ottawa, completed in August 1992. Cornelia Oberlander has been the President of the Canadian Society of Landscape Architects (1986-1987) and Environmental Chairman (1987-1989).

ANTHONY M. O'NEILL The firm of Anthony M. O'Neill was founded in 1967 by Anthony O'Neill and his wife Barbara who had trained together at the School of Architecture, National University of Ireland, Dublin, where they gained B. Arch degrees. Postgraduate studies were undertaken at the School of Planning, London University where they specialized in Town Planning/Civic Architecture and Landscape Architecture respectively. In 1957 they emigrated to Montreal, Canada, moving into private practice in 1961 when they co-formed the firm of O'Neill and Warshaw. Since returning to Eire they have won both national and international acclaim for their work as architects, planners and landscape consultants, resulting in 1987 in the American Society of Landscape Architects Honour Award for Glenveagh National Park. Their work emphasis is towards large-scale, regional landscape-planning works with clients including the Bord Failte and several county councils and corporations in Eire. Both Anthony and Barbara O'Neill belong to a selection of professional associations and advisory bodies such as the American Society of Landscape Architects and the Irish Institute of Landscape Architects.

PARENT LATREILLE ET ASSOCIÉS was founded in 1977 by Jean Marc Latreille and Anne Marie Parent. Their main areas of expertise are site planning, urban design and landscape architecture. Today the firm consists of a dozen professionals and technicians who have been awarded numerous honours on regional and national levels. Principal clients include federal and provincial governments, municipalities and private institutions.

GEORGE PENKER studied at the Technische Universitat München and opened his own office in Neuss, Düsseldorf in 1958, which employs at present twelve full-time designers. The majority of his work is in the areas of landscape design and environmental planning and his aim is to harmonize nature and civilization. Completed projects include the University of Düsseldorf, the Nordrhein-Westfalen Parliament in Düsseldorf and the Rhein Promenade in Cologne. He has received many national awards for his work and is a member of both the Bund Deutscher Landschaftsarchitekten (BDLA) and the Deutsche Gesellschaft für Gartenkunst und Landschaftspflege (DGGL).

(PSA) PROPERTY SERVICES AGENCY is one of the UK's largest multi-disciplinary design, project-management and technical advisory consultancies offering pre-design, project management, quantity surveying, construction, quality control and specialist advisory services. It currently manages most of the Government's major construction projects. Pat Bullivant is an architect/landscape architect who trained at the Architectural Association School and then at London University School of Landscape in the Peter Youngman era. She worked in several private architectural practices in London, notably that of Peter Shepard, before joining the PSA in 1978.

HEINER RODEL trained at the Fachhochschule für Garten und Landschaftsgestaltung, Freising-Wahenstephan, Germany, graduating as a landscape architect. He founded his own practice in 1977 having collaborated on many landscape projects, including the consultation for the landscape design of the Museum of Contemporary Art, Centre Georges Pompidou, Paris. Since 1977 he has worked in Saudi Arabia, Iran, Kuwait and Switzerland on public and private commissions. Recent schemes include a new five-star hotel complex 'Il Giardino' in Ascona, Switzerland and numerous private residences. In 1986/1987 he won first prize in a competition for the extension of a hotel and nautical club on the Comino Island of Malta.

ROLLAND/TOWERS was originally founded as Peter G. Rolland and Associates in 1963, changing its name in 1987, and today consists of a ten-strong landscape architectural practice, with emphasis on specific site design and master planning, while still being concerned with construction detailing and observation and continuing consultations. Their work ranges from private residences to corporate headquarters, university campuses, land developments, urban complexes, airports and, most significantly, the New Parliament House in Australia. The firm has been the recipient of twenty-five national and international design awards and their schemes have been widely published and exhibited. In 1982 Peter Rolland was made Fellow of the American Society of Landscape Architects and in 1990 was awarded the American Institute of Architects' Honours for his design achievements.

SASAKI ASSOCIATES. INC. has earned international recognition for planning and design since its foundation nearly forty years ago in 1953 by Hideo Sasaki. Schemes largely include services for college and university campuses, resorts and leisure environments, new communities, suburban mixed-use centres, parks and gardens, and recently the firm has added to its multi-disciplinary capabilities by employing interior and graphic designers. In 1988 Sasaki Associates formed an affiliation with Suter and Suter, a European consulting, planning, architecture and engineering concern based in Basel, Switzerland, which has opened up opportunities throughout Europe. Hideo Sasaki is a guest lecturer at many colleges and universities throughout the USA and Canada.

STODDART AND TABORA ARCHITECTS
John Godfrey Stoddart and Fernando Tabora Pena trained as architects at the Bartlett School of Architecture, UCL and the Catholic University of Santiago respectively. Stoddart and Tabora Architects was founded in 1964 and deals with environmental planning, civic design and landscape architecture throughout Latin America and the Caribbean. The practice has produced projects for new cities, master plans for green areas, civic designs for plazas, squares and parks, several university campuses, airports, international exhibition and fairgrounds, racetracks, five-star complexes and private residential work. The

partnership received the first National Award for Landscape Architecture in 1977 and has participated in many international exhibitions. John Stoddart was elected Vice-President of the Western Region of the International Federation of Landscape Architects from 1980-83. Today he is completing his chairmanship of the IFLA Latin American Regional Council and has recently been elected Fellow of the American Society of Landscape Architects. Fernando Tabora Pena was in charge of the development of the Master's Course in Landscape Architecture at the Central University and has recently been invited to become one of the directors of the Museum of Architecture which he helped to establish.

TAKANO LANDSCAPE PLANNING LTD.
was founded in 1975 by Fumiaki Takano, a graduate of the Hokkaido University in Japan with an MA in Environmental Design from the University of Georgia, USA. Prior to returning to Japan he worked as a landscape architect for a designers' collaborative in Athens, USA and for Simmonds and Simmonds in Pittsburgh, USA. His expertise lies in the design of parks and he works both in Japan and abroad. In 1980 he received the Japan Landscape Association design award for the Okinawa Marine Expo Children's Park. He is a guest lecturer at many universities, including Georgia, Carnegie and Cornell in the USA.

TOKYO LANDSCAPE ARCHITECTS INC. is a Tokyo-based design outfit with offices in fifteen cities throughout Japan and one in the United States. It offers a full range of services from research and study, and urban, regional, and environmental planning and development, through to the design of parks and open spaces, supervision of construction and future maintenance and administration. They also concern themselves with architectural and civil engineering design which takes into consideration ecological and landscape elements.

TTG (TRUPER AND GONDESEN) was founded in 1972 by Teja Truper and Christoph Gondesen and today employs twenty-two staff, practising in Lübeck, Germany. They work mainly in open-space design, environmental planning and resource management.

ANTHONY WALKER AND PARTNERS was founded by Anthony Walker in 1970 where today he is principal. He trained at Wye College, receiving a BSc in Horticulture in 1965, and later at the University of Newcastle-upon-Tyne where he undertook a postgraduate diploma in Landscape Design. His firm specializes in project planning and coordination, environmental impact analysis, consultancy management, minerals planning and restoration, and golf course design and management. Currently they have five offices in the UK and project offices overseas. Major schemes include township conservation and settlement, design in Saudi Arabia, motorway and trunk road projects in the UK, major urban renewal schemes, supermarkets and retail parks and mineral planning submissions. More recently they have become involved in recreational and leisure developments. Anthony Walker is a member of the British Institute of Agricultural Consultants and since 1980 he has been a Fellow of the Institute of Quarrying and of the Landscape Institute.

PETER WALKER AND PARTNERS The office of Peter Walker and Partners was formed in 1983 for the practice of landscape architecture with a particular emphasis on providing a personal service to clients desiring a unique design in the landscape. Their aim is to challenge traditional concepts of landscape design and this attitude has been applied to a variety of projects within the US, ranging from private residential gardens and parks to hotels, plazas, campuses, large-scale corporate headquarters, mixed-use developments and new communities. The firm has recently participated in three winning design competitions, the re-design of the historic Todos Santos Plaza, the Marina and Linear Park in San Diego and the Performing Arts Center in Fremont, California. Peter Walker has served as a consultant and advisor to a number of public agencies and institutions such as the Redevelopment Agency of San Francisco. He is the former Chairman of the Department of Landscape Architecture and acting director of the Urban Design Program and he currently holds an adjunct professorship at the Graduate School of Design, Harvard University. He is an Honorary Fellow of both the American Society of Landscape Architects and the Urban Land Institute.

PETER YOUNGMAN graduated from Cambridge University with a degree in history, after which he worked as an apprentice to a firm of garden contractors and as an articled pupil to a garden designer. There followed two years as a trainee/assistant for a town planning consultant, during which time he attended a part-time course at the London School of Planning and Research for National Development. Since 1946 he has been in private practice and has worked on number of

planning consultancies in the UK and abroad, as well as various design projects from small domestic gardens to large public commissions such as Gatwick and Heathrow Airports and Sizewell Power Stations. From 1948-78 he was a part-time teacher at University College London in the departments of Town Planning and Environmental Studies, as the first visiting professor in landscape design. He is a past president of the Institute of Landscape Architects and a fellow of the Royal Town

Planning Institute. He was appointed CBE in 1983 and was awarded the Landscape Institute medal in 1989.

ZEN ENVIRONMENTAL DESIGN was founded in 1959 and is involved in many facets of environmental design, from large-scale city-planning and the landscape architecture of resorts and parks, to street furniture and sign design. It has won both national and international acclaim for its work.

PROJECT ACKNOWLEDGEMENTS

1.1 SHA TIN PARK, Sha Tin New Town, Hong Kong
Landscape architect Brian Clouston and Partners Hong Kong Ltd. *Project team* Alan Tate (Director-in-charge 1981-1988), Arnie Coombs (Director-in-charge 1988-1990), Martin Jones, John Dainton, Neil Chapman; *Concept design* Henry Steed, Jennifer Steed; *Detail design* Peter McGowan, David Ausherman, Willie Cheng, Sidney Lui, John Dainton, Peter Sandover, Alyson Salkild, Chris Donovan, Ophelia Wong, Winnie Wong; *Client* Sha Tin New Town Development Office, Hong Kong Government; *Main contractor* Shiu Tai and Co. Ltd., Sung Foo Kee, Sui Chong; *Planting* Asia Landscaping Ltd.; *Electrical* Jardine Engineering Ltd.; *Fountain* P & A Engineering Ltd.; *Tensile structure* Helios Inc.; *Irrigation* Multiprop Ltd.; *Civil and structural engineers* Mannsell Consultants Asia; *Electrical and mechanical engineers* Ove Arup and Partners, Hong Kong, Ltd.; *Quantity surveyor* Clifford Webb and Partners (Faithsul and Gould); *Architectural consultant* Martin Iles Partnership.

1.2 RUHEGARTEN, The Enz Garden, Landesgartenschau, Pforzheim, Germany
Landscape architect S. Knoll Landscape Architecture; *Project team* Robin Winogrond, Büro Knoll; *Client* Pforzheim Landesgartenschau GmbH; *Main contractors* Ebel und Pross, Glasbau Liebherr GmbH; *Airbrush colour work* BGT Bischoff Glastechnik; *Aluminium contractors* Spittelmeister GmbH, Eloxal, Weil der Stadt; *Aluminium consultants* Aluminium Zentrale, Vereinigte Aluminium Werke AG, Oase Pumpen; *Glass supplier* Glasverarbeitung Bietigheim GmbH.

1.3 JOHN KNIGHT MEMORIAL PARK, Canberra, Australia
Landscape architect Denton Corker Marshall Pty Ltd.; *Project team* Adrian Pilton (Director), Paul Geehan; *Client* National Capital Development Commission; *Main contractors* Able Landscaping, A & A Construction Pty Ltd., Savo Stankovich Pty Ltd., Paul O'Brien Engineering Pty Ltd., Urban Contractors Pty Ltd., Arny Pty Ltd. (play structure); *Civil and structural engineers* Maunsells Pty Ltd.; *Hydraulic engineers* R A Young and Associates.

1.4 NACION PLAZA, Nishinomiya New Town, Japan
Landscape architect Heads Co. Ltd.; *Project team* Yasushi Ueno, Hiroki Nakanishi; *Client* Housing and Urban Development Corporation; *Main contractors* Rinkai Construction Co. Ltd., Kubota Construction Co. Ltd.; *Landscape contractor* Kuraray Ryokka Co. Ltd.; *Sculptor* Riera I. Arago.

1.5 PARQUE TEZOZOMAC, Acapotzalco, Mexico City, Mexico
Landscape architect Grupo de diseño urbano S.C.; *Project team* Mario Schjetnan, Jose Luis Perez, Jorge Calvillo; *Client* Delegacion Azcapotzalco and Federal District's Department; *Main and landscape contractor* Delegacion Azcapotzalco; *Historical consultant* Tomas Calvillo; *Graphic design* Jorge Sandoval.

1.6 THE FIELD OF BATTLE LANDSCAPE CONSERVATION, Battle, East Sussex, UK
Landscape architects PSA Services; *Project designer* Pat Bullivant; *Clients* Department of the Environment, Department of Ancient Monuments and Historic Buildings, now English Heritage; *Consultant architects* Donald Insall and Associates; *Landscape contractor* Wealdon Woodlands (English Woodlands Ltd.); *Term contractor* Turfsoil Ltd.; *Fencing* P. B. Fencing Ltd.

1.7 EURODISNEY MAGIC KINGDOM, Marne-la-Vallée, France
Landscape architect Derek Lovejoy Partnership; *Project team* David Blackwood Murray, Clive McDonnell, James Welch, Angus Robertson, Jessica Beattie, David Watson – CAD Manager; *Client* Euro Disneyland SA; *Main Contractor* Lehrer McGovern Bovis Sarl; *Landscape Consultant* Eurodisneyland Imagineering Area, Development (Bill Coan), API Cooperative (Michel Viollet); *Irrigation Consultant* Aqua Engineering Inc.; *Fleurs-de-lys hedgework* Bruns Nurseries; *Forecourt trees and clipped yews* Lorenz Von Ehrens Nurseries.

1.8 APPROACH ROAD TO MIKASA PARK, Yokosuka, Japan
Landscape architect Mitsuru Senda and Environment Design Institute; *Project team* Mitsuru Senda, Kazuharu Mori, Osamu Sakuma; *Main contractors* Tokyu Construction Company Ltd., Maeda Road Construction Ltd.; *Sculptors* Bukichi Inoue, Kazuo Yuhara, Masamichi Yamamoto, Keiko Amenomiya; *Artist* (mural) Eijin Suzuki.

1.9 AQUATOP, Travemünde, Germany
Landscape architect Büro TTG, Trüper and Gondesen; *Project team* Teja Trüper, Mareile Ehlers, Sabine Torper; *Client* Travemünde Board of Tourism; *Landscape contractor* Ernst Jolitz & Söhne, Ekhart Brun; *Roof terrace elements* Bauteile und Umweltschutzsysteme GmbH & Co. KG.

1.10 TOYAMA AIRPORT SPORTS PLAZA, Toyama City, Japan
Landscape architect Keikan Design Inc, Tokyo Branch; *Project team* Tooru Miyakoda (Principal-in-charge), Sumitaka Naka, Hiroshi Watanabe, Hiroshi Yokota, Hideo Takiura; *Client* The Environmental Pollution Service Corporation; *Main contractor* Fuji Ueki Co. Ltd.; *Landscape contractor* Tateyama Zoen Doboku Co. Ltd.; *Brick supplier* Azunick Co. Ltd.; *Signage* Chiyoda Kanban Co. Ltd.; *Cast stone and concrete* Kantou Concrete, Kogyu Co. Ltd.; *Metalwork* Sekina Konchiku Kanamono Co. Ltd.; *Sculptor* Mikio Nakajima; *Graphics* Kazunari Yoshida.

1.11 PARC SAUSSET, Paris, France
Landscape architect Michel and Claire Corajoud; *Project team* Michel Desvigne, Christine Dalnoky, Henri Bava, Marc Claramunt, Thibault de Metz; *Client* Seine-Saint-Denis Department; *Main contractor* Conseil General de la Seine-Saint Denis; *Architects* Pierre Gangnet, Edith Giraid; *Landscape contractor* Jacques Coulon; *Design consultants* Pascal Mourgue with Patrice Hardy, Bernard Rousseau; *Engineer* Tristan Pauly; *Agronomical engineers* Claude Guinaudeau, Marc Rumelhart; *Structural engineer* Marc Mimram.

1.12 NABESHIMA CERAMIC PARK, Imari City, Japan
Landscape architect Zen Environmental Design; *Project team* Zenichi Nakamura, Sinichi Misima, Kyuji Nakamura, Tatsuo Kishi, Shuichi Tanamachi, Kazuya Tsukada; *Client* City of Imari; *Main contractor* Kuroki Construction Co. Ltd.; *Consultants* Tokusu, So-Setsubi.

1.13 THE HANGING GARDENS, Newcastle-upon-Tyne, UK
Landscape architect Anthony Walker and Partners; *Project team* E. Winship, S. Hughes, C. Emmerson, N. Wright; *Client* Tyne and Wear Development Corporation; *Main contractor* John W & S Dorin Ltd.; *Landscape contractor* Charles Lambert (Lawns) Ltd.; *Consultant engineers* Hutter Jennings and Titchmarsh; *Quantity surveyors* Ian S. Clark and Associates; *Hardwood structures* Sarum Hardwood Structures Ltd.; *Irrigation equipment* Cameron Irrigation; *Lighting* Selux; *Mild steel railing* Tubular Barriers Ltd.

1.14 MANUKAU COURT, Manukau City, New Zealand
Landscape architect Boffa Miskall Partners; *Project team* Frank Boffa (Director-in-charge), Ron Flook (Designer), Steve Drakeford (Landscape architect); *Client* Manukau City Council; *Main contractor* Green and McCarhill; *Landscape contractor* Manukau City

Council; *Engineering consultants* Murray North Partners; *Quantity surveyors* Maltby Partners.

1.15 GRAND-MALL PARK, Yokohama City, Japan
Landscape architect Tokyo Landscape Architects Inc.; *Project team* Haruto Kobayashi, Susumu Yamanaka, Tsuneo Suzuki; *Lighting consultants* Mikiko Ishi Design Office; *Technical advisor* Nihon Setsubi Sekkei; *Lighted paving slabs* Kyosera KK; *Washed concrete slabs* Sanesu KK; *Stonework* Seiura KK; *Water features* Suikosha KK.

1.17 SHINAGAWA WARD PARK, Tokyo, Japan
Landscape architect AI Landscape Planning Co. Ltd.; *Project team* Kiyofsa Hiramatsu (Director), Koichiro Kamegai, Kunio Kurihara, Yoshinori Watanabe, Hachirou Sakakibara, Akiyoshi Manabe; *Main contractor* Shimizu Corporation; *Landscape contractor* Odukyu Landscape Gardening; *Technical advisors* Sunpu Civil Engineering Consultant, P. T. Morimura & Associates.

1.18 TSUEN WAN PARKS AND PLAYGROUNDS, Tsuen Wan New Town, Hong Kong
Landscape architect Denton Corker Marshall Pty Ltd.; *Project team* Adrian Pilton (Director-in-charge), Suny Yeung (Contract adminstration), Paul Geehan (Landscape architect/design), Bob Nation (Architect), Peter Bradon (Detailed design and documentation); *Client* The Hong Kong Government; *Main contractor* Fung Cheung Kee Construction Ltd.; *Mechanical and engineering contractors* Bylander Meinhardt Partnership; *Geotechnic and civil consultants* John Connell Associates; *Quantity surveyor* R. Brechins.

1.19 CHARLESTON WATERFRONT PARK, Charleston, South Carolina, USA
Landscape architects Sasaki Associates, Inc.; *Project team* Stuart O. Dawson (Design principal), Edward J. Fitzgerald (Managing principal), Jay B. Faber (Project designer), David C. Clough (Project manager, landscape architecture), Varoujan Hagopian (Project manager, civil engineering and construction services), Jeanne Lukenda (Project landscape architect), Bert Ferris (Construction administration); *Client* The Honorable Joseph P. Riley, Jr., Mayor – City of Charleston; *Main contractor* Ruscon Construction Co. Inc.; *Main landscape contractor* Micah Jenkins Nursery; *Landscape architecture* J. Edward Pinckney; *Urban design* Cooper Robertson and Partners; *Fountain consultant* CMS Collaborative; *Structural engineer* David Carsen (deceased); *Electrical engineering* Holladay, Coleman and Associates.

1.20 MICHINOKU LAKE WOOD PARK, Miyagi Prefecture, Japan
Landscape architect Takano Landscape Planning Co. Ltd.; *Project designer* Fumiaki Takano; *Client* Ministry of Construction; *Main and landscape contractor* Seibu Zoen Co. Ltd.

2.1 IBM FEDERAL SYSTEMS DIVISION, Pasedena, Texas, USA
Landscape architect Peter Walker and Partners Landscape Architecture Inc.; *Project team* Peter Walker, Doug Findley, Tony Sinkosky, Lisa Roth, Tom Leader, David Walker; *Client* IBM Corporation and Cadillac Fairview Development; *Architects of record* CRS Cirrine; *Landscape contractor* Ridgewood Landscape Inc.; *General contractor* Linbeck Construction Co.

2.2 REGENT COURT OFFICE BUILDING, Dearborn,

Michigan, USA
Landscape architect John Grissim and Associates; *Project team* Randall Metz (Project designer and manager); *Client* Ford Motor Land Development Corporation; *Main contractor* R. E. Dailey; *Landscape contractor* Chas. F. Irish Co. Inc. (autocourt), Skandia Landscape Inc. (building grounds); *Irrigation design* C. J. Colein and Associates; *Lighting design* Luminart Inc..

2.3 R & V VERSICHERUNG ADMINISTRATION BUILDING, Karlsruhe, Germany
Landscape architect Karl Bauer; *Client* R & V Lebensversicherung AG; *Architects* Schmitt, Kasimir and Partners; *Landscape contractor* Bohn & Worth GmbH; *Construction/metalwork* Schuler Metalltechnik.

2.4 PLAZA TOWER ONE, Englewood, Colorado, USA
Landscape architect Hargreaves Associates; *Project team* George Hargreaves, Glenn Allen, Mary Margaret Jones, Brian Costello; *Client* Chevron Land and Development; *Main contractors* B. L. Cohen, Yerkey Landscape, PCL Construction (fountain); *Consultant* Fountain Tech.

2.5 HARLEQUIN PLAZA, Greenwood Village, Denver, Colorado, USA
Landscape architect SWA Group; *Project team* George Hargreaves, Glenn Allen, Jean Schaffeld, Danny Powell; *Client* John Madden Company; *General contractor* Centric Corporation; *Structural engineers* NV Tsiouvaras and Associates; *Mechanical engineers* Hadji and Associates; *Electrical engineers* Garland D. Cox and Associates Inc.

2.6 RMC INTERNATIONAL HEADQUARTERS, Surrey, UK
Landscape architect Derek Lovejoy Partnership; *Project team* Michael Langlay-Smith (Consultant), David Blackwood Murray (Partner), Kevin Underwood (Senior associate); *Client* RMC (Ready Mix Concrete); *Architects* Edward Cullinan Architects; *Main contractor* Trafalgar House Management Construction Ltd.; *Landscape contractor* Waterers Landscapes Ltd.; *Roads* Roadstone Surfacing Ltd.; *Tiling* Carters; *PCC walls* Wootton Concrete Products; *Granite* Dimensional Stone; *Irrigation* Cameron; *Clipped trees* Arcangell Giavanni, Pistoria, Italy.

2.7 COURTYARD FOR BUSINESS PARK, Stuttgart, Germany
Landscape architects Bernd Krüger and Hubert Möhrle; *Client* Businesspark GmbH; *Architect* Geray und Reck; *Main contractor* Schüttkus, GST Bau; *Stone supplier* Firma A Schütz Naturstein GmbH.

2.8 SOLANA, Westlake and Southlake, Texas, USA
Landscape architect Peter Walker and Partners Landscape Architecture Inc.; *Project team* Peter Walker, Doug Findlay, Toney Sinkosky, Tom Leader, David Meyer, Lisa Roth, David Walker, Rob Rombold; *Clients* Maguire Thomas Partners, IBM Corporation; *Architects* Mitchell/Giurgola Architects, Ricardo Legorreta Arquitectos; *Main contractor* HCB Contractors; *Irrigation* Hall Sprinkler Co.; *Water feature* Rock and Waterscapes Inc.; *Stonework* Chief Benson; *Meadow planting* Wildseed Inc.

2.9 URBAN RECREATION AREA, UBS Administration Building, Zurich, Switzerland
Landscape architect Heiner Rodel; *Collaborators* Sergio Notari (Designer), Stephanie Knoblich (Landscape architect); *Client* Union Bank of

Switzerland; *Landscape contractor* SPROSS Ga-La-Bau; *Artist* Ivan Pestalozzi.

2.10 PACIFIC BELL ADMINISTRATION CENTER, San Ramon, California, USA
Landscape architect MPA Design; *Project team* Michael Painter (Principal-in-charge), Thomas Klope (Project designer), David W. Nelson (Project manager); *Client* Pacific Bell; *Architect* Skidmore, Owings and Merrill; *Main contractor* Swinerton and Walberg; *Landscape contractor* Cagwin and Dorward; *Irrigation consultant* Russell D. Mitchell Associates; *Horticulture* Barrie Coate.

2.11 REFUGE ASSURANCE PLC HEADQUARTERS, Wilmslow, Cheshire, UK
Landscape architect Building Design Partnership; *Project team* Phil Moss, Paul Taylor; *Client* Refuge Assurance PLC.; *Management contractor* Laing Management Contracting Ltd.; *Landscape contractor* Living Landscapes Ltd.; *Paving* Empire Stone Ltd., IMAG, Baggeridge Bricks; *Alkerplan geomembrane lake liner* Landline Ltd.; *Timberwork* Woodscape Ltd.; *Fountains and electronic controls* Water Techniques; *Courtyard boulders* Summerfield and Lang Ltd.

2.12 NORTH CAROLINA NATIONAL BANK PLAZA, Tampa, Florida, USA
Landscape architect Dan Kiley; *Project team* Dan Kiley (Partner-in-charge), Peter Walker (Partner), Peter Lindsay Schaudt (Associate), Caroline Kiley, Brian Smith, Laure Quonium, Joachim Kiley; *Clients* North Carolina National Bank, Faison Associates; *Architects* Wolf Associates; *Landscape architect* Odell Associates; *Lighting consultant* Jules Fisher and Paul Marantz, Inc.; *Soil engineers* Soil and Material Engineers, Inc.; *Surveyor* Heidt and Associates; *Marble suppliers* Vermont Marble Co.

2.13 COLONIA PARK, Cologne, Germany
Landscape architect Georg Penker; *Client* Colonia Insurance Company, Cologne; *Landscape contractors* Karl Leisten GmbH and Co. KG, Pilot Garten und Landschaftsbau GmbH, Rogross Garten und Landschaftsbau.

2.14 HARSTON MILL, Harston, Cambridge, UK
Landscape architect Jakobsen Landscape Architects; *Project designer* Preben Jakobsen; *Client* Cambridge Interactive Systems; *Architect* R. H. Partnership; *Mechanical and electrical engineers* Sibley Robinson Partnership; *Quantity surveyor* Davis, Belfield and Everest; *Landscape contractor* Frosts Landscape Construction Ltd.; *Concrete slabs and setts* Blanc de Bierges – Milner Delvaux Ltd.; *Timber retaining wall* Permacrib (Euro) Ltd.; *Slate boulders and beach pebbles* IMAG Ltd.; *Millpool liner* Landline Ltd.

2.15 THE BROADMOOR PARK, San Francisco, California, USA
Landscape architect Danielson and Associates; *Project designer* Robert Danielson; *Client* I. M. Liberman; *Architect* Richard Blanchard and Associates; *Main contractor* Granada Inc.; *Landscape contractor* Katsura Gardens; *Structural engineer* H. Robert Hammill.

2.16 RIVERWOODS OFFICE PARK, Befordview, Johannesburg, South Africa
Landscape architect Environmental Design Partnership; *Project team* Wendy Farrand, Garreth Singleton, Peter Dijkhuis; *Client* AECI Pension Fund; *Architect* Louis Karol Architects; *Building contractor* Kirchmann Hurry; *Landscape contractor* RSA Contractor; *Interior*

landscaping The Office Plant; *Developers* Oakwood Ventures; *Irrigation* Top Turf and Associates; *Drip irrigation* Countryline Drip Irrigation; *Superior large trees* Instant Trees.

2.17 THE GARDENS OF NORTH POINT, Useppa Island, Florida, USA

Landscape architect Burner and Co. Inc.; *Project team* Peter Burner, Theresa Artuso (Vice president), Valerie Corbett Burner (Design associate); *Clients* Mr and Mrs Jack James, Mr and Mrs Paul F. Miller Jr., Useppa Inn and Dock Company; *Main contractor* Safety Harbor Builders; *Landscape contractor* Useppa Inn and Dock Company.

2.18 PRADO HUMBOLDT COMPLEX, Caracas, Venezuela

Landscape architect Stoddart and Tabora Architects; *Project team* John Godfrey Stoddart, Fernando Tabora Pena; *Client* Architect Federico Beckhoff; *Specialist services* Beckhoff Associates; *Hydraulics engineer* Eduardo Santo Michelena.

3.1 COURTYARD OF THE CATHOLIC UNIVERSITY, SCHOOL OF BIOTECHNOLOGY, Oporto, Portugal

Landscape architect Andresen and Castel-Branco Arquitectura Paisagista Lda.; *Project team* Cristina Castel-Branco; *Client* Portugese Catholic University; *Architect* João Adão da Fonseca; *Main contractor* Hard landscape – Sociedalde de Constração, Alberto Leal SA, Soft landscape – Joaquim dos Santos; *Pumping and hydraulic system* Jorge Frois; *Engineering consultant* Adão da Fonseca and Associados.

3.2 ENID A. HAUPT GARDEN, Smithsonian Institute, Washington DC, USA

Landscape architect Sasaki Associates Inc.; *Project team* Stuart O. Dawson (Design principal), Neil J. Dean (Managing principal); *Client* US General Services Administration; *Architect* Shepley Bulfinch Richardson and Abott; *Main contractor* Blake Construction Company; *Granite suppliers* Cold Spring Granite Company, Rock of Ages Corporation.

3.3 NEW CANADIAN CHANCERY, Washington DC, USA

Landscape architect Cornelia Hahn Oberlander/Arthur Erickson Architects; *Project designer* Cornelia Oberlander; *Architects* Arthur Erickson Architects; *Client* The Canadian Government; *Main contractor* George Hyman Construction Co.; *Landscape contractor* Ruppert Landscape Co. Inc.; *Structural engineers* M. S. Yolles and Partners; *Mechanical engineers* R. David Mackay Engineering Ltd.; *Electrical engineers* BFH/Shawnigan; *Sculpture* Bill Reid.

3.4 GREVE KIRKEGÅRD, Greve Kommune, Udvidelse, Denmark

Landscape architect Andreas Brun; *Client* Greve Menighedsråd; *Main and landscape contractor* J & B Byggerprodktion AS.

3.5 NEW VICTORIA THEATRE, Newcastle-under-Lyme, UK

Landscape architect Prof. Chris Baines; *Client* New Victoria Theatre Trust; *Contractor – brick paving* G. Percy Trentham; *Light fittings* BEGA.

3.6 CEREMONIAL HALL AND CONFERENCE CENTRE COMPLEX, King Abdulaziz University, Jeddah, Saudi Arabia

Landscape architect Jogindar Judge Khurana; *Project team* Judge Khurana, Geoff Ricks; *Client* King Abdulaziz University, Project Directorate Office; *Main

contractor Daelim Industrial Company Ltd.; *Landscape contractor* Saudi Arabian Landscape Company; *Main consultant* Saudconsult, Architects and Engineers.

3.7 CANADIAN MUSEUM OF CIVILIZATION, Ottawa/Hull, Canada

Landscape architects EDA Collaborative Inc., Parent Latreille Associés; *Project team* Ronald D. Tatasciore (EDA Collaborative Inc.), Anne-Marie Parent, Jean Marc Latreille (Parent Latreille Associés); *Client* The Architectural Consortium DJC/TPL, acting for the Canadian Museums Construction Corporation; *Main contractor* Concordia Construction Management Co.; *Pavers* Brekon Masonry Inc.; *Soft landscape at park level* F. Leblond Cement Products Ltd.; *Landscape at plaza level* Meyknecht-Lischner Contractors Ltd.; *Large-tree transplanting* Douglas Wood, Large Tree Sales; *Fountain systems* Lambert Somec and Crystal Fountains; *Site lighting* Black and McDonald.

3.8 CITY HALL PUBLIC PARK, Hagen, Germany

Landscape architect Georg Penker; *Client* Hagen Town Council; *Landscape contractor* Büngen and Sieg GmbH and Co. KG.

3.9 NEW GRAPHIC WING, LOUISIANA MUSEUM OF MODERN ART, Humlebaek, Denmark

Landscape architect Lea Nørgaard and Vibeke Holsher; *Client* Knud W. Jensen, Louisiana Museum of Modern Art; *Architects* Jørgan Bo, Vilhelm Wohlert, Claus Wohlert; *Main contractor* Danbyg A/S; *Landscape contractor* Ebbe Dalsgaard; *Indoor planting* Lyng-Miljo; *Automatic irrigation* Delta Design; *Plant suppliers* P. Kortegaard's Planteskole af 1982, Vejenbrod Planteskole A/S.

3.10 FARNBOROUGH COLLEGE OF TECHNOLOGY, Farnborough, Hampshire, UK

Landscape architect Jakobsen Landscape Architects; *Project designer* Preben Jakobsen; *Client* Hampshire County Council – County Architect; *Main contractor* Kyle and Stewart; *Landscape contractor* Tilhill Landscaping; *Mechanical and electrical engineers* Dale and Goldfinger; *Quantity surveyors* Dearle and Henderson; *Structural engineers* Anthony Hunt Associates; *Irrigation systems* Irrigation and Slurry Services; *Fountain* Ustigate Ltd.; *Metal screens* Orsogril UK Ltd.; *Biological control* MF Koppert (UK) Ltd.; *Boulders and cobbles* Civil Engineering Developments Ltd.; *Golden amber marine gravel* Industrial Minerals and Aggregates Ltd.; *Circular concrete pavers* Blanc de Bierges – Milner Delvaux Ltd.

3.11 NEW PARLIAMENT HOUSE, Canberra, Australia

Landscape architect Peter G. Rolland and Associates; *Project team* Peter G. Rolland (Principal-in-charge), Peter Britz (Project manager), Catherine Brouwer, Mervyn Dorrough, Richard Horsman, David Kamp, Stuart MacKenzie, John Michel, Keith Reece, Andrew Tung; *Client* Parliament House Construction Authority; *Main contractor* Concrete Holland (specially formed for this project); *Forecourt fountain* Robert Woodward; *Fountain consultants* Richart Chaix/CMS Collaborative; *Landscape contractors* Ables Landscaping, Citra, Conturf.

3.12 UNIVERSITY SQUARE, Tromsø, Norway

Landscape architect Prof. Bjarne Aasen; *Artistic idea* Prof. Guttorm Guttormsgaard; *Clients* Directorate of

Public Construction and Property, The Foundation for Decoration of New Public Buildings; *Landscape contractor* Roar Marcussen; *Subcontractors* Electrical Installations – EB-installasjon, Water, drainage and construction – Nordgruppen Entreponør; *Consultants* Bjørn Vileid (construction technique and clerk of works), Sletten AS (heating and sanitary), El-prosjekt AS (electricity); *Suppliers* Johansen Granitt (stone), Skjalg Andreassen (steel in basin).

4.1 CENTENNIAL PARK AND RESERVOIR, Howard County, Maryland, USA

Landscape architect LDR International, Inc.; *Project team* J. C. Hall (Principal), Donald F. Hilderbrandt; *Client* Howard County, Department of Parks and Recreation; *Main contractors* Oak Contracting Corp., Cherry Hill Construction; *Landscape contractor* Ruppert Landscape; *Civil engineer* Rummel, Klepper and Kahl; *Electrical engineer* Turpin Wachter, Inc.

4.2 CHANNEL TUNNEL, UK TERMINAL, Folkestone, Kent, UK

Landscape architect Building Design Partnership; *Project team* Janet Jack, Kenneth Trew, Mike Martin, William Barter, Peter Austin, Michael O'Brien, Henry Mead; *Client* Trans-Manche Link; *Main contractor* Trans-Manche Link; *Landscape contractor* Economic Forestry Group plc.; *Consultant* Van den Berk Bros. Ltd.

4.3 FRANCONIA NOTCH STATE PARK AND PARKWAY, White Mountains National Forest, Concord, New Hampshire, USA

Landscape architect Johnson, Johnson and Roy; *Project team* Kenneth M. Cobb, James H. Page, Richard A. Rlgterink; *Client* New Hampshire Department of Transportation; *Main consultant and traffic engineer* DeLeuw Cather and Company; *Landscape contractors* Bartlett Tree Export Co. Ltd., Gatz Landscaping, Inc., Stewart's Nursery, Inc., A. J. Cameron Sod Farms, Inc., Green Carpet Landscaping, Salmon Falls Nursery, Inc.

4.4 RIVER STURA LINEAR PARK, Turin, Italy

Landscape architect Marisa Maffioli, Carlo Buffa; *Client* Municipality of Turin.

4.5 SIZEWELL B POWER STATION, Leiston, Suffolk, UK

Landscape architect Peter Youngman; *In association with* Ron Hebblethwaite and Peter Emberson of CEGB (up to 1990), Rendel and Branch (1990 to date); *Client* CEGB/Nuclear Electric; *Landscape contractors* Dew Group Ltd., C.D.C. Blower Contractors; *Consultant architects* YRM Architects and Planners; *Executive architects and engineers* Nuclear Design Associates; *Ecological consultants* School of Biological Science, University of East Anglia; *Forestry consultant* J. Workman, H. Barnett; *Agricultural consultants* Reading Agricultural Consultants; *Building and civil engineers* John Laing Ltd. (main site), Kier Construction Ltd. (foreshore cooling water works), Elliot Medway (Northern) Ltd. (public information centre).

4.6 NTSHONDWE CAMP, ITALA GAME RESERVE, Northern Natal, South Africa

Landscape architect Environmental Design Partership Inc.; *Project Team* Gareth Singleton, Wendy Seymour; *Client* Natal Parks Board; *Architects* Gallagher Aspoas Poplak Senior; *Main contractor* S. W. Van Heerden; *Irrigation* Water Plant; *Consultant engineers* Hill Kaplan Scott Inc.; *Quantity surveyors* Southby Bihl Detert Slade and Slade.

4.7 OLYMPICS, SUMMER 1992, Barcelona, Spain
For information contact Barcelona Holding Olimpic SA (HOLSA); *Client* National Government of Spain, City Council of Barcelona; *Urban planning* Institut Municipal de Promocio Urbanistica SA (IMPUSA); *Olympic village* Vila Olimpica SA (VOSA); *Montjuic development* Anella Olimpica de Montjuic SA (AOMSA).

4.8 STOCKLEY BUSINESS PARK, Heathrow, London, UK
Landscape architect Ede Griffiths Partnership; *Project team* Bernard Ede, David Coomes; *Master planners* Arup Associates; *Project team* Michael Lowe, Graeme Smart; *Client* Stockley Park Consortium Ltd.; *Main*

contractors Cinnamond Reclamation Ltd., Edmund Nuttall Ltd., Fitzpatrick and Sons Ltd., George Dew, Valetta Surfacing Ltd., Walcon Construction plc; *Landscape contractors* Artscapes Ltd., Berhard's Rugby Continental Landscapes Ltd., Craigwell Nurseries (Guildford) Ltd., Krinkels beplantings maatschappij b.v., Mostert de Winter, Stockley Park Management Ltd., Turfsoil Ltd., Walcon Construction plc, Waterers Landscape Ltd., White Horse Contractors Ltd.; *Landscape maintenance contractors* Horton Gravel and Restoration Ltd., Turfsoil Ltd.; *Suppliers* Arbor PVBA (semi-mature trees, hedging plants, containerized shrubs and groundcover), Oakover Nurseries (forestry stock), Vannucci piante (containerized evergreen and specimen shrubs),

Wyevale Nurseries Ltd. (small trees), Green Brothers (GEEBRO) Ltd., Sarum Hardwood Structures Ltd. (timber items); *Golf course construction* Land Unit Construction Ltd.; *Water feature* Water Techniques.

4.9 GLENVEAGH NATIONAL PARK, Glenveagh, Co. Donegal, Eire
Landscape architects Anthony and Barbara O'Neill; *Client* Parks Department, Office of Public Works; *Main contractors* Thomas McMahon Ltd., Kevin McMonagle; *Landscape contractor* Enda McMonagail; *Structural engineers* Michael Punch and Partners; *Quantity surveyors* O'Halloran, McLoughlin and Co.; *Mechanical and electrical engineers* Curry and Associates Ltd.

ADDRESSES OF DESIGNERS, CONTRACTORS & SUPPLIERS

Prof. Bjarne Aasen, Grensen 5-7, N 0159 Oslo, Norway

Able Landscaping, 89 Kendall Avenue, Queanbeyan, New South Wales 2620, Australia

ACB – Andresen and Castel-Branco, R.S. Joao da Mata 35-30, 1200 Lisbon, Portugal

Joao Adao da Fonseca, R. Delfrim Ferreira 424 2o E, 4100 Porto, Portugal

AI Landscape Planning Co. Ltd., YS-2 Bldg., 2-42-7 Matsubara, Setagaya-ku, Tokyo, Japan 156

Keiko Amenomiya, 1-25-26 Eifuku, Suginami-ku, Tokyo 168, Japan

Arbor PVBA, Provinciebarn 25, B3141 – Houtvenne, Hulshout, Belgium

Riera I. Arego, Nov. de Santa Eulalia 14, 08017 Barcelona, Spain

Arnya Pty Ltd., P.O. Box 193, Queanbeyan, New South Wales 2620, Australia

Artscapes Ltd., Silk Mill House, 24 Winchester Street, Whitchurch, Hampshire, UK

Asia Landscaping Ltd., 2/F Lok Moon Commercial Centre, 29 Queen's Road East, Hong Kong

Azmic Co. Ltd., 2-3-4 Ebisu-Nishi, Sibuya-ku, Tokyo 150, Japan

Prof. Chris Baines, P.O. Box 35, Wolverhampton, West Midlands WV1 4XJ, UK

Baggeridge Bricks, Sedgeley, Dudley, West

Midlands DY3 4AA, UK

Barcelona Holding Olimpic S.A. (HOLSA), Ronda Sant Pau, 43, Barcelona, Spain

Bartlett Tree Expert Co. Inc., Main Street, Box 246, Meredith, New Hampshire, USA

Karl Bauer, Killisfeldstrasse 42B, 7500 Karlsruhe 41, Germany

Bungen and Sief GmbH & Co. KG, Garten und Landschaftsbau, Floaweg 9, 5632 Wermeiskirchen, Germany

Bautcilo and Umweltschutzsysteme GmbH & Co. KG, Eichenstrasse 30-40, 2084 Rellingen, Germany

Beckhoff Associates, La Piramide, Complejo Prado Humboldt, Prados des Este, Caracas, Venezuela

BCP – Brian Clouston and Partners, 19/F Trinity House, 165-171 Wanchae Road, Hong Kong

BGT Bischoff Glastechnik, Alexanderstrasse 2, 7518 Bretten, Germany

Black and McDonald, 557 Cambridge Street, Ottawa, Ontario, Canada

Richard Blanchard and Associates, 746 3rd Ave., San Francisco, California 94118, USA

Boffa Miskell Partners Ltd., Rex Rotary Entrance, 109-113 Dixon Street, Wellington, New Zealand

H. A. Brechin and Co., 6/F 101 Wanchal Road, Hong Kong

Ekhard Bruhn, Segeberger Strasse 100, 2406 Stockelsdorf, Germany

Johannes Bruns,

Deutsche Export Baumschulen, Postfach 11652903, Bad Zwischenahn, Germany

Andreas Bruun, Quistgardsvej 4, 4600 Koge, Denmark

Building Design Partnership, 16 Gresse Street, London W1A 4WD, UK

Burner and Company, Inc., 8660-180 College Parkway, Fort Myers, Florida 33919, USA

Bylander Meinhardt Partnership (now known as BMP M&E Ltd.), Level 5 Wah Ming Centre, 421 Queen's Road West, Hong Kong

Cameron Irrigation, Unit 8B 24, Thorp Arch Trading Estate, Wetherby, Yorkshire LS23 7BJ, UK

A. J. Cameron Sod Farms, Inc., P.O. Box 536, Farmington, New Hampshire, USA

Cherry Hill Construction, 8170 Mission Road, Jessup, MD 20794, USA

Cinnamond Reclamation Ltd., P.O. Box 239, Watford, Herts WD1 7LZ, UK

Civil Engineering Developments Ltd., 728 London Road, West Thurrock, Grays, Essex RM16 1LU, UK

Ian S. Clark and Associates, 19 Lansdowne Terrace, Gosforth, Newcastle-

upon-Tyne NE3 1HP, UK

CMS Collaborative, P.O. Box 3565, Carmel, California 93921, USA

A. L. Cohen Construction Co., 6021 S. Syracuse Way, Denver, Colorado 80211, USA

Cold Spring Granite Company, 202 S. 3rd Avenue, Cold Spring, Michigan 56320, USA

Barrie D. Coate, 23535 Summit Road, Los Gatos, California 95030, USA

C. J. Colein and Associates, 817 Main Street, Rochester, Michigan 48306, USA

John Connell and Associates Ltd., 12/F Sun Hung Kai Centre, 30 Harbour Road, Wanchai, Hong Kong

Conseil de la Seine Saint Denis, Service des Espaces Verts, Cite Administrative No. 2, Batiment E, BP 193, 93000 Bobigny, France

Continental Landscapes Ltd., Whichwood House, 26 High Street, Kidlington, Oxford OX5 2DH, UK

Cooper Robertson and Partners, 3111 West 34th Street, New York, NY 10036, USA

Michel and Claire Corajoud, 34 rue Balard, 75015 Paris, France

Jacques Coulon, 93 rue de Tuzenne, 75003 Paris, France

Countryline Drip Irrigation, P.O. Box 782066, Sandton, South Africa

CRS Sirrine Inc., 1111 West Loop South, Houston, Texas, USA

Curry and Associates Ltd., 83 South Park, Foxrock, Co. Dublin, Eire

Daelim Industrial Company Ltd., P.O. Box 7007, Jeddah, Saudi Arabia

Ebbe Dalsgaard, Vejenbrodvej 45, Kokkedal 2980, Denmark

Danbyg AS, Naverland, Glostrup 2600, Denmark

Danielson and Associates, 474 Francisco Street, San Francisco, California 94133, USA

Dearle and Henderson, 4 Lygon Place, London SW1 WOJR, UK

Delegacion Azcapotzalco, Castilla Oriente y 22 de Febrero, Col. Azcapotzalco, 0200 Mexico D.F., Mexico

DeLeuw Cather and Company, 290 Roberts Street, East Hartford, Connecticut 06183, USA

Delta Design, Bdrnstofsvej 242, Charlottenlund 2920, Denmark

Denton Corker Marshall Pty, Ltd., Level 16, 109 Pitt Street, Sydney, New South Wales 2000, Australia

Derek Lovejoy Partnership, 8-11 Denbigh Mews, London SW1V 2HQ, UK

J. L. Detzy Ltd., 131 Jean-Proulx, Hull, Quebec, Canada

John W & S Dorin Ltd., Hadrian House, Airport Industrial Estate, Kenton, Newcastle-upon-Tyne, UK

Douglas Wood Large Tree Sales, R.R. No. 2 Rockwood, Ontario, Canada

Ebel and Pross, Sommerweg 31, 7530 Pforzheim, Germany

EB-installasjon, Skattoraveien 62, 9000 Tromsø, Norway

Economic Forestry Group plc, Forestry House, Great Haseley, Oxford OX9 7PG, UK

EDA Collaborative Inc., One Eleven Court, 10212 – 111 Street, Edmonton, Alberta, Canada

Ede Griffiths Partnership, 40 Market Place, Warminster, Wiltshire BA12 9AN, UK

El-prosjekt AS, Postboks 1159, 9001 Tromsø, Norway

Environment Design Institute, Mita Sonnette Bldg., 1-1-15 Mita Minato-ku, Tokyo, 108 Japan

Environmental Design Partnership, Unit 5, Tulbagh North, 369 Oak Avenue, Ferndale, Randburg 2194, Transvaal, South Africa

Euro Disney Imagineering/Area Development, Chantier Euro Disney, B.P. 13, Marne le Vallée, 77905 Montevrain Cedex, France

Firma A Schutz Naturstein GmbH, Steinstrasse 17, 7580 Buhl/Baden, Germany

Fuji Ueki Co. Ltd., 4-1-9 Kudan-Minami, Chiyoda-ku, Tokyo 102, Japan

Gallagher Aspoas

Poplak Senior, P.O. Box 31133, Braamfontein, South Africa

Gatz Landscaping, Inc., 1800 Sound Ave, Mattituck, NY, USA

Geray und Reck, Freid Architekten, Zettachring 12A, 7000 Stuttgart 80, Germany

Glasbau Liebherr GmbH, Julius-Holder-Strasse 50, 7000 Stuttgart 70, Germany

Granada Inc., 1499 Sutter St., San Francisco, California 94109, USA

Johansen Granitt, Postboks 2146, 1702 Sarpsborg, Norway

Green and MaCahill Group, 374 Church Street, P.O. Box 12 443, Penrose, Auckland, New Zealand

John Grissim and Associates, 37801 Twelve Mile Road, Farmington Hills, Michigan 48331, USA

Grupo de diseño urbano, S.C., Fernando Montes de Oca No. 4, Col. Condesa C.P. 06140, Mexico D.F., Mexico

Claude Guinandeau, 38 Ave. Franklin Roosevelt, 77210 Avon, France

Guttorm Guttormsgaard, 'Meieriet', N 1925 Blaker, Norway

Hall Sprinkler Co., 1127 Judd Court, P.O. Box 740397, Dallas, Texas 75374-0397, USA

H. Robert Hammill, 150 N. Wiget Ln., Walnot Creek, California 94698, USA

Hargreaves Associates, 545 Mission Street, Fourth Floor, San Francisco, California 94105, USA

HCB Contractors, 8050 Northwest Highway, Roanoke, Texas 76262, USA

Heads Company Ltd., 2-15 Sugawara-cho, Kita-ku, Osaka, Japan

Heidt and Associates, 2212 Swann Avenue, Tampa, Florida 33610, USA

S. W. Van Heerden, P.O. Box 1659, Vryheid, South Africa

R. Hepplethwaite, 13 Pennana Road, Falmouth, Cornwall, UK

Hill Kaplan Scott Inc., P.O. Box 4164, Durban, South Africa

Horton Gravel and Restoration Ltd., Benoyn Manor Farm, Stanwell Road, Horton, Berkshire SL3 8PE, UK

Hutter Jennings and Titchmarsh, 15 Portland Terrace, Newcastle-upon-Tyne NE2 1QQ, UK

George Hyman Construction Co., 7500 Old Georgetown Road, Bethesda, Maryland 20814-6135, USA

Image Ltd., 5/7 Mill Street, Congleton, Cheshire CW12 1AB, UK

Bukichi Inoue, 242-5 Meigetsudani, Yamanouchi, Kamakura, Kanagawa Prefecture 247, Japan

Industrial Minerals and Aggregates Ltd., 5-7 Mill Street, Congleton, Cheshire CW12 1AB, UK

Donald Insall and Associates, 19 West Eaton Place, London SW1X 8LR, UK

Instant Trees, P.O. Box 161, Randburg, South Africa

Institut Municipal de Promocio Urbanistica S.A. (IMPUSA), Ronda Sant Pau, 43, Barcelona, Spain

Irrigation and Slurry Services, Unit 6, The Bourne Centre, Salisbury Business Park, Southampton Road, Salisbury, Wiltshire, UK

Jakobsen Landscape Architects and Urban Designers, Mount Sorrel, West Approach Drive, Pitville, Cheltenham, Glos. GL52 3AD, UK

Jardev, Route Nationale 19, Santeny 94440, France

Johnson, Johnson and Roy Inc., 2828 Routh Street, Suite 600, Dallas, Texas 75201, USA

Ernst Jolitz und Söhne, Sibeliusstrasse 2, 2400 Lübeck 1, Germany

Katsura Gardens, 1825 Post Street, San Francisco, California 94115, USA

Keikan Design Inc., c/o Nitto Tochi, Kayabacho, Chuo-ku, Tokyo, Japan 103

Jogindar Judge Khurana, P.O. Box 9027, Jeddah, Saudi Arabia 21413

Dan Kiley, Office of Dan Kiley, East Farm, Charlotte, Vermont 06446, USA

Kirchmann Hurry Construction, P.O. Box 41189, Craighall, South Africa

Siegfried Knoll, Kurze Gazze 10a, 7032 Sindelfingen, Germany

P. Kortegaard's Planteskole, Ovej 10, Kappendrop, Landeskov 5550, Denmark

Kuoki Construction Co. Ltd., 1-100 Matsushima-cho, Imahri-shi, Saga ken, Japan

Krinkels beplantings maatschappij b.v., Plantagebaan 58, Postbus 5, 4724 zg wouw, Holland

Bernd Krüger and Hubert Möhrle, Gutenbergstr 41, 7000 Stuttgart 1, Germany

Kuraray Ryokka Co Ltd., Shibata-cho Bld, 1-4-14 Shibata, Kita-ku, Osaka, Japan

K.K. Kyosera, 6-27-8 Jungumae, Shibuya-ku, Tokyo 2, Japan

Kuroki Construction Co. Ltd., 1-100 Matsushima-cho, Imari-shi, Saga Ken, Japan

Laing Management Contracting Ltd., Management House, Alma Street, Luton, Bedfordshire LU1 2PL, UK

Charles Lambert (Lawns) Ltd., Blezard Business Park, Brenkley Way, Seaton Burn, Newcastle-upon-Tyne, UK

Lambert Somec and Crystal Fountains, 725 rue Lachance, Quebec City, Quebec, Canada

Latitude Nord, 44/46 rue de Domremy, 75013 Paris, France

LDR International Inc., Quarry Park Place, 9175 Guilford Road, Columbia, Maryland 21046, USA

F. Leblond Cement Products Ltd., 1360 Triole Street, Ottawa, Ontario, Canada

Lehrer McGovern Bovis Sarl, Le Pascal, 7-11 Boulevard Georges Melies, 94350 Villiers-sur-Marne, Paris, France

Karl Leisten GmbH and Co. KG, Garten-Landschafts- und Sportplatzbau, Rheinstr 41, 5160 Düren, Germany

Linbeck Construction Co., 3810 W. Alabama, Houston, Texas, USA

Louis Karol Architects, P.O. Box 6676, Johannesburg, South Africa

Luminart Inc., 404 North River, Ypsilanti, Michigan 48198, USA

Lyng-Miljo, Kong Georgsvej 17, Vedbaek 2950, Denmark

Thomas McMahon Ltd., Portnason, Ballyshannon, Co. Donegal, Eire

Enda McMonagail, Falcarragh, Co. Donegal, Eire

Kevin McMonagle, Gortahork, Co. Donegal, Eire

Maeda Road Construction Ltd., 3-14-12 Kamio Osaki, Shinagawa-ku, Tokyo 141, Japan

Marisa Maffioli, Dipartimento di Agronomia, Selvicoltura E gestione del Territorio, Universita Degli Studi di Torino, Via Giuria 15, 10126 Torino, Italy

Maltby Partners Ltd., 8-10 Whitaker Place, Auckland, New Zealand

Roar Marcussen, Ringveien 73, N. 9000 Tromsø, Norway

Maunsell Consultants Asia Ltd., 12/F Bank of Tokyo Building, 1 Kowloon Park Drive, Tsim Sha Tsui, Kowloon

Meyknecht-Lischner Contractors Ltd., 3856 Richmond Road, Nepean, Ontario, Canada

Eduardo Santos Michlena, Torre Norta, Of. 151, 15th Floor, Av. F. Miranda, Ed Banco, Caracas, Venezuela

Mikiko Ishii Design Office, 6 Rokubando 8, Chioda-ku, Tokyo, Japan

Russell D. Mitchell and Associates, 2760 Camino Diablo, Walnut Creek, California 94596, USA

Morimura and Association, 1-2-9 Yojogi Shibuya-ku, Tokyo, Japan

Mostert de Winter, Geluidwerendgroen bv, Riverdijk 18, Postbus 37, 3350 AA Sliedrecht, Holland

Pascal Mourgue with Patrice Hardy, 3h rue de Lappe, 75011 Paris, France

MPA Design, 562 Mission Street, San Francisco, California 94105, USA

Natal Parks Board, P.O. Box 662, Pietermaritzburg, South Africa

Nihon Setsubi Sekkei, Yokohama 'Excellent' 3, 3-35 Nakadori-Minami, Nakaku, Yokohama-shi, Japan

Lea Norgaard and Vibeke Holscher, Godthabsvej 7, 2000 Frederiksberg, Denmark

Nordgruppen Entrepenor AS, Postboks 810, 9001 Tromsø, Norway

Nuclear Design Associates, Booths Hall, Knutsford, Cheshire, UK

Edmund Nuttall Ltd., St. James House, Knoll Road, Camberley, Surrey GU15 3XW, UK

Oak Contracting Corporation, 3501 Sinclair Lane, Baltimore, Maryland 21213, USA

Oakover Nurseries, Callehill, Leacon, Charing, Ashford, Kent, UK

Oakwood Ventures, P.O. Box 784320, Sandton, South Africa

Oase Pumpen, Burgstrasse 15, D-7310 Plochingen, Germany

Cornelia Hahn Oberlander/Arthur Erickson Architects, 1372 Acadia Road, Vancouver, British Columbia V6T 1F6, Canada

Paul O'Brian

Engineering Pty Ltd., 29 Harris Street, Hackett ACT 2602, Australia

Odell Associates, 129 West Trade Street, Charlotte, North Carolina 28202, USA

Odukyu Landscape Gardening Ltd., 1-8-3 Nishisinjuk, Shinjuku-ku, Tokyo, Japan

The Office Plant, P.O. Box 2378, Northcliff, South Africa

O'Halloran McLoughlin and Co., 13 Fitzwilliam Place, Dublin 2, Eire

Anthony M. O'Neill, 8 Seafield Avenue, Monkstown, Co. Dublin, Eire

Ove Arup and Partners Hong Kong Ltd., 56/F Hopewell Centre, 183 Queen's Road East, Hong Kong

P and A Engineering Ltd., Room 8, 4/F Kinetic Industrial Centre, 7 Wang Kwong Road, Kowloon Bay, Kowloon

Tristan Pauly, 59 route de Boursonne, 02600 Villers Cotterets, France

PB Fencing Ltd., South Street, East Hoathly, Sussex BN8 6DX, UK

Permacrib (Euro) Ltd., 72/74 Bath Road, Cheltenham, Glos. GL53 7, UK

Georg Penker, Brahmsstrasse 11, 4040 Neuss, Germany

Ivan Pestalozzi, CH-8122 Binz/Maur, Switzerland

Pilot Garten– und Landschaftsbau GmbH, Garten, Landschafts und Sportplatzbau, Judenpfad 79, 5000 Köln 50 (Hahnwald), Germany

J. Edward Pinckney, 247 Meeting Street, Suite 200, Charleston, South Carolina 29401, USA

PREC, Newlife Ichiban-cho Bldg 201, 4-5 Ichiban-cho, Chiyoda-ku, Tokyo 102, Japan

PSA Services, C401 Whitgift Centre, Wellesley Road, Croydon, Surrey CR9 3LY, UK

Michael Punch and Partners, 6 Percy Square, Limerick, Eire

R. H. Partnership, 94 Chesterton Road, Cambridge CB4 1ER, UK

Reading Agricultural Consultants, 14a Honey Lane, Cholsey, Wallingford, Oxon, UK

Rendal and Branch, The Old Canal Building, East Challow, Wantage, Oxon, UK

Ridgewood Landscape Inc., 5625 Greenhouse, Houston, Texas, USA

Rinkai Construction Co. Ltd., 1-8-5 Kyomachibori, Nishi-ku, Osaka, Japan

Rock and Waterscape, 11 Whalney, Irvine, California 92714, USA

Rock of Ages Corporation, P.O. Box 482, Barre, Vermont 05641, USA

Studio Heiner Rödel, Via S. Gottardo, 61, 6900 Massagno, Switzerland

Rogoss Garten– und Landschaftsbau, Mülheimer Strasse 256-260, 5000 Köln 80, Germany

Rolland/Towers, 15 Purchase Street, Rye, New York 10580, USA

Bernard Rousseau, 13 rue des Miarimes, Paris 75003, France

RSA Landscapes, P.O. Box 2946, Honeydew, South Africa

Marc Rumelhart, 9 rue Claude Debussy, 78280 Guyancourt, France

Rummel, Klepper and Kahl, 5800 Faringdon Place, Suite 105, Raleigh. North Carolina 27609, USA

Ruppert Landscape, 17701 New Hampshire Ave., Ashton, Maryland 20861, USA

Safety Harbor Builders, 1705 Colonial Boulevard, Suite B3, Fort Myers, Florida 33907, USA

Salmon Falls Nursery, Inc., 300 Route 236, Berwick, Maine, USA

K K Sanesu, 4-322 Sakuragaoka, Higashi Yamato-shi, Tokyo, Japan

Joaquim dos Santos, Horto da Granja, 4405 Valadares, Portugal

Sarum Hardwood Structures Ltd., Suite 6, 124/126 Stockbridge Road, Winchester, Hampshire SO22 6RN, UK

Sasaki Associates, Inc., 64 Pleasant Street, Watertown, Massachusetts 02172, USA

Saudconsult, Architects and Engineers, P.O. Box 7352, Jeddah, Saudi Arabia

Saudi Arabian Landscape Company (SALCO), P.O. Box 12310, Jeddah, Saudi Arabia

Savo Stankovich Pty Ltd., 16 Bass Road, Queanbeyan, New South Wales 2620, Australia

SCAL (Sociedade de Construcao Alberto Leal) SA, R Vila Gualdina 30, 4560 Penafiel, Portugal

Schuler Metalltechnik, Robert-Bosch-Strasse 20, 7530 Pforzheim, Germany

Schuttkus GST Bau, Theodor-Hauss-Strasse 21, 7147 Eberdingen – Hochdorf, Germany

Seibu Zoen Co. Ltd., 1-16-15 Minami-Ikebukuro, Toshima-ku, Tokyo, Japan

Seiwa K K, Machobori Building, 4-10-2 Machobori, Chuoku, Tokyo, Japan

Shimizu Corporation, 2-16-1 Kgobashi, Chuo-ku, Tokyo, Japan

Subley Robinson Partnership, The Old Rectory, Church Lane, Fulborn, Cambridge CB1 5EP, UK

Skandai Landscape Inc., 18340 Middlebelt, Livonia, Michigan 48150, USA

Skjalg Andreassen, Fridtjof Nansens Plass 6, 9000 Tromsø, Norway

Sletten AS, Postboks 349, 9001 Tromsø, Norway

Sobetram, C.D. 1 Varney 55.000, Bar le duc, France

Soil and Material Engineers, Inc., 5909 Breckenridge Parkway, Tampa, Florida 33610, USA

Sony Sound Tech KK, 3-9-17 Nishi-Gotanda, Sinagawa-ku, Tokyo, Japan

So-Setsubi – Sekkei Office, 3-2-5 Maizuru, Chuo-ku, Fukuoka-shi, Kyushu, Japan

Southby Bihl Detert and Slade, P.O. Box 9045, Johannesburg, South Africa

AS Steinsliperiet, Postboks 68, Bossekop, 9501 Alta, Norway

Stewart's Nursery Inc., 135 Millers Falls Road, Turners Falls, Massachusetts, USA

Stockley Park Management Ltd., The Arena, Management Suite, Stockley Park, Heathrow, Uxbridge, Middlesex 11 1AA, UK

Stoddart and Tabora Architects, Avenida La Corniza, Ed. La Corniche 3B, Altamira Caracas 1062, Venezuela

Suburbaine de Travaux, Zone Industrielle des Mardelles, 75 rue Blaise Pascal 93 600, Aulnay Sous Bois, France

Suikosha K K, 2-8-16 Fukangawa, Kotoku, Tokyo, Japan

Summerfield and Lang, Ann Street East, Widnes, Cheshire WA8 OTA, UK

Sunpu Civil Engineering Consultant, 1-22-24 Hyakunin-cho, Shinjuku-ku, Tokyo, Japan

Eijin Suzuki, 3-1-7 Shinjuku, Zushi, Kanagawa Prefecture 249, Japan

Swinerton and Walberg, 580 California Street, San Francisco, California 94104, USA

Takano Landscape Planning Co. Ltd., 37 Nishi 1 Sen. Aza Mammen, Otofuke-cho, Kato Gun, Hokkaido, Japan

Tateyama Zoen Dobuku Co. Ltd., 244 Machimura, Toyama 930, Japan

Tilhill Landscaping, Greenhills, Tilford, Farnham, Surrey GU10 2DY, UK

Tokusu – Talks, Sekkei Office, 3-2-5 Maizuru, Chuo-ku, Fukuoka-shi, Kyushu-shi, Kyushu, Japan

Tokyo Construction Company Ltd., Shibuya Metro Plaza, 1-16-14 Shibuya, Shibuja-ku, Tokyo 150, Japan

Tokyo Landscape Architects, Meito Building, 16-4 Jingumae 1-chome, Shibuya-ku, Tokyo 150, Japan

Top Turf and Associates, P.O. Box 260, Alberton, South Africa

Trafalgar House Management Construction Ltd., Mitcham House, 681 Mitcham Road, Croydon, Surrey CR9 3AP, UK

Trans-Manche Link, Beachborough, Newington, Folkestone, Kent CT18 8NP, UK

Buro TTG, Trueper and Gondesen, Untertrave 17, 2400 Lübeck 1, Germany

Tubular Barriers Ltd., Washington, Tyne and Wear, UK

Turfsoil Ltd., Tunbridge Road, Teston, Maidstone, Kent, UK

Turpin Wachter, Inc., 8e Pennsylvania Avenue, Towson, DM 21204, USA

Tomas Calvillo Unna, Pedro Vallejo N. 893, Barrio San Miguelito, San Luis Potosi S.L.P., Mexico

Urban Contractors Pty Ltd., 8 Beltana Road, Piralligo, ACT 2609, Australia

Useppa Inn and Dock Company, Bocilla Island Club, 8115 Main Street, Bokeelia, Florida 33922, USA

Ustigate Ltd., 3 Berkeley Crescent, Gravesend, Kent, UK

Valetta Surfacing Ltd., 1 Main Street, West Wilts Trading Estate, Westbury, Wiltshire BA13 4JR, UK

Van den Berk Bros Ltd., Postbus 130, 5490 AC, St. Oedenrode, Holland

Vannucci Painte, Via Vecchia Pratese 238, Pistola 51100, Italy

Vejenbrod Planteskole AS, Vejenbrodvej 27, Kokkedal 2980, Denmark

Vereinigte Aluminium Werke AG, Georg-von-Boeselager-Strasse 25, 5300 Bonni, Germany

Vermont Marble Company, Proctor, Vermont, USA

Vila Olimpica S.A., Joan D'Austria, 7-21 3e Plta, 08005 Barcelona, Spain

Bjorn Vileid AS, Verftsgata 4, 9000 Tromsø, Norway

Viry, Z.1. du Fort B.P. 8, 88191 Golbey, France

Walcon Construction plc., Lakesmere House, Allington Lane, Fair Oak, Eastleigh, Hampshire SO5 7OB, UK

Anthony Walker and Partners, 42 Jesmond Road, Newcastle-upon-Tyne NE2 4PQ, UK

Peter Walker and Partners Landscape Architecture, Inc., 2222 Bush Street, San Francisco, California 94115, USA

The Water Display Specialists, Downside Mill, Cobham Park Road, Cobham, Surrey KT11 3PF, UK

Waterers Landscape Ltd., Nursery Court, London Road, Windlesham, Surrey GU20 6LQ, UK

Water Plant, P.O. Box 350, Paardekraal, South Africa

Water Techniques, Unit D3, Sandown Industrial Estate, Mill Road, Esher, Surrey KT10 8BL, UK

White Horse Contractors Ltd., Blakes Oak Farm. Lodge Hill, Abingdon OX14 2JD, UK

Wildseed, Inc., P.O. Box 308, Eagle Lake, Texas 77434, USA

Woodscape, Upfield, Pike Lowe, Brinscall, Nr. Chorley, Lancashire PR6 8SP, UK

John Workman, Far End, Sheepscombe, Stroud, Glos., UK

Wyevale Nurseries Ltd., Kings Acre, Hereford HR4 7AY, UK

Masamichi Yamamoto, 4-5-9 Kugenum Fujigaya, Fujisawa, Kanagawa Prefecture 251, Japan

Yerkey Landscape Construction, 8996 South Motsenbocker Road, Parker, Colorado, USA

Sir Peter Youngman, 60 Langley Hill, Kings Langley, Herts WD4 9HE, UK

YRM Architects and Planners, 24 Britton Street, London, UK

Kazuo Yuhara, 106-55 Kamisugeta-cho, Hodogaya-ku, Yokohama 240, Japan

Zen Environmental Design Inc., Yomimuri Fukuoka Bldg. 7F, 1-12-15 Akasaka, Chuo-ku, Fukuoka-shi, Japan

Z and Z Constructions Pty Ltd., 25 Barwon Street, Kaleen ACT 2617, Australia

Index